Spectacles

Sue is perhaps best known for being one quarter of double act Mel and Sue, where she plays the part of Mel. Together, the pair have bounced, shouted and gurned their way through countless hours of television, most memorably *Light Lunch* and its later counterpart, the imaginatively titled *Late Lunch*.

Over the years, Sue has worked on a wide range of solo projects, including documentaries on art, popular fiction and history. In 2008 she appeared on the BBC show *Maestro*, culminating in her conducting at the Last Night of the Proms. She has also collaborated with food-critic Giles Coren on the *Supersizers* series, where the duo power-ate their way through five centuries of lungs, livers and testicles whilst half-cut on sherry.

In the last couple of years, Sue has travelled extensively throughout Asia, driving the Ho Chi Minh trail, exploring the length of the Mekong River and getting felt up by a Cambodian hermit.

She is a regular contributor to *Have I Got News For You*, *Just a Minute*, *QI* and *The News Quiz* and has been crowned, officially, The World's Greatest Liar in a hard-fought contest in Cumbria.

Oh, and apparently she does some cake show on BBC1.

Spectacles

SUE PERKINS

MICHAEL JOSEPH
an imprint of
PENGUIN BOOKS

MICHAEL JOSEPH

UK | USA | Canada | Ireland | Austraila
India | New Zealand | South Africa

Michael Joseph is part of the Penguin Random House group of companies
whose addresses can be found at global.penguinrandomhouse.com

First published 2015
001

Text and images copyright © Sue Perkins, 2015

The moral right of the author has been asserted

Set in Dante MT Std
Typeset by Palimpsest Book Production Limited, Falkirk, Stirlingshire
Printed in Great Britain by Clays Ltd, St Ives plc

A CIP catalogue record for this book is available from the British Library

ISBN: 978–1–405–91856–5

10% of the royalties of this book go to The Serpentarium on the Isle of Skye.

www.greenpenguin.co.uk

For Scarlett Jukes

Heron   A reasonable effort.

The cruel beaked menace

Savage and ruthless, evil

Terror of all fish

                 S Perkins

B-

Contents

Most of this book is true.

I have, however, changed a few names to protect the innocent, and the odd location too. I've skewed some details for comic effect, swapped timelines and generally embellished and embroidered some of the duller moments in my past. I have sometimes created punchlines where real life failed to provide them, and occasionally invented characters wholesale. I have amplified my more positive characteristics in an effort to make you like me. I have hidden the worst of my flaws in an effort to make you like me. I may at one point have pretended to have been an Olympic fencing champion.

Other than that, as I say – I've told it like it is.

Preface

I've always wanted to be a writer; since I first felt the precarious wobble of a book in my hand, since I first heard the phrase 'Once upon a time', since I first realized that fairies, wizards and sea-farers could transport you from the endless grey of 1970s south London. I was a prolific child. By the age of seven, I had produced several anthologies of poems about God, death and aquatic birds. I was prolific right up to the point I received a B- for a haiku I'd written about a heron. The uninitiated can be so unkind.

As an adult I started writing articles, reviews and glib little pieces for glossy magazines. I'd hide away in my room on the days I wasn't on set and continue work on *Ra'anui and the Enchanted Otter*, the intense, magic-realist novel set in Tahiti I'd been working on for the best part of a decade. By the time it neared completion, it was clear that there was never going to be an appetite for it and that the book world had changed beyond recognition. Almost to prove that point, I had a meeting in the autumn of 2010 with a well-known publishing house to discuss the possibility of writing something. I'd been invited to a swanky restaurant in St Martin's Lane. I arrived late, as always, in full wet-weather gear to find a semicircle of unspeakably beautiful people sat at the table waiting for me.

'Hi, I'm Tamara,' said the immaculate blonde to my left, proffering a manicured hand. 'I'm head of talent acquisitions.'

I leant forward to greet her. Dried mud cascaded from my sleeve into the *amuse-bouche*. 'Sorry, I've been walking the dog on the heath.'

'I'm Sarah-Jane,' said the immaculate blonde to my right. 'I'm the publishing director.'

'Nice to meet you. Ooh, I wouldn't hug me – I'm a little damp around the edges.'

'Hi, I'm Dorcas,' said the immaculate blonde dead ahead of me. 'I'm the managing director.'

'Hello – oops!' I said, as a roll of poo bags unfurled from my coat pocket.

It wasn't the best first impression I'd ever made. I sat down and panic-nibbled on some artisanal micro-loaves.

'So, Sue . . .' said one of the immaculate blondes, staring at me as if I were a monkey smearing itself with excrement at the zoo. 'What would you like to write?'

It was the question I had been waiting all my life to answer. Twenty-five minutes later I finished speaking, having evoked, in minute detail, my proposed epic:

'. . . so Ra'anui finally tames the beast with his uncle's amulet and marries Puatea. It's essentially a meditation on climate change.'

There followed a long pause during which I awkwardly pushed some 'textures of artichoke' around my plate.

'Well . . .' said one immaculate blonde, breaking the silence, '. . . that's great!'

'Really, really great,' chimed the second.

'Great!' said the third.

This was going so well. All three had said 'great'. In a row! Then came the stinger.

Blonde 1: Now, you see, what *we'd* like you to write . . .

Me: Oh . . .

Blonde 2: No, hear us out . . .

Blonde 1: We've looked at what generates mass sales – you know, what really works piled up at Tesco and Asda. And we've developed a formula . . .

Blonde 2:   [*blurting*] Death is really hot right now . . .

Blonde 3:   And pets . . .

Blonde 1:   So either of those would make a great starting point.

By now I thought we were all having a laugh, that I was among friends. We'd ordered *sharing plates* for goodness' sake. I'd dug my fork into Blonde 1's sweet anchovies. Blonde 2 had tried my avocado tian. I mean, we were *mates*. In that spirit of fun I joined in.

Me: [*grinning*] Well, what about combining the two?

Blonde 1:   [*intrigued*] What? Death *and* pets?

Me: Yes, why not? [*Carrying on*] A kind of *Lovely Bones* meets *Lassie*.

Blonde 3:   [*squealing*] Amazing! Amazing!

Me: We could call it . . . *Angel Dog*.

Blonde 3:   Oh my God – *Angel Dog*!

Me: The dog dies, doesn't go straight to heaven – ends up in some kind of canine purgatory, depending on how deeply Catholic you want to get – and ends up guarding his owners from the plane of the undead. *Angel Dog*.

Blonde 1:   *Angel Dog* . . .

Blonde 2:   Wow. *Angel Dog*.

Blonde 3:   I love it. I love it!

I roared with laughter. Roared. It took me nearly a minute to realize no one else was roaring with me. The penny finally dropped – they were being serious.

Well, I'm sorry, but this book isn't *Angel Dog*. There is a dog in it, later on, although she was far from an angel, as you shall see. I doubt this book will ever disappear in huge numbers from supermarket shelves, or that shoppers will scuffle over the last discounted copy in a frenzied Black Friday riot. But neither is it the Polynesian pan-generational epic I pitched all those years ago. It's something in the middle. Mid-range. Comfy. The sort of book that turns up to a meeting covered in mud and shit having not changed into something more appropriate.

Something a little more me.

It's October 2014. My family are gathered together at my parents' house in west Cornwall. Rain relentlessly spanks the windows. There is the grumble of a distant tractor. My dad, brother and sister are bunched up together on the sofa watching a marginal American sport on a marginal subscription channel. Mum is perched on the armrest, jabbing at her iPad with a stiff finger, ET-style, muttering 'Well, I never!' in a loop.

It's at this moment I decide to tell them about the memoir. It's important to do so, I think, because memories are prismatic. I have my recollections, but they may well be totally different from those of my family. I want to see if I can integrate our perspectives so we can all be happy with the end result.

Me:	Hey, everybody, listen – I'm writing a book.
David:	What?
Me:	I'm writing a book.

Mum:	What kind of a book?
Me:	Well, sort of an autobiography.
All:	Oh God . . .
Dad:	Who's it about?
Mum:	Bert!
Me:	Hilarious, Dad.
Michelle:	Do I have to be in it?
Me:	Well, yes. You've been in my life for thirty-eight years, so you feature pretty heavily . . .
David:	Don't you mention that incident with the honeydew. I was just a teenager . . .
Michelle:	Can't you just say you've only got one sibling?
Me:	Not really. It'd just be weird.
David:	I'm serious – it was just experimental.
Dad:	What kind of book is it?
Me:	Dad, I've just told you. It's a memoir.
Dad:	Who the bloody hell wants to read that?
Mum:	Bert! [*To me*] Will there be swearing in it?
Me:	I don't know. Maybe.
Mum:	I don't think you should swear in it. People will realize you're not classy.
Michelle:	Surely you could just not mention me?
Mum:	Will we come across as mental?
Dad:	You are mental!
Mum:	BERT!
Me:	I don't know. How do you want to come across?
Michelle:	I don't want to be in it.
Dad:	I'd like to be taller. Like, really, really tall. Can I be six foot five?
David:	Can I be incredibly handsome and not a Lego nerd?
Me:	All right . . .
David:	I want every girl to fancy me. Can you do that?

Mum: Will there be swearing?

Me: I said I don't know!

Mum: Well, I'd like it to be clean. I don't mind what you say,
         but keep it clean.

Dad: [*to the telly*] Hit it, you little shit! Oh for Christ's sake.

Mum: Bert!

And so, with that in mind – taking into consideration their thoughts and wishes – I started writing the memoir my family and I had agreed upon.

ONE

Croydon

Chapter One

My first memory of Dad was him approaching my cot. I must have been around two years old at the most. I remember this towering figure coming towards me, blocking out the light as he bent forward to pick me up. We're not known for being especially tall in our family, but Dad was the exception. He stood at just over six foot five high – a magnificent oak of a man – born, as he was, from countless generations that never got beyond thin and weedy saplings.

'Hello, pumpkin,' he whispered, gathering me tightly to his chest, before standing back upright and knocking his head, hard, on the light fitting.

'Goodness gracious me, that was painful!' he said, and then carried me down the stairs for breakfast.

I was three when my brother, David, came along – and from the get-go we realized he was headed on a single-track road marked ADONIS. Wherever we went, pensioners, young mums and kids alike would peer into his pram and exclaim, 'What a stunning boy! I've never seen a child like it! He's an angel!'

He was born cool and grew up cooler. While children his age played with Scalextric and Lego, David would be programming computers and dabbling in abstract painting. Girls worshipped him, of course, but he'd only known what it was to be beautiful, so he took it in his stride. At the age of nine he was signed to a modelling agency, after being spotted at the local shopping centre, and by the time he hit puberty he had become the face of a well-known luxury goods brand.

By sixteen, David had queues of women following him – meaning, unlike his peers, he had no need whatsoever to masturbate into large round fruit while fantasizing about the opposite sex. Sexual opportunities afforded themselves at every turn. His popularity with women was so overwhelming that it even affected our family time. I have to admit it was hard growing up alongside him – alongside such perfection – and I would go through phases of resentment. Why does *he* get all the girls? Why did *he* get the beautiful genes and not me?

Mum had always wanted another baby, but she was so busy with her high-flying job as obergruppenadviser at Deutsche Bank that it never happened. Sometimes, when we'd get together as a four, and Dad and David were larking around, she'd wistfully remark in my ear, 'Wouldn't it be nice if I'd had another girl – you know, so we could outgun the boys . . .'

Sometimes I too longed for a sister, but it was never to be. What would she have been like? Would she have been as poor at relationships as I was? I doubt it. Would she have had the same issues with eye bags, anxiety and sugar addiction? Of course not. She would have been a younger, better and brighter version of me. And then, as I thought of her, I was glad she wasn't real. Because having a sister as amazing as that would have been *seriously* infuriating.

I remember clearly the day David introduced us to his first serious girlfriend after years of playing the field. It was Christmas Eve. Dad was tending to the logs on the fire as the doorbell rang.

'Mind your head, Bert!' shouted Mum.

Too late. Dad stood back, and there was a loud crack as his skull made contact with the ceiling.

'Gosh! That hurt!' he exclaimed. 'If only I wasn't so ruddy tall all the time!'

He went to the door. Standing there was David with wife-to-be Lynne on his arm. They made the perfect couple. They had matching luggage and everything.

'Finally, another daughter!' cried Mum, one eye on dinner, the other on the progress of her global equity derivatives. 'Come on – give me a hand with these giblets!'

I watched as Dad and David sat down together. Each cast a shadow over the other. A marginal sport was playing on a marginal subscription channel.

'Gosh, I do wish this fellow would make a better job of scoring!' bellowed Dad, and we all laughed. The fire crackled and the room pulsed with warmth. I looked over at my family and . . . and . . .

. . . and I thought, *This is ridiculous*. Honestly. Let's just say it as it is. Dad, you're a little bit squat. David, you still like Lego and you're a forty-two-year-old father of two, and, Michelle, sorry, but you *do* exist and you're a part of this mental, mental family. Deal with it. Oh, and people swear, so – and I mean this in the nicest possible way, Mum – fuck you. I'm doing this book my way.

The Museum of Me

When I began writing this book, I went home to see if my mum had kept some of my old stuff. What I found was that she hadn't kept some of it. She had kept *all of it* – every bus ticket, stub, programme, letter, postcard and picture, every school report, essay, poem and painting – all filed. From the moment I was born to the moment I was able to have the confidence to turn round and say, 'Why is our house full of all this shit?'

It's fair to say, Mum's 'collecting' (hoarding) has become a problem. She's probably only one back copy of the *National Trust Magazine* away from being the subject of a Channel 4 documentary. Every trip home I try to help out by bringing a skip with me. I'm best friends with the regional managers of at least four civic amenity sites, and I can separate paper, plastic and glass quicker than anyone I know.

We realized things had got out of control when, whilst helping her with a recent house move, we discovered that she had washed, and packed, over a hundred margarine cartons and taken them with her.

Me: [*eating a Müller Light*] Mum, why do you need these?
Mum: To put things in.
Me: What things?
Mum: Just, you know . . . *things*.
Me: Do you think collecting tubs to put things in might be encouraging you to collect yet more things to put in them?

Mum: No. Yes. Maybe. [*Pause*] Have you finished with that yoghurt
       carton?

And so there is this museum – a museum of me. It's not a
museum I'd pay to enter. Or one with artefacts of any interest
– not even, in many cases, to the very person to whom they
relate. The exhibits aren't pretty. They aren't even exhibited;
they lie in countless large plastic tubs, stacked four feet high.
Endless boxes full of bone-dry papers that hurt my fingers
almost as much as they hurt my heart to go through. Because
it is painful – it has been painful – to go back and see in such
forensic detail and with such unimaginable clarity the person I
was, trying to become the person I wanted to be.

Sometimes we don't want to be tethered to yesterday. It's
nicer to forget. Maybe the gaps in our memory are there for a
reason, evolutionary perhaps, to give us the space to grow, to
get away from childishness or childish things. Or maybe it's so
we have the chance to invent, or at least include, some magic
in our yesterdays. Surely the consolation of getting older, of
moving away from youth, is that we can shape our past to our
fantasies. So, even if the present isn't going the way we want it,
we can stand back and remember our earlier selves as exciting
and funny and daring.

I don't have that luxury. I have it all laid out in front of me.
No magic. No mystery. No possibility that I was ever fun or
dynamic. The mundanity of me writ large in endless lever-arch
files and black bin bags.

Sometimes, when searching, I have come across things which
cut deep. An innocuous cardboard box with 'I love you' scribbled on it in the carefree scrawl of an old boyfriend. A sorry
note from a little girl to her parents, a little girl who hadn't yet
done anything to be sorry for. There were so many sorry notes

in fact that nowadays, in arguments, when I'm being intractable and defensive, I wonder if I didn't use up all my apologies as a kid, leaving me nothing left to use in adulthood.

I started going through everything a few months ago in preparation for writing this. I became my own curator. I picked key pieces that I could display in this Museum of Me, arranged them and put them in a bag for safekeeping. The rest I stuffed into bin liners ready for recycling.

'Are these bags to go?' shouted my mum from the top of the stairs.

'Yep,' I shouted, idly, back.

Two days later my bag of treasures was no longer there.

It didn't take me long to realize that my mum had misunderstood me and taken the wrong bag. She had left countless sheaves of junk* and dumped the gems. If that doesn't sum up my family, I don't know what does. Good intentions – annoying outcomes.

Even though I hadn't seen any of it for nearly forty years, it felt like a bereavement – like something had been taken from me. It was good stuff. Funny stuff. Meaningful. I felt emotional and wobbly.

Mum, on discovering what she'd done, cried for two hours non-stop. 'I've ruined everything,' she bawled.

Me: No, you haven't. Besides, there's loads of other stuff. I can turn my attention to the remaining forty-two boxes . . .
Mum: I have! It's ruined! The book is ruined!
Me: No, it's not. I'm just going to have to . . . well, I'm now going to have to actually *write* it.

---

* Including a bad drawing of a wizard, a poem about corn on the cob and a series of pressed flowers Copydexed to pink cardboard.

In truth, she'd done me a favour. A memoir, after all, is as much about what you don't shine the light on as what you do. It's about judicious choices and edited picks. With that much primary and secondary source material, it would feel more like I was writing a biography than an autobiography. A biography of a shy person with limited social skills who collected pebbles and wrote bad poems and, bewilderingly, was obsessed with wearing kilts. That person was documented in so much detail, it didn't feel like me any more. I've outgrown me. I keep on outgrowing me.

Onwards . . .

If Mum makes herself feel safe by hoarding things, then Dad gets his sense of security from shedding them. For Mum the endless documents and pictures she keeps are like keys, keys which unlock emotional memories in extreme and dizzying detail. Dad's idea of hell is an emotional memory – for him life needs to be stripped bare of anything and everything extraneous. Dad experiences life through the prism of one thing – DATA.

Data is safe. Data does not lie. Data can be controlled. And that's why the world of patterns, information and numbers is the world my dad is happiest in.

Dad is basically the Matrix in human form. Every morning he wakes up, notes and logs the time of his waking, the atmospheric pressure on his barometer and the rainfall radar as indicated on the Met Office's website. Whereas I might be captivated by the skeins of pink in the heavens at dusk, he will be looking at his watch to check the exact moment the sun leaves the horizon. Whereas I'll be entranced by the sight of a wood-pecker boring into the ash tree in the garden, he'll be counting the exact number of pecks per minute.

It's not that Dad is emotionless. Quite the opposite. He is overwhelmed by emotion. He feels *too* much. And the thought of being overcome by sensation is so frightening that struc-tures need to be put in place to stem and control the flow.

Ever since I was a child, I've watched Dad codify his sur-roundings, obsessing over numbers and patterns, using stats and facts as a way of self-soothing. Nailing his life down to a series of fixed points gives him a sense of calm. It's perhaps inevitable that his eldest responded by being rule averse, dis-interested in boundaries and perpetually chaotic.

Since he first learned to write, Dad has kept a diary. He pre-fers a five-year diary as he doesn't need a great deal of space for his entries, which are, in essence, factual one-liners about events, climactic conditions and his children's height. When he turned seventy-five, he collected the data from the assembled diaries and boiled it all down into one single Mega-Journal. Finally, his life has been reduced to a series of clear, simple stats: 30 degrees, David born, Gerbil died, got cancer.

But more of that later.

I don't say all this to judge him; I say it (and he'd love this) as a matter of *fact*. I love him whatever. We all have our peccadil-loes. But the saddest thing is it doesn't matter whether I say that I love him or not as he will never read this book. Why? Well, certainly not because he's unsupportive. I can't think of anyone who has allowed me to be myself more. No. The fact is, reading this would make him uncomfortable. Squeamish even. He doesn't know how I'm going to tell the story, how many surprises the pages might contain. There would be too much emotion, too many twists and turns; the journey would make him anxious. He prefers Science Fiction. He likes his stories comfortably displaced to another galaxy.*

So there you have it. My parents. I grew up with the Hoarder Indoors and Rain Man.

* To my great surprise and delight he has read this. His comment? Good, but a few spaceships would have livened it up no end.

When Two Became One

My parents met in Brockley, south London, on 4 June 1966 at a party organized by my mum's school friend Christine Cavanagh. It's at this point I'll let the lovebirds take over and tell their own story, romantic and heart-warming as it is. This is taken, verbatim, from a recording made of them in the summer of last year.

I have asked my parents to recall the night they met. Mum tilts her head upwards, picking tiny sensory jewels from the black sky of memory. Dad has stomped into the study and fetched his diary.

Dad: Why have I got 'poaching' written in my diary?

Mum: *Pochin*. Pochin was Christine's maiden name.

Dad: Oh, right. [*Spends the next minute fastidiously cancelling and amending the entry*]

Mum: Your dad arrived on a motorbike. He was very memorable. He was wearing an orange Bri-Nylon shirt and very tight synthetic slacks.

Silence.

Me: What was Mum wearing, Dad?

Dad: Clothes. And a very heavy fringe . . .

Mum: Well, it was actually a hairpiece. Trouble was, I was laughing so much –

Dad: [*muttering*] Drunk.

Mum: – that it fell forward and got stuck there, low on my fore-head, for the rest of the evening.

Dad: What's the name of that character from *Planet of the Apes*?

Mum: Anyhow, your father came over to chat –

Dad: Cornelius. That's who she looked like.

Mum: He came over and his opening line was 'Hello, I'm a misogynist.'

Me: What?

Mum: 'Hello, I'm a misogynist.'

Dad roars with laughter.

Me: Was that your chat-up line?

Dad: Yep.

Me: What, always?

Dad: Yep.

Me: And how often was it successful?

Dad: Never.

Me: Ever think of changing it?

Dad: Nope.

Mum then embarks on an epic monologue, during which Dad closes his eyes and drifts off. After fifteen minutes of listening, I feel like I have drunk liquid morphine and every cell in my body is shutting down. I am now cutting to the end of her tangential mutterings to spare you, Dear Reader, the pain of the whole thing. Although I might release it as a download for people suffering from insomnia.

Mum: Anyway, his shirt was vile, and it created static when we danced . . . then we sat and had a chat and things went on from there . . . and then he got up and said, 'Well I have to leave, my mum will have done breakfast.'

I am suddenly alert again. Something in that last sentence hinted at potential gossip and/or excitement.

Me: What? Why? Why did he say that? Was it morning when he left?

Mum: No. His mum used to put his breakfast out the night before. And he needed to get back for it.

Me: Right . . .

Dad: [*looking in his diary and suddenly bellowing*] Seventh of October 1967!

Mum: We got married, and we had our honeymoon in Majorca at the Hotel Bahia Club in Paguera.

A profound and awkward silence as they remember.

Me: So . . . Did you enjoy it?

Long pause.

Dad: It was certainly the best honeymoon I've had.

Opening Night

I was born on 22 September the following year at East Dulwich General Hospital – ironically in the same ward that my father ended up in fifteen years later after another one of his 'accidents'.*

Me: Was I premature?
Mum: Yes, you were a week early.
Dad: I'm still not ready for you.
Mum: You were very little and thin but very beautiful.
Dad: You were a red mess.
Mum: And then a yellow mess.
Dad: Jaundice.
Mum: And that awful acne . . .
Dad: Waxy head, that's what I remember.
Mum: You fed every three hours.
Dad: She still does – have you seen the size of her?
Mum: We had to get your weight up to five pounds before you could leave the hospital.

A slight pause for Mum to catch her breath.

Dad: [*reading*] One foot five inches.
Me: What?

* Dad is notoriously clumsy. Notable accidents include: falling out of the loft head first, severing his finger on a ham tin lid and leaping backwards into a greenhouse while playing catch.

Dad: That's how tall you were when you were born.

Me: What? You measured me? You measured me when I was born?

Dad: No, the hospital measured you. I didn't want to go any-where near you.

At this point Dad buries his head in his stats book and produces a graph of my height and weight from birth right up to the age of twenty-two. At twenty-two I obviously found the strength to tell him that grown women don't tend to stand against an architrave and have their parents draw a pencil line above their heads. Again, he had nothing emotional or personal written down about that time, merely raw data. I'd been stripped to my essentials. Rationalized. Rendered. Made Statistic.

I understand it now – after all these years of raging I get it. The more he could associate me with mere facts, the more reassuringly distant I became. The less he had to engage with the idea of me being a living, breathing human being that he loved – that he might have to see hurt or ill or heartbroken. I wanted to say to him – I've always wanted to say to him – *There's nothing you can do, Dad. That's what life is. You can't just cherry-pick the nice bits and block your ears to the painful bits. Plus, in insulating yourself against the bad stuff, you miss so much of the good stuff. Don't you see?*

Mum had fallen suspiciously quiet. I always think something is seriously wrong if she goes without speaking for longer than thirty seconds.

Finally she punctured the silence. 'I think I've still got it.'

'What?'

'My diary from when you were born.'

What? You've got a diary as well. Oh God . . .

'I'll go hunt for it.'

'Mum, it's OK, really . . .'

She disappeared for some time. There was a scraping of boxes on the upstairs floor, then she reappeared brandishing a yellowing piece of paper.

It's rare that I'm lost for words, but this was one of those occasions. It turned out that my mum is *so* good at cataloguing, she even managed to keep an hour-by-hour account OF HER OWN LABOUR. You don't see that very often on *One Born Every Minute.*

The maternity unit of a busy London hospital. A fixed-rig camera looks down on a woman in the advanced stages of labour. There is the sound of medical equipment beeping.

Midwife: That's right, keep pushing!

The woman screams in agony.

Midwife: Come on, you can do it! Nearly there . . .
Woman: [*panting*] Please –
Midwife: Remember, push *down*.
Woman: Please, could you –
Midwife: Push *down*.
Woman: [*getting weaker*] Could you . . .
Husband: She's asking for something.
Woman: Please . . .

The husband goes over to her.

Woman: Please, my diary . . .
Husband: She needs her diary!

He rushes over to a bag in the corner of the delivery room and retrieves a small notebook. She lets out another bellow as the pain rises again. He hands the diary over; she opens it and starts writing furiously.

Midwife: I can see the head!
Woman: [*screaming*] What time is it?
Husband: It's 19.31.

She writes this down. Then screams again.

Midwife: Nearly there!
Woman: What's the name of this ward again?
Husband: Magenta Four.
Woman: Thanks.

She writes this down. One final, long wail of pain.

Midwife: There you are! You did it! It's a girl. It's a lovely little girl.
Woman: [*to husband, pen poised ready for the answer*] How would you describe the furnishings in here? Mustard? Taupe? Plain beige?

That's how stoical my mum is. A mere seven stone in weight, slap bang in the middle of labour pains, shoved in a cold bath and left there until nearly eight centimetres dilated – and she *still* manages to get in a diary entry. Screw you, Samuel Pepys, you lightweight. Try commentating on the Great Fire with a bowling ball pushing its way out your arse with just a little gas and air, and no man, woman or child to comfort you.

Here is Mum's entry.

21/9/69   6.00 pm mild backache.

10.30 pm bed but only
slept till 2.00 pm Backache
& tummy pains. Up again at
3.0.0 & 4.00. Then back to bed

4.45 – 8.00.
Made tea for Mum. Then went
into her bed. Bath.
Got up for breakfast at 10.00
went back to bed at 11.00 am.
Got up for lunch at 1.00 approx
But went back to bed at 2.00 –
pains more intense but not regular.
2.30 Bilious attack
3.30 ate orange
4.00 Bilious attack
Left to come up to London
Arrived DH Hospital 5.30 approx
5.45 Waters broke while waiting
in admissions

6.00 - 6.30 was palpated, shaved + had enema. Show of blood - rush after enema. Frightened me. Bath + then up to ward. Contractions every 3 or 4 minutes.

Into labour ward on F3.
Want to push (approx. 7.15)
Moved to Delivery room — can push. Used gas + oxygen. All very quick. Marvellous staff.
Baby born 7.50 pm 4 lbs 6½ ozs
Stitches put in by Dr. Handler about 8.45 pm. Then bed bath + entered ward at 9.45 approx.

Detailed, isn't it? Except for the actual *baby* bit, you know, the *important* bit. That part, well – it's just 'Baby born.' Notice I don't even get an adjective. The staff do. The staff are 'marvellous'.

'Baby born.' Ha ha ha.

Imagine. I *lived* with that.

I still think my favourite bit is when she has a bilious attack at 2.30 p.m. and thinks the best thing to do is have an orange. My mum is allergic to oranges. Always has been, always will be. Yet she thought that moment, that specific moment, was the right one in which to play Russian roulette with her digestive system. Unsurprisingly she has another bilious attack an hour later.

Question, Mum. Would an anaphylactic decide to have a handful of cashews just before their baby was born?

No wonder my sister Michelle thought twice about being associated with us.

Kindergarten and Junior School

Here are the things I learned from playgroup:

- If you spend the whole of the lunch break cutting the heads off Barbie Dolls, you tend to be left alone by everyone for the rest of the afternoon.
- If you know Anthony, then you are part of the cool gang.
- If you are Anthony's girlfriend, YOU RULE THE WORLD.

Anthony owned that playgroup. So much so, he didn't even need a surname. Like all true leaders – Hannibal, Alexander the Great, Chico – a second, family name was superfluous.

The playgroup that Anthony presided over was brutal – feudal – like a toddler's version of *Game of Thrones*. Justice was swift and merciless. Get on the wrong side of Anthony and he would bite your face, drive a buggy into your knees or smash a Fisher-Price My First Medical Kit over your head. The day he did the latter was, coincidentally, the day I discovered irony.

I don't know why Anthony and I hit it off. Perhaps I was the much-needed moderate queen to his despotic king. Perhaps my pudding-bowl fringe screamed, 'I was put on this earth to be your henchman.' Perhaps he was just looking for someone happy to go around saying 'Sorry' after he'd battered and smacked his way around the group. I don't know. All I know is that he hated everyone else. But he loved me.

Anthony's modus operandi was to be the first to everything: every toy, every experience, every break-time snack. I remember the teachers once organized a tea party. A vast array of sandwiches and scones and cakes sat on a gingham tablecloth behind glass doors in a prescient sign of what awaited me in adulthood. No sooner had those glass doors opened than Anthony steamed in, elbowing everybody out of his way, whereupon he firmly pressed his dirty thumbs into every snack in sight. There wasn't an egg-and-cress bap without his DNA on it, nor a square of Nimble without his fingerprints embedded deep into the dough.

I looked on with a mixture of awe and dread. It was like watching a rogue Staffie cock his leg against the opulent *fruits de mer* display at Harrods Food Hall – half of me was appalled, the other half applauded the sheer, glorious chutzpah of it all.

Anthony's finest hour came when the playgroup's new slide arrived. We'd been promised this new toy for weeks, and there it was in all its magnificent wooden glory. His eyes burned as he saw it wheeled into place. I could hear the cogs of his brain whirring, trying to figure out how best to stamp his authority on his peers once and for all. The teachers moved the slide into its new home, and just as they stood back to admire their work Anthony launched himself at the steps for the inaugural descent. Before the teachers could so much as shout his name, he had made his way down the chute and was standing for applause at the bottom.

Immediately I knew something was wrong. Pure instinct. Like when a rabbit sits up, alert in a field, and knows it's being stalked. Something told me I didn't want to go down that slide any more, and so I let my friends jostle past me to the front of the queue. Sure enough a few seconds later there was a loud cry. We all crowded around the slide to find a poor girl called Melissa stranded midway down, legs akimbo, buttocks seemingly glued to the wood.

I shot a glance at Anthony. The front of his trousers was soaked through. He had wilfully, deliberately pissed himself all the way down the slide. One thing I did know: wet slide, no glide. Not so much a scorched earth as a damp chute policy. And very effective it was too. Nobody but Anthony ever went on it again.

I don't know what happened to Anthony. He disappeared from my life as forcefully as he'd arrived. Back then he was deemed a 'little character'; nowadays he'd go by the slightly longer label of 'attention deficit hyperactivity disordered, oppositionally defiant'. I imagine he's now either in a penthouse office at Canary Wharf running Europe's finances or drawing pictures with crayons using his feet in a rubber room somewhere in a secure facility. With Anthony it could have gone either way.

After playgroup, Mum and Dad decided to send me to the local Catholic school.

Dad: Ronnie Corbett's children were at that school with you.
Me: Is that pertinent?
Dad: No, it's name-dropping.

The school in question was a little convent outfit in Sanderstead, just where the concrete of Croydon met the manicured park life of Surrey suburb. There were trees and front lawns and everything felt neat and clean.

The most exciting thing that could possibly happen at our school (or indeed I imagine at *any* school) was someone cracking their head open on the playground. We'd heard about this – someone said, 'Nicholas fell and cracked his head open.' *Open.* We imagined a head split in two, with blood and brains spilling out of it, and sat around in gangs at break praying for it to happen until the sight of a wimple sent us rushing back to class.

The nuns were a terrifying bunch led by Head Horror Sister Mary Dorothy. Sister Mary was old-school strict with an old-school belief in right or wrong – and by old-school I mean MEDIEVAL. It was bad enough I was a brunette (mildly satanic) with short hair (sorcerer's overtones), but the crunch point came when she discovered I was also left-handed (aka the full Beelzebub). Every time I sat down to eat in the school hall I found myself surrounded by wimpled women telling me to swap my cutlery around. Nineteen seventies beefburgers were rigid offerings at the best of times, but try cutting into one with a weak right hand that has never used a knife before. My brain would hurt and my fingers ache, but every time I tried to swap the utensils back, the nuns would descend again until I became exhausted and confused and tearful.

I started getting skinny. I started resisting going to school of a morning and became paranoid at mealtimes, wondering why my parents didn't swoop on me when I picked up my knife and fork in my usual fashion. Finally, Mum managed to get the truth out of me. Dad went very quiet. You only ever worried about Dad when he went very quiet. The next day he went in and 'had a word' with Sister Mary Dorothy, which involved backing her against a wall and telling her to leave his daughter alone. Effectively, he went a bit Liam Neeson on her ass. It's easy to see why – ask my dad to splay his fingers, and two on each hand are battered out of shape courtesy of the ceaseless rectifying ministrations of the Brothers of Holy Joe's School for Boys in 1940s Beulah Hill.

The other thing the nuns loved to do was make you finish your food. Not because there were starving kids in the world – oh no, they didn't seem too concerned with all that. No, they simply wanted to see a five-year-old face down in cold tapioca or collapsed in a puddle of viscous, greasy gravy.

One day I got locked into a war of attrition with a starchy ball of Smash instant mashed potato, which had been delivered lovelessly from the clutches of an ice-cream scoop. It sat there, and so did I. Neither of us moved. Neither of us was going anywhere. Sister Mary Dorothy did her rounds of the hall, wordlessly peering at our plates and dismissing those lucky enough to have finished. I had not finished. As she walked by, I nonchalantly flicked a lump of potato off my fork, which landed, by accident rather than design, just feet in front of her.

She carried on, polished shoes clicking on the polished floor, until her toes hit the tattie slime.

The rest was pure poetry.

My classmates watched as the Bride of Christ skidded, feet outstretched, until the wall provided a brake. There was a crunching sound and then silence.

'Has she cracked her head open?' said Thomas, the kid next to me.

'Maybe.'

'I think she has. She's cracked her head! She's cracked her head!'

A ripple of excitement went down the table.

I quietly picked up my fork with my right hand and let a little smirk cross my face. If you're going to be treated like a devil, you might as well behave like one.

Lesson learned.

Pets

A girl in a psychedelic dress, sporting a pudding-bowl haircut, approaches her father. She looks like Damian from *The Omen*, if Damian were a girl and liked psychedelic dresses.* Her father is busy 'doing stamps'. No one in the family knows what 'doing stamps' means, but it seems to involve him spending a lot of time in the box room drinking whisky and sobbing.

Girl: Dad?

Dad: What is it?

Girl   Can I have a dog?

Dad: No.

Girl: Dad, pleeeeease.

Dad: I said no!

Girl: [*a single tear forming*] But why?

Dad: Because pets die and leave you despairing and alone. [*Pause*] Pets are pain, Susan.

There is a profound silence. The girl walks slowly away.

I was six years old.

   Over a decade after I left home I discovered that my dad, as a boy, had owned a cat. He fed it raw fish every day, and it

* Don't believe that anyone could actually look like that? Turn to the next page.

slept on a rug at the foot of his bed every night. I don't know the name of the cat, because even seventy years on he finds it too sad to talk about. It is merely Cat. Nameless. Generic. All I know is that when Cat died, my dad never, ever got over it.

That's what pets were to him – unimaginable solace and unimaginable pain – in sparing us the latter, I guess it never crossed his mind he might have denied us the former.

I grew up in a nondescript road in a nondescript borough of London.

Croydon – twinned with Mordor.

It's less of a place, more of a punchline.

Croydon was like an airlock in the middle of the A23, a place neither one thing nor the other. It wasn't close enough to the city to feel like London proper, nor far enough away to feel like the bosom of green-belt Surrey. It was the poor relation of both town and country, mocked, maligned but with an enviable degree of office space. It was a place you went to get to somewhere else. It's all relative, of course. We'd come from Peckham, so it was paradise.

To give you an idea of what Croydon felt like . . . Every year there was a funfair on the Rotary Field. A sense of torpor hung in the air. The skinheads couldn't be arsed to spin the waltzer. Candy didn't floss. Bunting wouldn't flap in the breeze. Kids would risk injury standing under the swinging pirate ship in order to catch the coins as they dropped from upturned pockets. Every year we all queued religiously for the centrifuge ride. You know the one – it looks like a giant salad spinner in the sky. We queued and we queued and we queued. Why? Because word had got out that John Daniels' dad had detached his retina on that ride. That's the kind of place Croydon was in the 1980s. You joined a long queue of people waiting to spin themselves blind.

We lived on a wide road lined with silver birch trees, which held sway from my earliest memories right up to the time Michael Fish murdered them in 1987. A jumble of bungalows, 1930s semis and mid-century monstrosities lined the route like broken, wonky teeth. It must have all looked rather lovely once upon a time, when the suburbs were in bloom, but this was the 70s, and now concrete was king.

We moved there when I was barely nine months old, but I've seen photos of what our house looked like when my folks took possession of the keys. The outside was a dull cream, with coils of paint hanging from the bay windows like Hasidic curls. Green slate tiles, which resembled fish scales from a distance, decked the roof, and inside sagging ceilings held on to antique brass light fittings as if for dear life.

My parents set about getting rid of all that 'old stuff' as soon as possible – after all, it was the 1970s, and the phrase 'original features' was right up there with 'Baader-Meinhof Gang' and 'Vietnam War'. So out went all that junk and in came proper stuff – polystyrene ceiling tiles, neon strip lighting, endless miles of teak sideboards and a swirling Axminster carpet that gave you a window into what mild epilepsy might feel like.

Only one thing could make this concrete metropolis more perfect for a kid.

A dog.

Not even my dad's epic three-quarters-of-a-century grief was going to stop me in my mission to get a hound. So I wore my parents down with the most toxic weapon in my arsenal. My personality.

I tried again.

29 March 1976

A girl in a tartan kilt and thick tights with a pudding-bowl hair-cut approaches her mother. She looks like a Scottish version of Damian from *The Omen*.

Girl: Mum, can I have a dog?
Mum: No.

Girl: Mum, pleeeeeeease.
Mum: I said no.
Girl: [*plug of snot forming in nostril*] But why?
Mum: Because . . .
Girl: But why?

If my dad's reason for not having pets is that they will die and make you sad, then my mum's excuses are way more comprehensive . . .

Mum: Well, for starters, they're dirty. They're unpredictable. They transmit diseases. They can give you asthma, hives, ring-worm, roundworm, heartworm, tapeworm –

I am going to stop her in her tracks because that list goes on and on. What you need to know about my mum right now is this: she is a weapons-grade catastrophizer.* That is to say, she's a professional mountain-maker when only a molehill is called for. Give her an inch, she'll panic about running the mile. OK, let's return to the list.

Mum: – hookworm, toxocariasis, campylobacter, Lyme disease, scabies . . . oh . . .

Here it comes – the Big One.

Mum: . . . and rabies.

* Me: Mum? How many catastrophizers does it take to change a light-bulb?
    Mum: Change it? Are you out of your mind, Susan? You need a qualified electrician to do that. Sandra Harvey tried that and she was in hospital for a week.

Yep, just to reinforce the point, she'd dropped the R-bomb. Anyone who was a child during the 1970s understands the knee-jerk horror created by the mere mention of rabies. We grew up watching endless public service announcements – the whole of my childhood in fact felt like one long cautionary tale voiced by Donald Pleasance dressed in a Grim Reaper outfit. Many of these 'Charlie Says' information films were specifically about the dangers of slathering wild dogs (usually from France, of course), which could, at any time, cross the Channel and bite us into insanity.

The rabies thing worked. It was a while until I asked about dogs again.

My mum actually liked dogs. When she was little, her parents had bought her a poodle called Tracy, who turned out to be the only hypo-allergenic thing to have come out of the 1960s. After Tracy shuffled off her many mortal coils, Mum's folks invested in a series of ever-larger beasts, culminating in Dusty and Clyde – two vast and menacing Alsatians that looked like they'd run straight from Berchtesgaden. I was four years old when I first clapped eyes on them and was fascinated by Dusty in particular, especially when she was feeding. There was something about her powerful jaws as she crunched through lamb bones that intrigued me. So I decided to take a closer look. One dinnertime, as her bowl was put down, I decided to saunter over and get a worm's-eye view of her mouth in motion.

As my mum entered the kitchen, she was greeted by the sight of her four-year-old daughter lying on the floor, back of her head in the dog bowl, with Dusty's vast teeth clamped either side of her face.

Mum: [*suddenly very quiet*] Susan, what are you doing?

Me: I can see inside!

Mum: There's a good girl, Dusty, good girl. [*Trying to prise the dog's jaws apart*]

Me: It's dark. And it smells weird. Where does the food go?

Mum: [*sound of growling*] Easy now, easy now.

Me: [*pressure in my head growing*] My ears feel bursty, Mummy.

A pop as my head is released. There is a moment of calm, followed by the time-honoured Ann Perkins battle cry.

Mum: Bert! Get the Dettol!

As far as my mum is concerned, there isn't a single situation that can't be cured by either a.) a bath in Dettol or b.) gargling with TCP. Her anxiety is constant. Oftentimes I'll come home and she will have left a message on the answerphone like this one, which is taken, verbatim, from a recording in 2011.

'Hi. Just to let you know that I've heard from Jean about a new Yardie scam in London. They flash their headlights at you, and if you flash yours back, they'll steal your car and kill you. Thought you should know. Oh, it's Mum, by the way.'

Recently, while visiting them in Cornwall, I chucked a handful of dog biscuits on the lawn for my pet hound to sniff out. Mum immediately starting fretting.

Mum: Will they sprout?

Me: What?

Mum: Only your father and I have spent ages on that grass.

Me: Mum, they're dog biscuits.

Mum: Yes, but will they sprout?

Me: Yes, Mum, they'll grow into kibble trees, with pelletized dog-food fruit that will drop onto your lawn all summer.

There is no situation, however banal, that my mum can't infuse with dread. To read about a promotional credit card offer is to have it completed, sent off, card received, maxed to the limit and thence be whisked to debtors' prison. During the anthrax scare of 2001 she opened all her mail wearing Marigolds. One day, on returning home to visit, I found her bent over the steps to the front door, daubing the edges with luminous white paint.

'What are you *doing?*'

'These steps are a trip hazard!' she replied.

'What? Suddenly? Since last week?'

'Yes. Your dad's not getting any younger, you know.'

'He's *fifty-five!*'

'Yes, he's fifty-five *now*,' she replied – and carried on painting.

And yet, for all her anxiety, she didn't see the threat that lurked just outside her home. Despite all the consternation about poisoned Royal Mail packages and credit card debt, my mum seemed oblivious to the fact that she and Dad had chosen to buy a house *right next to* an electricity substation – a brick bunker hung with daisy chains of barbed wire and stock-proof fencing. There was even a massive sign, replete with skull and crossbones that said:

WARNING!
KEEP OUT!

But no. She was so concerned with what was happening within a six-foot radius of herself, she never even noticed I was living my entire childhood within sight of a sign reading:

DANGER OF DEATH

And thank goodness, because what I discovered for myself is that when the DANGER OF DEATH is permanently on your doorstep, it takes an awful lot to freak you out from further afield. I was fearless.

Pinky and Perky

A couple of years later my parents relented and got us two gerbils. Even though I was not the sharpest tack in the box, I was aware that the furry sausages shitting in the cage in front of me were not the Dalmatians I had asked for. My mum christened them Pinky and Perky because apparently (as I was duly informed) Christopher and Reeve were not appropriate pet names.

Never owned gerbils? Want to know a little more? At this point I defer to world-renowned gerbil expert Susan Elizabeth Perkins, aged seven. I have asked for the author's permission in publishing these extracts . . .

WHAT IS A

GERBIL?

What is a Gerbil?

A Gerbil is a member of the Rodent family.
It is a small creature and looks abit
like a Mouse or Hamster. Their fur is a
sandy coloured and the end of thier tail
is tipped with black. They also have soft
small ears, black inquisitive eyes and
fine whiskers. Gerbils are rather like miniture
Kangeroos.

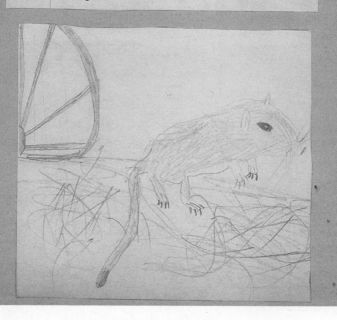

BREEDING.

Baby Gerbils.

Baby Gerbils look more like pink sausages than Gerbils at all. When they are born they are hairless and blind. The usual number of Gerbils born is about 5 though the female can have 1-10 babies in a litter.

When the Gerbils are born the Mother is always alert. If someone came in she would dart to the nest to cover them. She also is very aware of what her babies are doing and if one strays out she will pick him up by the scuff of its neck and gently puts it back.

The babys open their eyes in about 16-20 days and the fur starts to appear at about 10-12 days

My Gerbils have had 27 children. ✓

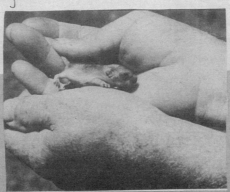

Now, my rule of thumb when it comes to choosing a pet is simply this: am I ever going to see it? In the case of the gerbils, the answer was clearly NO. Gerbils are nocturnal. And I, at the age of seven, was not. (Unless I'd been on a Robinson's orange squash binge, in which case this little soldier was going on a four-eyed 24/7 rampage.)

Our incompatible sleeping regimes meant I probably only spent about twenty minutes of quality time with our pets in just under four years. I say quality time; I mean grabbing them from their slumber and squeezing their back ends till their eyes bulged. The gerbils' main hobbies were eating a plastic wheel and defecating in a nest, both of which they appeared to excel at. I say 'appeared' – I have no idea, since everything they did was performed in the dead of night when I was out for the count.

In fact, the only time I ever saw my gerbil do anything, was when she ate one of her babies after my brother bombed down the stairs while giving a spectacularly rousing version of the *Batman* theme tune. This act of casual infanticide was the only thing I witnessed my pet doing in all the four years of its life. I was distraught. I was disturbed. But mainly I was confused.

Me: But why? Why did it do that?
Mum: Well, Susan, the mummy was protecting her babies.
Me: What? By EATING them?
Mum: [*leaden pause*] Yes.

I'm forty-five years old now, and I still can't see the logic in that. It's like worrying that your child might get bullied at school, so beating them to death to protect them.

They've got a lot to learn about motherly love, gerbils. Even now I can't listen to the opening strains of the *Batman* theme without thinking of that fat infanticidal mamma licking her lips in a now empty cage.

She may have been a slouch when it came to childcare, but Perky was certainly game in the procreation stakes. My mum had made it clear to Helen Banks' parents that she wanted two of the same sex. And yet, just a few months after taking receipt of them, in a miracle of same-sex breeding, six babies were born. And then another five. Then six again. Then seven.

Always one to turn tragedy into profit, I sold the babies to the local pet shop for sixty pence a pop. What began with a pair of nocturnal siblings, ended in a thriving cottage industry. Every month was like Christmas. I'd come down the stairs to find a writhing mass of pink four-legged sausages, like recently severed still-twitching fingers.

Once, a tiny baby escaped and made a bid for freedom behind the piano. We hunted high and low and finally had to assume it was dead. We lit a candle, said prayers – I may have even made a cross out of lollypop sticks. Those who say Catholicism can be easily sloughed off have never seen a seven-year-old give full burial rites to what basically amounts to a posh mouse. Two weeks later it turned up, alive and well, behind the sofa, where it had grown fat on a diet of discarded Marmite sandwiches and fluoride tablets. It was fat, feral and happy – with a set of gnashers more gleaming than Donny Osmond's. When I handed it over to the pet shop, I couldn't help but think they'd got a bargain.

My lack of interaction with them notwithstanding, when Pinky and Perky died in quick succession, I grieved like a drama-school Medea. Not only had I grown to love them, I had made a total of £23.40 out of them in a mere three years. Their death brought not only emotional pain, but my own personal credit crunch.

Dad knelt in the garden, Farah action slack stretched against beefy thigh, flicking the rigored corpses into an ice cream tub and thence into a hole in the garden.

'See, I told you,' he said, fixing his beady blue eyes on me. '*Pain.*'

Later the postman arrived and seemed to pay an awful lot of attention to Dad's frantic digging.

Mum: It was the time of the torso murders, so it looked very suspicious.

Me: What kind of torso could fit into a one-litre tub of Wall's non-dairy solids ice cream?

Mum: Oh, you'd be surprised. They can be very devious, these serial killers . . .

After Pinky and Perky we went through a period of what can only be described as pet surrogacy. Here are the creatures that passed through our doors.

Rollo the budgie

Dad was obsessed with Rollo the budgie and used to spend hours every day training him to say 'You bastard'. However, Rollo did not *want* to say 'You bastard' and therefore remained mute for the entire period of his stay. The next, and last, time Rollo came to stay with us, Dad renewed his efforts – staying up late into the night repeating the same phrase over and over and over again. Still nothing.

Rollo's owners came to collect him the next day. As his cage crossed the threshold, I heard Rollo mutter something. I couldn't be sure, but it sounded an awful lot like 'Thank fuck for that.'

Tasha/Kara

Kara, like her sister Tasha before her, was a Samoyed, a bright white husky as gormless as she was cute. And she was very, very cute. She belonged to our beloved family friends the Szilagyis, and we'd look after her when they went on their summer holidays. To say Kara shed fur was an understatement – she'd drop hairballs the size of fairground candyfloss wherever she went. Her finest hour came following a long walk after she had been put in the back of the car. Suddenly she caught sight of a squirrel and leaped straight through the back windscreen, leaving it in shards behind her. She didn't even feel it. Told you, gormless.

Unnamed hamster

I don't remember this creature's name – just his testicles. That's me for you. He arrived one autumn, and it became immediately clear the poor thing had a serious case of elephantiasis of the gonads. He looked like two beanbags attached to a pipe cleaner. We spent a few weeks watching him gamely lug his junk from one end of the lounge to the other, until his owners came back from a fortnight in Magaluf and our fun was over.

Polly the cat

Polly, or Pog as we called her, was our neighbours' cat – but as with most cats the concept of home was a movable feast. She used to occasionally pop round for some chicken and a cuddle, but she decided to come and live with us full time in the winter of 1999. She made her home on my dad's stomach as he lay sleeping on the downstairs couch. His insomnia had become increasingly bad, and he'd set up camp in the lounge so as not to disturb Mum.

Shortly after Pog started making pilgrimages to his tummy, he was diagnosed with colon cancer. There were operations which cut his already scarred belly into ribbons. Then there were the ridges of incisional hernias which followed. During this time Pog seemed to understand she shouldn't sleep *on* him, so lay beside him, purring like a pair of bagpipes cranking into life – a contented wheeze that was the soundtrack to his long road to recovery. After the hernias there were more ops. Radiotherapy. A year of chemo delivered through a Hickman line into his heart. She purred while his nails went black and fell out, while he bloated with steroids, as he crunched endless mints to get the metal taste from his mouth. She purred through the whole damn thing.

The Christmas after Dad got the all clear, Mum took a whopping seven-kilo turkey out of the chest freezer and stood it in a large bucket to defrost. We went out en masse to do some last-minute shopping and returned to find Pog in a state of some distress, dragging the bird around the floor, her fangs fused to the frozen meat. We didn't shout at her; Mum merely got out the electric carving knife, hacked off the entire breast that she'd punctured, popped it in the microwave and gave it to her to finish at her leisure.

A few weeks later Pog took herself off to die. We never got the chance to thank her, or to let her know that any one of us would have happily lain next to her, like she did with Dad, in her hour of need.

I did finally got the dog I'd always wanted. At the age of thirty-one. It turns out that Dad was right – animals are pain.

But what a joyous, joyous pain.

Nineteen

Describing how sound recording equipment worked in the 1980s to a teenager today is like a *Homo habilis* explaining how he used to slap mammoths to death to the *Homo erectus* who has just invented the spear. Even as you describe the process, you feel as obsolete in the world as the technology you're describing.

Well, kids, in the olden days, if you wanted to listen to music and most importantly find out what was number one, you had to wait until Thursday nights and *Top of the Pops*. For those too young to remember, *Top of the Pops* was a documentary about a group of predatory paedophiles set against a backdrop of disco music and early electronica.

My brother received a Prince cassette deck for Christmas in 1985 and immediately set about taping every *TOTP* he could. To do this, you had to get your recorder, depress the Play and Record buttons together and hold the machine directly against the TV speaker for the duration of the programme. The main problem with this method was that not only did it record everything on the television, but everything that went on in the background too.

What strikes me, listening back to these tapes, is not the quality of the music, but the relentlessness of my family's pesterings, particularly my mother, who made a beeline for us any time *TOTP* was on. Partly out of interest, partly out of an instinctive feeling that there was something not quite right with the presenters.

Spectacles

Transcript of tape recording made 28 February 1985
featuring Paul Hardcastle's '19'

Narrator: In 1965 Vietnam seemed like just another foreign war. But it wasn't. It was different in many ways – and so were those who did the fighting. In World War II, the average age of the combat soldier was twenty-six. In Vietnam he was nineteen.

In-in-in-in-in-in-in in Vietnam he was nineteen. [*Repeat*]

Mum: [*shouting from nearby room*] David!

Narrator: The shooting and fighting of the past two weeks continued today twenty-five miles west of Saigon.

Mum: David, are those your trousers in the bathroom?

Soldier: I really wasn't sure what was going on.

Narrator: Ni-ni-ni-ni-nineteen, ni-nineteen, ni-nineteen, nineteen.

David: Mum, shut up – I'm taping!

Narrator: In Vietnam the combat soldier typically served a twelve-month tour of duty, but was exposed to hostile fire almost every day.

Mum: Can you please come and pick your trousers off the bathroom floor?

Narrator: Ni-ni-ni-ni-ni-ni-ni-ni-ni-ni-ni-ni-ni-

Singers: Nineteen!

Narrator: Ni-ni-ni-ni-ni-ni-ni-ni-ni-ni-ni-ni-ni-

Singers: Nineteen!

Mum: They're a trip hazard, and you know what will happen if your dad gets his foot caught in them.

Narrator: Ni-ni-ni-ni-ni-ni-ni-ni-ni-ni-ni-ni-ni-

Singers: Nineteen!

Narrator: In Saigon a US military spokesman said today more than seven hundred enemy troops were killed last week in that sensitive border area. Throughout all of South Vietnam the enemy lost a total of 2,689 soldiers.

Mum:	He could put a toe into the gusset and fall. You know how clumsy he is.
Singers:	All those who remember the war They won't forget what they've seen Destruction of men in their prime Whose average was nineteen.
Mum:	David! Are you listening?
Singers:	De-de-de-de-de-de-de-de-destruction.
Mum:	This isn't a hotel.
Singers:	De-de-de-de-de-de-de-de-destruction.
Mum:	I'm not a chambermaid, you know. You're thirteen years old . . .
David:	Mum!
Narrator:	According to a Veterans' Administration study, half of the Vietnam combat veterans suffered from what psychiatrists call post-traumatic stress disorder. Many vets complain of alienation, rage or guilt. And some succumb to suicidal thoughts.
Mum:	You're big enough to bend down and pick up your own trousers, aren't you?
David:	Mum. SHUT UP!
Narrator:	Eight to ten years after coming home almost eight hundred thousand men are still fighting the Vietnam War.
Mum:	Don't you talk to me like that! You're not too old for a wallop, you know . . .
Singers:	De-de-de-de-de-de-de-destruction. De-de-de-de-de-de-de-destruction.
Mum:	I'm coming down. I'm leaving your trousers for you to deal with. Bert!
Narrator:	None of them received a hero's welcome.
Singers:	Ni-neteen.
Narrator:	Saigon Saigon Sa-Sa-Sa-Sa-Saigon Saigon.

Singers: Ni-neteen.

Soldier: I really wasn't sure what was going on. [*Repeat*]

Dad: What now, Ann?

Mum: There's a trip hazard in the bathroom! What on earth are you listening to, David?

Narrator: Ni-ni-ni-ni-ni-ni-ni-ni-nineteen.

Mum: Is there something wrong with the sound or does that man have a stammer?

Narrator: Vietnam Sa-Sa-Saigon Vietnam Sa-Sa-Saigon.

Mum: [*sound of heavy footsteps coming into the room*] And that's enough of that.

Tape ends.

Bitten

Everyone's first, and sometimes last, experience of acting is the school Nativity play. Remember the part you played? It's pretty easy to recall, isn't it, seeing as the cast of characters has remained unchanged for over two thousand years. Take a guess at what I played.

You: How about Mary and Joseph?

Me: Oh, don't be silly.

You: Little Baby Jesus?

Me: Per-lease.

You: The three shepherds around the manger?

Me: Nope, not even close.

You: [*getting exasperated*] The Three Kings who came from the east, bringing gold, frankincense and myrrh?

Me: Still wrong . . .

You: One of the angels?

Me: Now you're just taking the piss. Come on! There's only one character left . . . Yes?

You: Sorry, I've no idea.

Me: The fox! Yeah, you remember! The fox! You know, the fox. The fox at the Nativity? Come on, you must remember. Just to the left of the crib. The fox. You know – *the fox*.

Yes, that's who I played. A fox. I was the imaginary vermin that might have bitten the boy child Jesus and given him rabies *had I existed*. Though God only knows, had I been allowed to extend my role into biting the Saviour, I might just have done it, such was my frustration at the pitiful nature of my role.

A year later, after much jostling I graduated to fourth shepherd. Out of three. I didn't care; I got to wear a tea towel with a bit of old rope wrapped around it. I was living the dream.

Finally – after frantic lobbying bordering on stalking – I got the big one. An angel. Once again I rocked the Damian fringe, which made me look, in retrospect, less Right Hand of God and more Left Armpit of Satan.

It's no wonder I didn't get plum roles or perfect casting opportunities: I was freakishly pale and perpetually odd. Added to which, I was terribly shy with a mild stammer, and I couldn't look anyone in the eye. I know – fun, eh? Don't you want to invite the young me to *all* of your parties?!

So there I was, a weird conflicted kid, split down the middle, as riven as a floor tile. Desperate to be at the centre of it all but too afraid to do anything but loiter on the margins. A friend once described me as 'backing into the limelight', which is about the most accurate description of me I can imagine hearing.

At the edge of the school playing field, where grass met path, there was a run-down shed which went by the genteel description of 'the Pavilion'. The name conjures a village green – young men with oiled moustaches and pressed flannels endlessly rushing at one another, the soprano hurrahs of the assembled wives, the *chink* of bone china as the sun sets on Empire.

Our pavilion, however, amounted to a single cold room – no heating – with a desk at one end and a few chairs at the other.

At that desk, one day a week, sat Ms Carole Schroder, manicured and perfect, the sort of character you find in a Roald Dahl novel – suspiciously prim at first but who turns out to unexpectedly save the day.

I walked into that room a gibbering wreck. Week after week I was encouraged to stand up and read out painful, faltering renditions of Shakespeare, Wendy Cope and Pam Ayres. I began to learn about breathing. Cadences. Intonation. I began to relax. My voice became less staccato. I raised my head and looked out at the world. A few years later I walked out of that room able to speak clearly. Fluently. Finally, the voice coming out of my mouth matched the chattering inside my head.

Ms Schroder gave me the gift of speech.

And in doing so she created a monster.

In the early spring of 1983 the school production was announced, something modest that would befit our tiny little educational establishment in south London –

The Hobbit.

When J.R.R. Tolkien wrote his fantasy dystopian masterpiece, I believe he knew, deep down, in the back of his mind it could only *truly* be realized by a gang of thirteen-year-olds. I also feel *The Hobbit* was a particularly appropriate choice for a single-sex girls' school, since there are just *so many* women's parts in the book.

It became clear early on in rehearsals that we were all merely pawns in a much larger game, namely fulfilling the hitherto failed ambitions of a litany of English and drama teachers that had gone before us. Ambitious simply wasn't the word. Ridiculous, however, comes close.

Now I was able to speak properly, I had hoped for a starring role, a Gandalf or a Samwise Gamgee, but, as always, I ended up with something derisory – in this case third dwarf from the left. I was incandescent. This was, remember, WAY before Peter Dinklage as Tyrion Lannister made smaller folk sexy. In 1983 they were just, well, small.

I was Oin, brother of Gloin, distant cousin of Thorin Oakenshield (if you're interested). I had read the book and noted that they were northern dwarves, so gave my character a rich Yorkshire twang, based on a guy I'd seen birthing a calf in *All Creatures Great and Small*.

My line, and it was JUST ONE LINE, was:

'Never any sun.'

As parts go, it was pretty weak, though I fared better than my friend Sarah Ebenezer, who played a sheep. Now I don't especially remember sheep in Tolkien – though I'm sure some media student will have done a meta-critical study of ungulates in the Shire and will let me know otherwise. Having said that, I don't remember foxes in the Christmas story, and this casting came from the same imaginative source. Sarah's role, as the unnamed grass-muncher of the piece, was to wear a zero-visibility wire-mesh animal head festooned with cotton wool and make it through 'the forest' without shattering her coccyx. Crucially, she managed this for only two out of the three performances.

There were several problems with the show from the outset, not least my costume – a millefeuille of heavy woollens, with hessian pedal pushers that rode dangerously high up my dwarfish arse crack. Added to which my make-up made speaking virtually impossible. I say, make-up; it was essentially orange panstick and a beard.

Yes, a beard.

This was basically wire wool fashioned into Brian Blessed-style face-fuzz and glued to my chin with spirit gum. For those not used to spirit gum, let me illuminate – it's an industrial resinous adhesive with a high alcohol content. It's a solvent. My dwarf was about to become a glue sniffer.

So . . . to the show. My job was simply to say my line, then crouch down and hold a piece of cardboard battlement next to a load of other dwarves holding battlements. Together we formed a vast, yet ultimately recyclable, wall designed to with-stand an orc invasion. And, indeed, the sight of a line of schoolgirls about to hit puberty would have been enough to repel *all* marauders.

Finally, after what seemed an age of crouching and listening to other people mumbling through facial hair, it was my turn. I was baking hot, mouth dry and cracked, and feeling woozy from the glue fumes. I got up to speak and immediately wanted to vomit.

'There's never any t'sun!' I roared in a broad, generically northern burr. Silence. The silence I now identify with so many of my subsequent performances.

I waited. Nothing. I waited a little longer. Sadly, it seemed the udders of appreciation were dry.

I sank back down behind the cardboard battlements and once again felt the thick material of my costume chafing my Middle Earth.

'What the massive fuck was that?' hissed my friend Karen Flanders – also in full beard.

'What do you mean?'

'You're increasing your part!'

'What are you talking about?'

'You're supposed to say, "Never any sun," said a goblin who may or may not have been Helen Renwick.

'You said, *"There's* never any sun,"' spat Karen.

'So *what*?!'

'That's a 25 per cent increase!'

'And what's your point?'

'Actually, that's a 33 per cent increase,' said a nearby elf, helpfully.

'SHUT UP!' yelled the hobbit to my left. 'And hold that battlement straight, you twats.'

'Don't call me a twat,' said Karen.

'You *are* a twat,' I ventured, cleverly.

And so it went on.

As the Battle of the Five Armies raged above us, a battle of our own was developing behind that cardboard wall, which was now shaking with a mixture of hysteria and righteous rage.

'Some of us are holding our fortifications still,' said a smug little dwarf further down the line.

'Good for you! GOOD FOR YOU!' I responded.

'Your wall is wobbly.'

'Well, so is your goatee!'

'At least it's not real, like yours,' said Karen, still fuming.

I can't remember who won that day, but we can safely say it was not a victory for theatre.

That production stayed with me for a very long time – or at least the beard did. It took nearly three weeks to remove it completely, despite the best ministrations of my mum. Her medicine cabinet had been stocked with weapons-grade exfoliants in preparation for its removal, but that glue was stubborn stuff. For weeks afterwards my jawline was mottled with reactive red lumps and residual grey wisps. I looked like a pensioner with PCOS. In the end Mum went back to basics.

'Bert! Get the Dettol!'

Subsequently, I have watched the Peter Jackson films. I liked them. Although for me they will never have the rich dramatic resonance, the dizzying emotional range of that glorious, definitive 1983 stage adaptation.

The next year at school we did *Finnegan's Wake.**

After *The Hobbit* I graduated to something a little simpler – *Peer Gynt*, a five-act play in verse by Norwegian dramatist Henrik Ibsen. I played Peer's mum, Ase, an ageing peasant. If that wasn't already way beyond my range, this particular production was set, for reasons still unknown to me, in Northern Ireland. For three and a half hours the cast roared at one another like kids doing an impression of an adult doing an impression of the Reverend Ian Paisley.

My dad, under duress, came to the opening night and promptly fell asleep. Mum woke him every hour or so – 'to avoid him getting pressure sores' – whereupon he'd bellow, so the whole auditorium could hear, 'Bloody hell – is it *still going?*'

Some two hours into the play my character met her tragic end. My sister, eight at the time, was the only one of my family remotely moved by my death scene. As I extravagantly wheezed my way into the afterlife (screw you, Karen Flanders) Michelle shouted out from the audience, 'Daddy! Susan's dead!'

* This is a lie. We did Homer's *The Odyssey.*

Dad woke in an instant.

'Thank God. Does that mean we can we go now, Ann?'

I learned two things from this experience. Firstly, I wasn't cut out to be a proper actor. Secondly, when your co-star, a seventeen-year-old boy, says he wants to drive you to the woods for a walk, he doesn't really mean a *walk*.

Next on the list, after Tolkien and Ibsen, came Bizet's *Carmen*, a four-act tragic opera with full orchestra and vast cast. We didn't have a full orchestra; we had our brilliant music teacher Lora on an old out-of-tune piano. We didn't have a vast cast, so we joined forces with the neighbouring boys' school (who also didn't have an orchestra).

Of course, it didn't matter that there was no band. We weren't doing it for that. We were in the show because we were going to meet *boys*. Real, actual *boys*. Essentially this production was a 1980s Tinder, with arias.

The show was the passion project of a man called Roland, an unspeakably glamorous Italian teacher with olive skin and slicked-back hair. I imagine he wore pomade. Even though I have no idea what pomade was or is, it's exactly the type of unguent he would have smeared himself with. Rowland had all the zeal of Alec Guinness's character in *The Bridge on the River Kwai* – creating a doomed edifice to reflect his own inner glory, dragging a pack of disinterested kids with him. It didn't matter to Roland that none of us could really sing or play an instrument or speak French. It didn't matter. What mattered was that we gave it a go – and that was enough.

The boys and girls rehearsed separately for the first few weeks. We girls were mainly playing prostitutes, if memory serves – although we decided, tacitly, that we would play these prostitutes as kids who had Latin lessons, wore uniforms and were terrified of touching boys. I like to think it was a novel and refreshing take on the classic trope. If I thought *we* seemed uncomfortable, it was nothing in comparison to the lads. Instead of playing football, they found themselves being squeezed into gold bolero jackets, mouthing some homoerotic badinage about smuggling.

A fortnight before the show the two schools came together for rehearsals. The boys flooded into the school hall, and we gasped and giggled as their energies met ours. Lora thumped away at the piano, and Roland barked things in Italian, like '*Staccato*' or '*Lento, lento*'. We had no idea what he was talking about but were surfing a sea of hormones, so details like that didn't bother us.

And then *he* walked in. Late. Scruffy. Laughing.

Rob.

It was love at first sight – at least for me. Now I look back on it, he didn't so much as glance in my general direction, so it's fair to say Cupid didn't strike us with his arrow at the same time. Maybe the arrow went through me and clipped him a bit as it exited – collateral damage – so it took a while for him to notice I even existed. Who knows? Love is strange, and all you can do is go where it takes you with a modicum of grace and gratitude.

Rob was like Tom Cruise, only visible without an electron microscope. He had an unruly mop of black hair and stooped slightly, the way that tall men do when they are kind and self-aware enough to realize they are taking up too much space.

Our relationship proceeded like most other relationships do when you're that age. We met in car parks and drank cider. We sat for hours until our sciatics thrummed with cold, chatting and snogging. We broke up at parties after litres of Southern Comfort. We got back together after more Southern Comfort and woke together on floors, wrapped around each other, forgetting that there'd ever been a cross word. We dragged family and friends into dramas that burned themselves to nothing in a heartbeat. Yet it worked. It worked for over five years. I had no idea why.

In my last year of college we drifted apart into sharper versions of ourselves. Rob went away to Florida to work. I was supposed to go out and visit in the holidays, but the night before I was due to fly he called me and said he didn't want me there. He wouldn't say why. He sounded small. Far away. Much further than the 4,594 miles that lay between us.

I flew out anyway.

For the first night we were close. Intimate. The next day he seemed choked, like something invisible had him by the throat. On the third day he cried and then fell into a silence. On the fourth day he started talking. And talking. And talking.

It turned out that Rob was having a breakdown. It turned out that Rob thought he might be gay. It turned out that Rob had cheated on me.

The last time I truly recall us being together, as a couple at least, was in 1991, at our HIV test in a humid sexual health clinic in Florida. A video on the dangers of pubic lice was playing in the background, a monotonous voice-over laid on top of some crude animations of genital critters.

A big Southern mamma filed her nails and sang tunelessly into the hot, static air.

Bitten

Take the ribbon from your hair
Shake it loose and let it fall.

I sat on the porch as the receptionist typed up my notes. *Tip tap, tip tap.* The sun cowered behind the low-rises in the distance. The cicadas began to own the night.

Time to grow up.

High Days and Holidays

As a child my summers were spent freewheeling the pavements on my bike or loitering on corners trying to master the art of blowing bubblegum. Occasionally, if I wanted an extra adrenalin rush, I'd mix it up a bit and opt for a spot of low-level shoplifting. I only ever worked the small-time con – I left the big stuff to the pros – in fact my thieving ambitions didn't ever stretch much beyond the odd Yorkie bar, Sherbet Dip Dab or packet of sugar cigarettes. But damn, I was good. Real slick. I had perfected what I believed to be a fail-safe, as well as highly original, technique. I would take my brother David to the newsagents with me. He was young and cute and therefore beyond reproach. I would make him wear his heavy-duty parka come rain or shine, and I would secrete the stolen items in his fur hood. Then we would walk out of the shop bold as brass.

David was basically a cocoa mule – a kind of Klepto-Kenny from South Park. It was the perfect scenario – my hands were clean, his hood was full. What on earth could go wrong?

On the way home I'd pick the chocolate bars out from the folds of fur lining and eat them. Occasionally, he'd hear me munching, look up at me sweetly and ask, 'Chocolate! Where did that come from?'

'It fell from the sky,' I'd answer, and break him off a chunk by way of a reward.

'I'm really, really hot, Suzy. Can I take my coat off now? Please?'

As so often happens in these situations, I became a victim of my own success. I got cocky. I pushed my luck, started playing with the big boys – family packs, large Toblerones and my ulti-mate nemesis, the Terry's Chocolate Orange. You see, unlike a Caramac or a Milky Way, a Chocolate Orange doesn't nestle discreetly in the fake fur of a parka hood. No. It sticks out like a sore orange. A sore Chocolate Orange.

In retrospect, I got a few things wrong. Firstly, and most importantly, it never occurred to me to actually *buy* anything in the shop. A kid in a sweet shop *not* buying sweets – I mean, *repeatedly not* buying sweets – was only ever going to arouse sus-picion.

One particular afternoon, as Klepto-Kenny and myself made our casual bid for freedom, the light was suddenly blot-ted out. Mr Wesson, the shopkeeper, was standing in the doorway, barring our exit.

'Now then, I think you might be leaving with some things you haven't paid for . . .'

It's in these testing moments you truly know what you're made of. It transpires I am made of the yellowest custard of cowardliness, with a slight back note of chicken.

'It's him!' I squealed, pointing at David. At that moment, as I stared at my brother accusingly, I realized just how much I had overdone it. His hood resembled a bulging Santa sack, stuffed full of confectionery. So much so that the weight of it was pulling the whole coat back, causing the fabric around his neck to choke him a little.

'What? What?' squeaked David, his larynx crushed by the weight of a dozen Bounties and a box of Milk Tray.

'Now let's have a look here then,' hissed Mr Wesson, delving into David's hood and producing fistfuls of contraband. David was visibly confused; on the one hand traumatized that a burly stranger was rootling around in his coat, on the other, relieved that his airways were now becoming clearer.

'Well, I have no idea how those got there,' I asserted, followed by an accusatory 'David, what have you *done*?'

David began to wail – one of those soundless wails, all cartoon tonsil wagging. Boulevards of green snot appeared under his nose.

I wondered how bad it could get. There would be a custodial sentence, of course, but for how long? Weeks? Months? A year? But Mr Wesson was way more vengeful than that. He did something far worse than call the police. He demanded I went home and told my mum – *my mum* – and that the three of us returned to the shop to see him.

I remember the slow plod home – David, silent save the odd pained gulp and viscous sniff. My mind was racing. How the hell could I get out of this one?

I let myself in and wandered upstairs. I could hear her in the bath.

Me: Mum . . .?

The occasional splosh. Faint humming.

Me: Mum . . .?
Mum: What is it?
Me: Mr Wesson wants to talk to you . . .
Mum: Why?
Me: It was an accident. You see, some sweets, *accidentally* –

Mum didn't hang around to hear the rest. She leaped out of the water like Glenn Close at the end of *Fatal Attraction*. There was a blur of wet dugs and blind rage as she launched towards me. Game over.

One thwacked arse, a trip back to Mr Wesson and a thousand public apologies later, I returned home. Then my mum told my dad. Another thwacked arse and a thousand apologies later, things calmed down.

That evening Mum was busy cooking dinner. The reassuring reek of fried onions and grilled cheese floated from under the kitchen door.

'Susan! Hang up your brother's coat and come and sit down for tea, please,' she shouted.

I bent over to pick up the anorak. As I stood upright, there was a rustle as a Twix, hitherto hidden undetected in a fold of the hood, worked its way loose and fell to the floor.

Revenge is sweet.

We didn't go abroad as kids. Abroad was a dangerous place, which my mum would often mutter about.

'Felicity went to Tenerife and came out in terrible hives after going in the pool.'

'Did you hear about Muriel? I don't think her stomach will ever be the same after that mussels incident in Majorca.'

My childhood holidays were brutal one-day affairs that invariably involved the pebbled beaches and sub-zero waters of 'summertime' Brighton as their endgame. Mum and Dad shared a loathing of traffic and a love of driving in the pitch black, so we would leave at the crack of dawn, around 5.30 a.m. There we'd be, deep in REM, when we were plucked from our beds and bundled into the car barely conscious. It was essentially a kidnap with a holiday twist.

'Dad . . .' I'd mumble, my mouth still furry with sleep, 'why's it so early?'

'We want to miss the traffic.'

'I've made sandwiches,' said Mum, by way of placation, brandishing a wonky Marmite doorstop.

Even at that young age there were two key points I wanted to raise. Sadly, I was always too shattered. Let me now, as an adult, make them . . .

Firstly – and this one's for you, Dad – we lived in *Croydon*. Croydon is a mere forty-three miles from Brighton. We didn't need to leave at 5.30 to get there in good time. Next up, Mum, this one's for you. My digestive system, it's fair to say, has evolved into a fairly robust beast. But no one, no one *on this planet* wants to eat Nimble bread slathered in yeast paste AT DAWN.

By 5.33 a.m. we'd be bundled into the back seat and Dad would start the Austin Princess, which would rumble into life just loudly enough to mask the screams of the neighbours it had by now woken from their slumbers. A strong petrol reek filled the car.

Dad: [*cheery*] We're off!
Mum: Bert! [*Screaming*] MIND THE SIDES!

Mum and Dad never had a lot of cash, but my God they were wizards on a budget. It's fair to say that for them the Age of Austerity began at birth and will only truly end once I've taken full responsibility for them in their dotage. Then it'll be the full Werther's Original all the way, guys. Mum was born into the culture of make do and mend and has never quite left it. Dad, for his part, was unnaturally good at saving, and so, between them, they would occasionally have enough funds to embark on

MAJOR WORKS.

Every few years or so Dad would announce that he was 'doing something to the house'. This filled us with terror. Dad's only contribution to the canon of interior design was to insist on bright swirly carpets everywhere. Ev-er-y-wh-ere – including up the side of the bath. Rad, eh? Eat your heart out, Kelly Hoppen.

When Mum and Dad embarked on

MAJOR WORKS

disaster was never far behind.

One year they decided to spend all their savings repainting the exterior of the house.

Mum: I want it white
Dad: White is boring
Mum: It's traditional!
Dad: I don't like traditional. I'm not traditional. I hate tradition!

So they decided to get some swatches. So far, so reasonable. Paint swatches, however, are notoriously misleading, due to the fact they are

- Printed facsimiles that don't always bear much relation to the actual colour you'll get from the tin.
- Are usually about one centimetre long and three centimetres wide, so it's very hard to work out how a larger area might look.

What happens with 'normal' people is that they pick a couple of swatches, then buy a tester pot, then paint a largish section of wall so they can gauge how the colour works within the environment.

Not my parents.

Mum and Dad waited for a nice rainy day, just as dusk was falling, to look through the swatches. The perfect light, you'll agree, in which to make a large-scale paint decision.

Dad: [*giving a cursory glance, before returning to the football*] I like that one.
Mum: Oh, Bert! It's white!
Dad: No, it bloody isn't!
Mum: You said you didn't want white.
Dad: It isn't white!
Mum: Have a look at it!
Dad: You're bloody blind, woman! It's not white! It's white*ish* . . .

The clue was in the 'ish'. We should have known. Ish! You never trust an 'ish'. You don't go with an 'ish'. You don't let a sleeping 'ish' lie. This much I have learned.

So the masonry paint was bought, dozens upon dozens of litres of the stuff. No tester pots, no trial runs – they just flat-out went for it.

I remember coming home from school with Mum that afternoon. I remember turning the corner and being met by the sight of our house. Our nice, discreet little house was discreet no more. The formerly shy, shabby 1930s nonentity was suddenly and shockingly transformed into something you might find at Disney World, or in the grounds of a Victorian stately home whose owner had been driven to folly by the ravages of tertiary syphilis.

Even Mum stopped talking for a split second. As if on cue, Dad appeared from around the side of the house.

Dad: [*cheerily*] What do you think?
Mum: Oh, Bert! BERT!
Dad: What?
Mum: It's pink!
Dad: No, it bloody isn't!
Mum: Have a look at it!
Dad: It's not pink!
Mum: Yes, it is!
Dad: It isn't! It's pink*ish* . . .

Yes. As pinkish as blancmange. As pinkish as baby sick. Pink. Ish.

So, back to our 'holiday' to Brighton. We are in the car and my mum is screaming, 'Bert! MIND THE SIDES!'

Here is the thing. When Mum and Dad decided more
MAJOR WORKS
were needed, they opted to splash some cash on a garage. Our local builder Pat, as always, was on hand to help. Now Pat was a lovely man, but on the official cowboy scale he ranked somewhere between Billy the Kid and Buffalo Bill. He had many skills, but mathematics was not, it transpired, one of them.

In his build calculations Pat had made a key error. He made the garage too narrow at the front, and *even more narrow* at the rear. Once constructed, we discovered that the inside of the front half of the garage was just four centimetres wider than the total width of the car, but hey, that was roomy compared with the back.

'Shit. Want me to bin it and start again, Ann?' Pat had said blithely on discovering his mistake.

'Not at all, Pat,' said Mum, with a passive aggression I have, apparently, gone on to inherit.

Mum and Dad could have parked the car outside the house, on the roadside, but no. They had paid for that garage and they were damn well going to use it. Parking meant painstakingly edging the nose of the car inside, until the backs of the wing mirrors hit the entranceway. Only the bonnet was hidden from view, the rest of the car stuck out, proudly, arse to the elements.

In order to exit safely without scratching the paintwork, it would routinely take my dad a good two or three minutes from turning on the engine to finally hitting the road.

Back to our 'holiday'. It's 5.33 a.m.

Dad: We're off! [*Putting the gearstick into reverse*]

He edges out of the garage at roughly the speed of evolution.

Mum: [*shrieking*] You're clear on the left! Watch the wheels!
Dad: We're off! [*Again, as if trying to convince us*]
Mum: Bert! MIND THE SIDES!

5.36 a.m. The excitement of departure over, tiredness would hit me, whereupon I'd black out.

We would arrive in Brighton around 6 a.m.

Let me tell you, 6 a.m. wasn't the romantic time it is now, with people making artisan bread, taking Bikram yoga classes and sipping on their barista's best Chai latte. NO. This was the 1970s, and 6 a.m. was a brutal hour. Nothing was open, no one was out, and no fun whatsoever was to be had.

'Are we here?' I murmured.

'Is it morning yet?' whispered Michelle.

'Would anyone like a Marmite sandwich?' said Mum brightly,

holding aloft something brown and sweaty wrapped in cling film.

'What now?' moaned David, in and out of consciousness.

'We wait,' said Dad like some kind of Fair Isle-wearing ninja. And wait we did. We waited and we waited. Occasionally we'd drift off, only to be woken by a savoury waft as Mum unwound the cellophane to check on the mummified sarnies beneath. We waited for THREE HOURS until the shops opened. I say shops; it was actually only one shop we were interested in – the fudge shop.

Finally, nine o'clock would come and the fudge shop would open. We'd run in, buy a block of rum and raisin and rush out. Thirty seconds later it was all gone.

Then came the sugar rush.

As we hit peak hyperglycaemia, we'd get booted out of the car for some enforced 'fun'. This took the form of swimming. Brighton is famed for its sole-splitting pebbled beaches; what's perhaps less well known was the sheer volume of dog shit and used needles on them in the mid 70s. We'd pick our way through the obstacles, with the promise of the black sewage-streaked waters of the English Channel in front of us. Happy days.

'Help me, Mum. Please! I'm dying!' I'd say, shivering piti-fully on the shingle after my brief dip.

'Nonsense, it's refreshing,' said Dad, who hadn't set foot anywhere near the water.

'Sandwich?' said Mum, proffering a boomerang of bent dough with Stork margarine oozing from its sides.

It took me the best part of a decade to realize why we'd leave so early. It wasn't because Dad wanted the A23 to himself (and he's welcome to it), and it wasn't because they were wor-ried all the fudge from the fudge shop would get eaten if we didn't queue outside from six in the morning. No, Dad wanted to leave early so he could be home in time for 12.15 and *Grand-stand*.

By the time midday struck we'd all be back home, coma-tose, with ripped feet and spiked insulin levels. Whereupon we'd pass out again until the sound of the vidiprinter and Dad's wailing (as Charlton Athletic got held to another no-score draw) echoed round the lounge.

By 5 p.m. we were awake again, somewhat bewildered, won-dering if we'd made the whole thing up.

'You ready for tea?' said Mum. 'It's Marmite sandwiches . . .'

Old south Wales and the newsagent of doom

One year, we tried to have an actual holiday. You know, a *holi-day* – where you go away for somewhere *longer than six hours*. Dad had decided it was high time we visited his favourite place in the whole world – Wales – specifically the Gower. So far, so glorious. But, because this is Dad we're talking about, this wasn't going to be your normal tourist pilgrimage to the gor-geous sands of Pobbles, Three Cliffs or Rhossili Bay. No. Dad wasn't interested in beaches or countryside or scenery or any of that nonsense. The only reason he was going, and by exten-sion *we* were going, was because he wanted to find a newsagent.

'What do you mean, a newsagent? We've got one of those down the road,' shouted Mum, on learning of our destination.

'It's a special one. In the Gower.'

'Why on earth do you want to find that?' said Mum.

'I went there as a boy. I want to see if it's still there.'

'Was it a particularly *nice* newsagent?'

'Perfectly pleasant, thanks. Now I'm going to get the car out. I'll see you outside in ten minutes.'

And that was that.

Our accommodation was a static in a 1970s caravan park. For those unfamiliar with statics, they have all the worst aspects of caravanning without the one redeeming feature: mobility. I can remember the tang of chemical toilet, the endless grey concrete, but most of all I remember the rain. I have never known rain like it. It started raining the moment we arrived and it did not stop for one single second until we left. It was the sort of rain that ate at your bones. The sort of rain that turned the sky to slate, so that day was indistinguishable from night. It drummed relentlessly on the roof and hit the windows like hysterical toddler tears.

It rained so hard that my eardrums held the memory of it for weeks. You know when people have a leg removed yet still have a sense of it being there, post-amputation? A phantom limb? Well, I had the same sensation with the sound of rain. Even after the deluge the echo of it lingered faintly in my eardrums.

In these conditions the static caravan quickly went from what we had hoped it would be – an occasional base – to a full-time prison. Within hours of our incarceration, the five of us had descended into open warfare. We screamed and shouted and lashed out. After one particularly fraught exchange, Dad chased me in circles around the minute lounge area with a hair-brush, like a coiffeur Jack Nicholson in *The Shining*. Mum ended up having to pacify him with a lukewarm Fray Bentos pie.

After three days of breathing each other's stale air, we finally donned full waterproofs and headed out for our trip. The fury of the rain on the car roof meant that all conversations inside had to be bellowed at full volume.

Mum: WHERE IS THIS NEWSAGENT?
Dad: WHAT NEWSAGENT?

Mum: THE ONE YOU'VE DRAGGED US HERE TO SEE.

Dad: I TOLD YOU – IT'S IN THE GOWER.

Mum: BERT, THIS *IS* THE GOWER! THE GOWER IS SEV-ENTY SQUARE MILES! YOU'RE GOING TO HAVE TO BE MORE SPECIFIC!

Dad: WELL, I THINK WE SHOULD KEEP LOOKING – TRY SOME OTHER STREETS. I MAY HAVE GOT IT WRONG.

We carry on. Mum lapses into silent fury. Dad circles the roads for hours, slowing at every shop.

Mum: [*barking, as dusk starts to fall*] DO YOU THINK IT MIGHT HAVE SHUT DOWN? IT WAS THE LATE 1940s LAST TIME YOU VISITED . . .

Dad: FINE. WE'LL STOP THEN. LET'S JUST PULL OVER AND GET THE KIDS SOME CRISPS.

We drive for another hour. It transpires every single newsagent in Wales is shut.

Dad: I WONDER IF THE CHIP SHOP I USED TO GO TO IS STILL HERE?

Not one of us replies.

Sometime in my early teens my maternal grandparents decided to move, like so many other nouveau riche, to the Costa del Sol. I never really understood how they made their money, only that they ran a car dealership in south London and that my granddad was in the Masons. To my mind, the Masons was an organization so scary it ranked somewhere between Opus Dei and the Ku Klux Klan, where hooded men sat around and whispered about the Rotary club or how to influence the planning guy at the council.

I loved the idea of Granddad being in a secret society, especially since someone at school told me the Masonic induction ritual involved holding a compass in your right hand while dropping your trousers. Why I had no idea. Perhaps Masons were required to be able to find north in all situations, including when caught in flagrante. Anyway, if it is true, it's one in the eye for all those who say that men can't multi-task.

From looking at my granddad, you'd deduce one of two things: he was either a car salesman or a Caucasian Huggy Bear impersonator. He was permanently encased in sheepskin and always behind the wheel of a Mercedes. On Sunday he and Grandma would turn up for lunch in a brand-new car, straight off the forecourt. Next week a different one would get a spin. I am not one for cars, but even to this day I get a visceral thrill from seeing a vintage Benz – the bulky SEs, the pillar-less coupés and my favourite, the 1969 280SL in black with cognac interior. Strange how we fetishize our past. I couldn't give a monkey's about the car I drive, but the thought of that one . . .

My grandparents bought a flat several floors up in a whitewashed high-rise in Torremolinos. Yes, my friends, they were living the expat dream. England had gone to the dogs, while Spain was a promised land of whitewashed high-rises, displaced bank robbers and knackered beach donkeys.

We visited just before my fourteenth birthday. It was my first time on a plane. It was the first time I'd seen the sun. I immediately went from Nosferatu to lobster, before peeling and turning Nosferatu again.

We lived off rugby-ball-shaped loaves of *pan rustico*, which would go from fresh to stale in twenty minutes. We drank Fanta through straws, which made it automatically 100 per cent more exotic than the same stuff we'd guzzled out of cans back home. At night we would wander in T-shirts along La Carihuela staring at the craftsmen and their stalls – a toothless man selling statues made from torn Coke cans, a hippy with amber eyes and skin like tobacco leaves, weaving strips of leather into bracelets. It was unbearably exciting, the bustle, the heat, the energy. What's not to love about a country where even the question marks fly in the face of convention¿

By the time I finished school I had travelled to London, to Edinburgh and to most of the fast-food outlets of the Costa del Sol. That was it. I was no different from my parents, whose sole lifetime excursion, excluding those I've mentioned, was a brief trip to Malaga. I'll let them take over.

Dad: We were on a bus.

Mum: It was heaving. Full. Rammed full of Spanish.

Dad: Who else was it going to be full of? We were in Spain . . .

Mum: I had you [*Me*]. You were ill.

Dad: She's always ill . . .

Mum: I think it was whooping cough.

Dad: It was a cold.

Mum: It was whooping cough. I did all the checks.

Dad: Anyway, I had David. And he suddenly started kicking off and screaming, so I thought I'd pick him up. I held him up in the air. Cut a long story short, he pissed in my face.

Me: Pissed in your face?

Dad: Yes.

Me: What? What, did he have no nappy on? Was he just a naked baby on a bus?

Mum: You have to remember, Susan, it was the 70s.

Me: Well, what happened after that?

Dad: Well, everyone stared at me. And I smelled. And then it dried. And then I think we went back home. Is that right, Ann?

Mum: [*very quietly*] Yes.

Their honeymoon they also recalled in loving detail.

Dad: [*getting down his dossier from the shelf and reading from it*] Seventh of October 1967, Paguera in Majorca.

Me: Thanks, Rain Man.

Mum: The Hotel Bahia Club. We still have the ashtray from it.

Me: Why?

Dad: Good question.

Mum: Because it hasn't broken yet.

I love that. That sums up my mum in one sentence. Why keep something? Because it isn't broken. Retain until destroyed. Cling on until obliteration. Never give up, never surrender. Ann Perkins is the veritable Buzz Lightyear of all things, including love. I often think to myself, *Why do they stay together, these two people – through thick and thin, through depression and anxiety, through sickness and health?* And there is the answer. Because, as stretched as it may be, it simply hasn't broken yet.

It was my relationship with Rob that really opened the doors to international travel. He was a man of the world, having been to Portugal and everything. A year before the sadness of that clinic in Florida we headed off for a holiday in Los Angeles.

Rob and I decided to visit all the theme parks we could while we were there. Perhaps subconsciously we wanted to do something innocent and childlike together in the midst of the increasingly grim realities of adulthood. It was a terrible idea. I'd had an overwhelming fear of roller coasters ever since John Daniels' dad detached his retina that time so anything more rigorous than a teacup and saucer ride is guaranteed to render me giddy with terror. As we approached the entrance to Six Flags Magic Mountain, I started to feel anxious.

Me: I hate rides, you know I hate rides . . .
Rob: This isn't a ride, I promise you.

We join a snaking queue of hopped-up adolescents, nervous and not sure what to expect. Sure enough, as we get nearer the entrance, I see the telltale health disclaimers.

Me: [*suspicious*] What's this ride called?
Rob: It's not a ride! Stop worrying!
Me: Yes, but what's it *called* . . .
Rob: ISN'T THIS FUN! [*He shouts in what I take to be an attempt to mask the screams coming from above*]
Me: Why does it say you have to declare if you have a heart condition?
Rob: Oh, you know Americans . . .

It was too late. No sooner had my eyes seen the legend FREE FALL than I was bundled by a joyless teen in a branded T-shirt into the cart. As we started to move, all became clear. Rob had got me there on a technicality. No, it wasn't a ride, it was a drop. A sheer drop. A high-speed zero-gravity drop to the centre of the earth. The bars clamped down on my knees, and up we went, up to more than a hundred feet.

'Isn't this fun?' screamed Rob again, quickly followed by 'Don't cry.'

Once we reached the top, the cage came to a violent halt. Then it moved forward a little. I could see the whole of North America laid out in front of me. There was a grinding of metal, a slight pause and then we were let loose.

You know those cartoons? Where the character suddenly drops, but leaves something of themselves behind? That's what happened with my stomach. As my body fell, my guts resolutely remained in the same place. They passed up my windpipe and seemed to hang in the breeze, until some complex bit of intestinal wiring forced them back down and inside again.

We ended up upside down, braking sharply, the roots of my hair stiff with fear.

'That was great!' roared Rob, quickly followed by, 'Susan, would you like me to call someone?'

The next day we went to Universal Studios, where it was agreed we'd do something more sedate. The ET ride seemed like a decent compromise. There was an element of roller-coaster elevation (albeit at 0.2 mph) for him, with a good dose of the sentimental and the infantile for yours truly. Now, the best thing – the *wonderful* thing – about the ET ride was that you got to say your name into a voice-recording machine as you went in, so that ET could say goodbye to you, personally, when you left.

So I said, 'WANKER.'

It really is impossible to overestimate how thrilled I was as I mounted that bike and slowly ascended to the bright moon above. Fibre-optic stars glittered in the black drape of night as the sound stage swelled with the luscious sounds of John Williams' strings. And, as I began my descent, there he was – ET, arm outstretched, finger lit.

As I glided past he murmured in that distinctive timbre, 'Goodbye . . . WANKER.'

There was a moment, just a moment, when I felt like the funniest person in the world. I was poleaxed with laughter, tears running down my face. And then I heard ET continuing, behind me:

'Goodbye, dickwad!'

'Goodbye, flange face!'

'Goodbye, numb nuts!'

That wizened foul-mouthed alien was spewing the most awful filth. It turns out I wasn't the only one who'd had that idea. Word had got out and now EVERYONE IN THE WORLD WAS DOING IT.

They've shut it down now – that ride – something to do with 'people abusing the system'. It's terrible, really. People are awful, truly awful. But, as ET would say, 'Fuck 'em.'

Nowadays I love nothing more than holidaying in the UK. I love the landscape, the people, even the weather, Nothing beats Sennen Cove in December, with the wind whipping at that empty curve of white sand. The Dales, shrouded in autumnal mist. Glencoe at dusk. I often stay in National Trust or Landmark Trust properties – mainly because they're beautiful, but also because I get to play my favourite game of all time, Spook the Tourist.

The beauty of this game is it requires only three things – a pen, the visitors' book and your imagination. The aim of the game is to unnerve the next guests as much as possible by detailing you've experienced ghosts or paranormal phenomena during your stay. If you're playing this game for the first time, here are a few sample suggestions, taken from entries I've made.

- Lovely comfy bed, gorgeous views – but what was scratching at the bedroom door all night long?!
- Great cottage, although I avoided the lounge. Had the feeling I was being watched in there!
- Came here for a long weekend with the rest of the investigative team. Can't believe we finally saw the infamous Grey Lady! With love from the Solihull Paranormal Society.
- Sorry for the breakages. We came down to see the plates flying off the dresser! PS Where are the cushions in the main bedroom from?

Enjoy!

TWO

Cambridge 1988–91

Go East

I was far from a model pupil at school – not badly behaved as such, just . . . well, *distracted*. Sadly, *distracted* looks an awful lot like *badly behaved* to members of the teaching profession.

I can be devastatingly obtuse when the mood takes me. I certainly wouldn't want me in my class. Recently I was handed a children's book called *All Dogs Have ADHD* by a friend of mine. It was an OK read – I got through most of it in twenty seconds to be honest. Sadly, I didn't get the chance to finish it as a squirrel caught my eye in a nearby tree. It was only then I realized it had been less of a reading suggestion and more of a diagnostic tool. Oops.

I'm an all-or-nothing student. I get As or Es, distinction or fails, firsts or thirds. If I'm interested in something, then I'm fanatically interested. If I'm not, then I'll make my excuses and leave, disrupt the lesson or try to make a large hat or makeshift cape out of any bits and bobs to hand.

Chemistry interested me right up to the point I was banned from setting anything else on fire. Biology interested me until they wanted me to toy with the insides of a dead frog. Arithmetic started well but hit a dead end once they got our art teacher, Mrs Samson, to stand in for our maths teacher for a term. Mrs Samson was, I believe, the first maths teacher to wear a smock, and certainly the first to do equations in watercolour. Crucially, she knew exactly as much about maths as the eight-year-olds she was teaching.

In our first lesson we examined the relationship between

fractions and decimals. In that lesson I learned that half of something equates to 0.05.

Yes, 0.05.

It all went downhill from there.

In my penultimate year at school a careers adviser from London came to visit us for the day. The idea was she'd briefly interview us about our likes and dislikes, then give tailor-made suggestions for our potential life journey. My classmates filed in one by one, and one by one she told them, in a bored monotone, that they'd make good secretaries. All of them. She told *every one* of the thirty people in my class that – except me.

She told *me* I should be a dentist.

When I said that I didn't want to be a dentist, and that I had almost zero interest in teeth, she gave me a long hard stare and scribbled something in her notebook. When her report came back, it said that I should maybe apply to a polytechnic to do a subject other than English.

That was the exact moment I decided to study English.

I've never really responded to peer pressure. What I do respond to, however, is someone categorically telling me I can't do something. I trill at the sound of a gauntlet going down. It feels like a dare. And I've *never* been able to resist a dare.

That night I vividly remember going home and asking:

Me: Mum, what's the best university?
Mum: [*carving a Viennetta*] I don't know. Ask your dad.

I wander into the lounge, where Dad is shouting at the Charlton Athletic result.

Me: Dad, what's the best university?
Dad: How would I know? One of the rowing ones, I guess. Cambridge? Yes, Cambridge, I think.

So that sealed it. That's where I was going to go. I was going to Cambridge to study English.

I have no idea why Cambridge took a punt on me and asked me for an interview. My O-level results had been average at best (As for the subjects I enjoyed, Cs for the subjects I didn't). I suspect my wonderful music teacher Lora stuck her neck out and gave me a decent reference. Either way, in the autumn of 1987 I received notice that I was to come to New Hall and be interviewed by the senior tutor.

There are three parts to getting into college: the interview, the offer, then getting the grades. I was now one third of the way there.

Or 0.03 of the way, if you prefer it in decimal.

That morning Dad woke me at first light and inched out the dun-coloured Peugeot so I could climb in.

'BERT! MIND THE SIDES!' shouted Mum from the front door, still in her nightie and slippers.

I'd barely slept but felt awake, skin prickling with excitement – the first flickering of my now constant colleague adrenalin, I guess. I'd never been east before. I'd never really been anywhere before – so I nestled back into the faux-suede seat and watched the landscape flattening to greet the rising sun.

Looking back, whether it's true or not, that day feels like one of the very few times as an adult that Dad and I spent any proper time together. He was ever-present in my childhood – waking us every morning before he went to work, returning in time for dinner at 6 p.m. sharp to share some jokes from his day. He bookended my life from the moment I had a conscious thought right up to the point I left home. The morning routine never varied in all that time. At 6.30 a.m. exactly there'd be his lumbering tread on the stairs and the clank of cups on metal tray. Slowly we'd stagger like zombies (in varying states of annoyance and doziness) into our parents' room. We'd sit on the carpet and I'd sip on cold milky tea each and every single morning until I was old enough to tell him I actually liked it strong with one sugar and just a splash of the white stuff.

Dad was particularly good when I was sick, which was often when I was little. There'd be the comforting sounds and smells of Mum busy in the kitchen, and then Dad would materialize out of nowhere, brandishing a bottle of Lucozade. I remember the rustle of gold cellophane, the dizzying fizz as it opened, that particular stinging sensation in my nostrils. Then he'd settle himself down on the side of the bed to deliver the next instalment of my favourite story, Sammy the Squirrel.

There wasn't much to Sammy, other than he appeared to live a relatively uneventful woodland life in a support group for alliterated animals. Other members of this group included Henry the Hedgehog, Richard the Rat and Deirdre the Deer – not forgetting their nemesis, Wicked Willie the Wolf.

I loved those stories as much as I loved him, although strangely they have left me with a pathological fear of chains of words with the same first consonant. These feelings will often overwhelm me, particularly in the refrigerated section of an M&S Food outlet. I can't tell you how incendiary I find those pre-packaged tropicals – Mango Madness, Fabulous Fruity Fingers, the Perfectly Pointless Pip-Riddled Pomegranates. It makes me want to commit a Motherfucking Murder Medley.

When we finally arrived at New Hall that October morning, I thought I'd just be an hour or two – a quick 'Hello, yes, I know I don't belong here, goodbye' – but it transpired I needed to do an interview, an exam, another interview and then an analysis of the exam. I'd never been so scared. Dad stood there, looking lost in his threadbare camel coat. What would he do in a place he didn't know – for a whole day? His answer was:

1. Locate the nearest tea room.
2. Analyse the height, depth and width of the scones on display at the counter.
3. Order the scones with the largest surface area.
4. Eat scones.
5. Leave the tea room, carefully counting the number of steps between there and the next available tea room.
6. Order scones at the next tea room.
7. Using a stopwatch count how long the scones take to arrive.

8. Eat the scones.
9. Pay for the scones while calculating how much they would cost in francs, Deutschmarks and pesetas.
10. Leave the tea room and head off in search of another tea room, keeping note of how many blue cars seen on the way.
11. Repeat from 1.

At 5.30 p.m. he came to pick me up, his arteries lined with clotted cream and his collar caked in scone dust. By that point my head was buzzing with the possibilities of a brave new world: Marxist dialectics, post-structuralism – a subsidized bar! We drove home in the rain, the earth rising to greet the setting sun. I knew some-thing had changed – that I was about to let loose my family moorings and become my own person. I didn't think that exact thought, as such; I was just aware of that moment being tinged somewhat, that moment of being a kid, in the car, with her dad – and how goddam transitory and precious it all was.

On 5 January 1988 I found out I'd been offered a place, but it wasn't until a summer's morning six months later that I found out I'd actually got the grades I needed to get in. These were still the halcyon days of the Royal Mail – when something you sent arrived at its destination rather than boomeranging to a depot in an industrial estate on the A406. These were the days when you knew the name of your postman (Bill), and that Bill would be there at 8.20 every morning and 12.30 every afternoon.

The morning my exam results were due I leaped from my bed at dawn, crept downstairs and made a beeline for my par-ents' drinks cabinet. I instinctively knew this wasn't one of those moments when you could countenance being sober. My arm snaked past the dusty decanters and old sherry bottles to the very back, where I pulled out a neglected bottle of cheap whisky.

I loaded up a tumbler and sneaked back to bed. By the time Bill arrived at 8.20 on the dot, and the metallic snap of the letterbox rang through the house, I was properly, properly blotto.

I still remember opening that letter. I remember every second of it. I remember how small the envelope was, and how thin the paper inside – as if it had done everything it could to belie its own significance. I remember the black punch marks of the typewriter and the indented lines and curves that spelled my future. I remember the thump of my pulse in my neck.

It felt like my whole life was on that page.

I read its contents and breathed out. I noticed a peaty stink as I exhaled. I wandered into my parents' room. They were both in bed with the sheets up above their heads, waiting – as terrified as I was. I guess I knew, and they did too, that this wasn't just a certificate. It was a passport.

I remember saying my grades out loud, woozy with booze, and them leaping into the air like the Buckets in *Charlie and the Chocolate Factory*. There was a sudden blizzard of threadbare sheets and handmade quilts. It wasn't just my joy, it was our joy. It wasn't just me heading off, it was all of us – the Perkins and Smiths and beyond – the countless generations of car dealers, midwives, soldiers and charladies. Here we all go, onwards and upwards, until the next generation comes along and mercifully outdoes us all.

Finally I could start to make plans for the intervening year. But that was going to cost money, so I had to resort to the worst thing imaginable to any seventeen-year-old.

WORK.

I'd had a Saturday job since I was fourteen, chambermaiding at a family friend's hotel. It mainly involved hoovering architraves and cleaning toilets. I earned £7.50 for a morning shift, which I'd spaff on fags, vodka miniatures and pick 'n' mix sweets. Once, after cleaning a particularly unpleasant bog bowl, I realized the Arab gentleman responsible for the eruption was still in the room, dozing under a pile of blankets.

'You. You come here,' he growled exotically as I made to leave. I approached the blankets. His breath smelled of something I can, with hindsight, now identify as halloumi. He grabbed my hand and opened my fingers. 'You take this. For your trouble.' Christ, but his intensity was captivating.

Something heavy fell into my palm. We locked eyes for a moment. I headed for the door, but it wasn't until I was outside that I allowed myself to look at my booty.

A kilo of half-eaten pistachios.

It was then I realized the service industry was not for me.

In 1988 Sherratt and Hughes bookshop was a rare jewel in the brutal concrete coil that was the Whitgift Centre, Croydon. It was an independent outfit, struggling to avoid the clutches of increasingly expansive chainstores. Most importantly, and most memorably, you could smoke on the shop floor. Baby, you could smoke *all over it*.

Smoking was my hobby. It remains the only thing I have ever been really good at and truly committed to, so working there was my dream job. It was a dream job, with dream colleagues,* but with a business model doomed to failure as the dark shadows of corporate branding and mega-bucks bullshit loomed.

Every day I'd pitch up around 9.30 a.m. and sit at the till,

---

* One employee, Stephen, ran the Business Books section downstairs. We were all a little in awe and in love with him. He was older, in his early twenties, and a graduate. Impossibly cool. He introduced me to the short stories of a new writer called Ian McEwan, who he suspected would go on to great things. Stephen now runs one of the most august publishing houses in the world. I'm so proud one of us at least has gone on to do something decent with our lives.

puffing away like a bastard. There was no dress code and we were actively encouraged to read at our stations. I never once took my eyes off the page. I read and read. Then I smoked and read some more. This approach had its pros and cons. On the plus side, customers never felt pressurized by any of the staff and browsed at their leisure. On the down side, the store had one of the highest rates of shoplifting in the south-east. Apparently one bloke would come in every week, regular as clockwork, carrying a large empty cardboard box. He'd proceed to fill it to the brim with bestsellers, then walk out, bold as brass, with it over his head. We only found out a year later when we had CCTV installed. We hadn't even noticed.

Every Tuesday we'd open the shop late, and instead of serving customers spend that first hour telling each other what books we'd read. We'd take notes, get recommendations, widen our horizons. It meant that when someone asked us to suggest a damn good read, we were better equipped to answer them. See? I told you. *Terrible* business model. With that level of care and love it could *never* have worked.

My regular dealings with the general public meant I got an awful lot better at lateral thinking.

Shop doorbell goes. Customer enters.

Woman: Excuse me? Do you have *Tess of the Duracelles*?
Me: Absolutely, madam. [*Heads for Thomas Hardy's* Tess of the D'Urbervilles]

Shop doorbell goes again. Another customer enters.

Man: Do you have *Rogit the Dinosaur*?
Me: Rogit the dinosaur?

Man:	Yeah. I'd never heard of it. I think it's a kids' book.
Me:	[*thinks for a second*] Here you go. [*Hands over* Roget's Thesaurus]
Man:	Cool. [*Looks inside*] Where's the pictures?

After nine months there it was time to go on my travels. I'd earned enough cash to get me on a plane to New York and thence on an Amtrak train down the East Coast. I went with my wonderful friend Polly, who had friends in America. This was unbelievably rad. The furthest-flung friend I had was from Caterham.

It was the little things – chewing on a bagel in Grand Central Station, looking out from the top of the Empire State, seeing steam billow from the street vents. When you're young you don't care that you're chasing clichés. You're unfettered by embarrassment, the need to feel 'unique' or 'independent'. You just pick the lowest hanging fruit, and it tastes bloody great. We spent two days in Manhattan, too overwhelmed and jet-lagged to venture beyond Midtown. Before we knew it, it was time to get to Penn Station for our ongoing train.

We were only a few blocks into our walk when I experienced my first and, thankfully, only mugging. As a woman of the world (and my mother's daughter), this was one of four dangerous scenarios I'd been preparing myself for while in the States – alongside rodeo riding, gunslinging showdowns at High Noon and being held hostage by a family of inbred rural banjo players.

This turned out to be no ordinary mugging, however – this was America's Most Benign Mugging.

As we trundled our suitcases along Avenue of the Americas, we were joined by a tall guy with a salt-and-pepper beard and dark, tatty clothes, who ambled alongside us.

| Man: | Morning, ladies. Can I carry your suitcases? |

Me:	[*brusque*] No, thanks. We're fine.
Man:	Come on now . . .
Polly:	Really, we're OK.
Man:	Now, ladies, I think you should let me.
Me:	We can manage.
Man:	I said, I think you should let me, you know?
Polly:	Don't worry.
Man:	[*getting exasperated*] Girl, are you getting me?
Polly:	Not really.
Man:	I'd like to have your bags, please.
Me:	That's not necessary; we can carry them.
Man:	[*increasingly menacing*] Don't make me ask you again.
Polly:	You don't need to ask us again. We've said no . . .
Man:	Damn it, girl!
Me:	Really, we're just fine. They're on wheels.
Man:	Jesus. I'm gonna have to get old school with you . . .

And with that, he grabbed my shoulder bag and ran off.

I was left with a confusing set of emotions. On the one hand, I was relieved that we hadn't been the victims of America's Most *Violent* Mugging, on the other, curiously furious that he'd been so polite.

Me:	I mean, he *asked* for our bags. *Asked for them.* What's that about? It's confusing. He's being a gentleman and a thief at the same time. Talk about mixed messages.
Polly:	[*wisely*] Americans are weird.
Me:	I mean, if you're a criminal, just be a criminal. It's them and us. Perpetrator and victim. There should be a moral distance between the two.
Polly:	It's confusing.
Me:	Yes! He asked our *permission.* Like he was getting us to collude

with him. I feel dirty. I feel like I'm an accessory to my own crime . . .

Polly: Mmm. Can we get on the train now?

In reality, all the Gentleman Mugger got away with was a handful of traveller's cheques (good luck cashing them, even in the 1980s) and a selection of hand sanitizers provided by my mother.

'You'd better take them. I bet there's threadworm in the Big Apple, and you know how that's spread – from toilet seats to bums to hands to *your hand*. YOUR HAND!'

I like to think of him, the Gentleman Mugger, back at his underground lair, tipping out the contents of my shoulder bag and examining the booty before exclaiming wisely, 'The English are weird.'

Two months before my first term at college, my reading list arrived – on *headed notepaper*. Suddenly it was official. In celebration, I headed to the shops to buy the next best thing to books – chocolate, fags and whisky miniatures – none of which, I noted sadly, seemed to feature as course requirements. Dad volunteered to come with me, which I remember thinking was odd. Dad never went with me *anywhere*. We headed there in silence, bar the adhesive tug of our shoes on the hot summer pavement.

'Well done,' he finally said. 'Well done.'

'Thanks, Dad.'

He stopped and turned to me.

'One thing.' I could see that his eyes were brimming. 'Make sure you don't become posh, eh?'

New Hall

I didn't know what he meant until I arrived. You can't underestimate what a shock it was for a girl born and swaddled in the
concrete of south London to see something as truly beautiful
as King's College, Clare Chapel or the Cam River wreathed in
mist. How impossible it was to try to accept, even for a
moment, that you might belong there. (I didn't. I don't. I
won't.)

New Hall, as it was then (it now has a new name – Murray
Edwards College, named jointly after the inventor of Murray
Mints and Huw Edwards*), was rumoured to have been built
according to the designs of a Swedish prison. Yes, Dear Reader,
you heard correctly – a Swedish prison. Apparently, the specifi-
cations were originally intended for a jail outside Stockholm,
but the Swedes rejected them. I'm not sure why. Had they
hoped for something a little more classical? Doric columns?
Pediments? Balustrades? Or maybe something stucco? Mock
Tudor? Perhaps I'm just being snotty in assuming that people
would have stipulations for penitentiaries that involved anything more ornate than a.) very high walls and b.) A MASSIVE
LOCKED DOOR.

Anyway, for whatever reason, the Swedes turned down the
plans. Fair enough. It's the next stage that interests me. What
on earth made someone then think, *OK, we're not going to use
this design for a maximum security stronghold, so . . . let's use it for*

---

* This has not been fact-checked.

*a single-sex college in Cambridge! It's a directly transferable struc-
ture, after all. Both sets of needs are exactly the same, aren't they?
Aren't they? Anyway, the girls won't mind – they've only been allowed
to take degrees at the university since 1948. They're just delighted to
be there. Plus, worst-case scenario, if they do kick up a fuss, we can
just LOCK THE MASSIVE DOOR on them.*

To give you an idea of the look of the place, think brutish St
Paul's. Or concrete Taj Mahal. In modern architectural par-
lance you might get away with saying it had 'clean lines' – but
this was the late 1980s, and back then it was simply 'ugly as all
shit'. Long wide concrete boulevards stretched from the
entrance. A murky shallow pool ran parallel to the main walk-
way, decked with algae and pigeon shit – in the days before
Pigeon Shit was an aspirational paint colour.

The college's main claim to fame (other than being the only
guaranteed escape-proof structure in East Anglia) was that it
had a hydraulic canteen. I am not sure whether this particular
feature was part of the original Swedish schematics. Perhaps it
was a ploy to distract and entertain the inmates with an ascending buffet. We shall never know. Certainly, *Orange is the New
Black* would be a very different show had the Federal Department of Corrections had an ascending buffet. No one would
give a toss about stalky ol' Suzanne 'Crazy Eyes' Warren or the
evangelical mutterings of Tiffany 'Pennsatucky' Doggett;
everyone would just drop their makeshift weapons/dildos and
watch in awe as Galina 'Red' Reznikov mechanically rose from
the bowels of the refectory.

Dinner took the form of classic mass catering, but with a
few twists. Firstly, once weekly, there was Formal Hall, which
essentially meant same food, different outfits. New Hall prided
itself on being a more relaxed and informal college: larger state
school intake, less traditional in its outlook. Even so, every

Thursday we had to don long black gowns when we ate in a nod to wider university etiquette. It was all a little Harry Potter, but without the fun of the Sorting Hat after dessert.

The catering team were veritable spin doctors. Their primary skill lay in creating a deeply mediocre pile of food and then putting a lady's name on the end of it – think Chicken Barbara, Lamb Diane and Guinea Fowl Cynthia – as if somehow that addition would work a kind of culinary alchemy. That suddenly the viscous puddle of grey gravy cosseting even greyer meat would become interesting. Romantic, even. In reality, each and every plate that hit the table was a triumph of hope over experience.

I'd specified on my application form that I would prefer to share a room in my first year, thereby acknowledging I considered loneliness a fate far worse than the possibility of being hacked to death by a total stranger while sleeping. Although I had seen the college at my interview, I'd never actually visited the halls of residence. So it was a surprise when I first clapped eyes on my accommodation.

F18 was a split-level room, with steep open concrete treads leading to another room upstairs. At the foot of the treads there was a large glass window. Waiting. Inviting me to get drunk and fall through it. I smashed against it many a time, but with too little force to shatter the glass, although my friend Jamelia went one better and leaped clean through hers during a heated debate at a Black Causus meeting. Her brave political gesture became the stuff of legend – tempered only by the fact she lived on the ground floor and was therefore able to break her fall with a gentle forward roll.

Essentially, our digs were open plan – affording roughly the same level of privacy as a flannel wash in Paul Dacre's office. I arrived first, no room-mate in evidence, so decided to climb the treacherous stairs and make my nest in the mezzanine. In fact it was pointless worrying about where to put my stuff, because there would have been no boundary strong enough to keep out the woman I ended up sharing with. Enter the irrepressible Shayla Clare Walmsley.

Shayla was unlike anyone I have ever met before or since. The term 'whirlwind' isn't wild or chaotic enough to describe the mass of raw energy she was fashioned from. Quixotic? Yes. Maverick? For sure. Welsh? Utterly.

Shayla was the first person I'd met in my life who was genuinely *different*, something other than the nice, monochromatic, lower-middle-class girls I knew from Croydon. Her otherness thrilled me to the point that ever since I met her, I've been looking for that shock of the new in everyone else I've encountered. She stormed in that afternoon, a corona of cigarette smoke over tangled red hair. Then, emerging from the fug, came a pair of Deirdre Barlow glasses and a syrup-thick Caerphilly burr.

'Who the fuck we go' ure?'

It turned out that Shayla had never met anyone from the south-east before and therefore had a few preconceptions. It was only when she asked whether I owned my own pony that I felt I needed to disabuse her of one or two of them. What started out as an awkward, self-conscious cultural exchange developed seamlessly into a unique and peculiar friendship. I say peculiar; it must have looked like abuse from the outside, she and I permanently slagging and jostling one other. Robust. Honest. No prisoners. And just bloody, bloody wonderful.

Shayla gave me two key things – firstly, a working knowledge of Spanish. She was a light sleeper and most nights would wake bellowing, '*¿Donde está, Eduardo?*' in a gruff and thoroughly convincing Andalusian. She had spent her year off riding horses in the Spanish hills. I'd worked in a bookshop in the Whitgift Centre. That sort of sums us both up, really.

Secondly, she loaned me some of her derring-do. Shayla threw herself at everything with an almost suicidal force. 'DO IT!' she would shout if I expressed the faintest interest in something – often accompanied by an impromptu grab or slap. 'DO IT! DO IT! DO IT!'

'I'm thinking of invading Nantwich.'

'DO IT!'

'I've always wondered what it might be like to milk a pig.'

'DO IT!'

'I'm thinking about forming a funk and soul collective with Eamonn Holmes.'

'DO IT!'

By the end of the first week of the first term Shayla had spent her entire grant (yes, we had them back then, children – as we basked on the sunny plains of state funding) on a box of contact lenses, a semi-permanent wave and a pair of stone-washed dungarees. This was back in the days when contact lenses needed to be hand-rinsed in a vat of chemicals and hung on a washing line to dry overnight.

Shayla had never had money before, and boy could she burn through it. Within seven days of starting college, all she had left to her name was a tenner.

That night, as we sat eating potatoes out of a can ('I spect you're used to caviar, love'), I expressed a mild interest in going to watch some comedy later at the Footlights Club Room.

'DO IT!' she said. 'Do a spot, an open spot!'

'What? No! Don't be silly.'

I could feel her fingers digging into my bicep.

'Ten quid. I'll give you ten quid. Go on! DO IT!'

By now she'd worked out I couldn't resist a dare.

'Go on. DO IT!'

So I did.

I loved her. I loved the bones of her.

Cambridge was also the place I met my brilliant beloveds, Nicola and Sarah. Nicola hailed from Essex and wore a full hunting outfit to her interview 'so they won't forget who I am'. (They didn't.) Sarah spent most of her undergraduate years in a pair of orange tie-dyed trousers bellowing, 'Who's got weed?' They're family, but without the burden of my genetic material. They're my rocks, my touchstones, my sounding boards. Together, we're proof that good things can come in triangles. Together, we're the unholy trinity of silly. Lucky me.

As for Shayla, we had a spat – over a boy. The three of us got close in our final year. It turned out that the boy liked me. It turned out she liked the boy. I bowed out, and they ended up dating for a while after we graduated, but the damage was done.

Stupid kids.

I saw her sporadically after we graduated. Well, twice. Twice in all those years, and yet not a week went by when I didn't think of her. There would always be something: a Welsh lilt, a raised, excitable voice, the impetus to do something wild and rash. It all reminded me of her. I'd go online and find hints of what she was up to: community work, teaching in Tower Hamlets, fostering big 'bad' Staffies. She could and would love the unlovable with a fire you couldn't put out. The more I heard about her good heart, following itself so clearly and purely, the more shame I felt about my rather tawdry and venal one.

I got the call last year as I was heading into the garden to hang out some washing. I vaguely recalled the voice at the end of the phone – as faint as all yesterdays. An old acquaintance from college seemed to be telling me that Shayla was dead. How very strange. If my brain didn't quite register it, then my body did. I lost my legs. I lost my legs and sat slumped on the floor, sobbing, with a wet bra slung over my shoulder and a tea towel hanging somewhere round the back of my head.

Oh Shayla. Oh Shayla, what have you gone and done now?

Shayla can't be dead. Not Shayla, with her lioness heart and flaming hair and bottle-top glasses. Not her, with that firm grip on my forearm, leading me off to try something daring and life-affirming. Who will push me now? Who will tell me to DO IT if not the Architect of Crazy herself?

A week after the news, and just before her funeral, I sat at my desk as I had often done over the years and tried once again to see if I could find her online. I typed in her name. In the blink of an eye I got 19,000 results. I looked through the first few pages, only to find the same out-of-date references and articles. Nothing I could have used to connect with her. I'd tried. I'd tried before – I'd sent emails into the ether – and nothing.

And then, halfway down the page, I saw it. Her Twitter account. She'd had a Twitter account. I clicked on it and up popped the face of my beautiful larger-than-life friend – head thrown back, mid-roar, as always. I could still hear that husky laugh in my ears. And then I saw, underneath her photo, two words:

FOLLOWS YOU

If I think about it too much, I cry. I cry because after all those years of silence she was one simple click away. She was only ever and always one click away.

I owe you, you infuriating, brilliant Caerphilly nightmare. I owe you always. Because if you gave me my first gig, then you also gave me the greatest gift that came with it:

Melanie Claire Sophie Giedroyc.

Melanie

I met Mel at that first open spot gig in the October of 1988. I had been at college less than a week. Here are a few basic things you need to know about her:

1. She is two years older than me.

Actually, that's it. That's all you need to know.

So where were we? Ah yes.

'DO IT,' said Shayla, when I told her I might, at some point, want to give performing a try. 'I'll give you a tenner if you do.'

DO IT. DO IT. DO IT.

And so I did.

That night I headed down to the Footlights, Cambridge's comedy club, with a few random jottings in my hand. The Footlights is one of the most talked about, and most shrouded in mystery, of all university societies. How do *you* picture it – if, indeed, you care to picture it at all? Perhaps you see it as a sort of light-entertainment wing of the Bullingdon Club, where men with red cheeks and even redder chinos bray at one another like coked-up donkeys.

Toff 1: Hugo, is your pa still running *The Times*?

Toff 2: Totally, but he's off to Deutsche Bank in the summer. Is yours still selling arms to Sierra Leone?

Toff 1: God, yah. Now listen. Lollo and his chums are coming for sups at my rooms tonight. Fancy it? There'll be totty for sure. We're talking about some new thing called a dot.com start-up. You game, old chum?

Toff 2:   Yah, bloody yah.

The truth is way more prosaic. The Footlights Club was a tatty little room in the basement of the Cambridge Union. It had a dusty, beer-stained carpet and benches upholstered in fake leather ran along each side. These were invariably decked with a multitude of props – rubber chickens, Swedish-blonde wigs, moustaches and sombreros. All the important stuff. And there, at the back of the room, was the stage, a slightly raised dais onto which a spotlight was trained. Maybe two. A deep fug permeated everything, no matter what time of day you entered the room – a perma-stink of booze, fags, fun and shame, the key notes of any comedic perfume.

I cannot overstate what an unprepossessing space it was (and most likely still is). It didn't resonate with a sense of its own history. It didn't feel momentous or special. It was just another damp, stinking student hole. The posters on the walls, some from the 70s, were tatty and unframed, the black curtain hanging at the back of the stage as ripped as a witch's hem. But I loved that. It's not a museum – it doesn't look backwards. It's a clubroom. It's for the *now*. It's a dirty bustling hive of success, failure and silliness.

History is reality distilled, events boiled down to a manageable partisan narrative we can easily remember. The Cambridge Footlights history has been duly reduced to the select list of those who 'made it' (Cleese, Cook, Idle, etc.), whereas the real lifeblood of the club came from the vast numbers who went on to do proper jobs. Oftentimes those people were the funniest – the ones who went on to be vets or gynaecologists or chemical engineers. My business isn't, as I'm forced to admit daily, a meritocracy.

To be part of the Cambridge University arts scene, and the Footlights Society in particular, was a pure privilege. The *people* weren't particularly privileged; they were just nerds with good A-level results. The absolute privilege came from the ability to experiment. To do *anything* you wanted. Want to tour Europe in urine-coloured leggings with a same-sex production of *King Lear*? Here's the cash. Want to put on Lorca's *Blood Wedding*? In Spanish? Naked? Knock yourself out. Hell, if I had the power, I'd make every community, college and university arts society as well funded as the ones I was lucky enough to be part of as a student.

At night the place came alive, transformed from generically unpleasant basement to Britain's most exciting underground lair. And on one of those evenings, in the middle of October 1988, I walked down there, scrap of paper in hand, and took that single step onto the stage. It often still strikes me how small a distance it is, that walk from real to heightened – from normality to performance. One small step for a woman, one giant leap for your adrenal system. How quickly we can move from one part of ourselves into another. How performance formalizes that. How, if you're not mindful of the gap, it can split you in two.

I remember the singular glare of the spotlight, blocking out everything. I remember my ramblings being accompanied by the drunken burble of the crowd, sometimes listening, sometimes not. I remember I was wearing a hot, red lambswool jumper and that my neck starting itching furiously mid-routine.*

But most of all, I remember Mel.

She was standing at the back of the room at the end of the

* Because I'd not had the time, skill or indeed motivation to craft anything in advance, this 'routine' mainly consisted of wry observations about the journey from college to clubroom that I'd taken some thirty minutes beforehand. On the plus side, no one could say it wasn't fresh material.

show, a shock of white hair and wayward teeth. She wore pink DMs and ripped jeans and was gassing with a gaggle of students wearing what looked like pyjamas.

She sidled over to me and introduced herself like some postpunk Svengali, and we got chatting. I couldn't tell you what we chatted about. All I can tell you is that there was just a feeling – that most perfect of feelings – a slow, unfolding understanding that I had met a person that I would know for the rest of my life.

Mel and I didn't work together much at college – on account of her being *so much older than me*. In my second year (her third) she went off to Bologna and power-ate spaghetti for a year. In many ways this was training for what was to come in our later careers. While she was gone, I spent my days trying to bluff my way through Jacobean tragedy and Anglo-Saxon, Norse and Celtic (boy, is it hard to bullshit in Norse). I spent my nights in the Footlights basement. By the time I hit my final year and Mel returned, I pretty much lived in that comedy bunker and rarely saw daylight.

I ended up becoming president of the club, a presidency defined by the fact that on my watch we received sponsorship from a beer company. I still have no idea how that happened. I don't remember 'reaching out' to them, 'establishing core values' or 'cascading information with a view to establishing value-generating paradigms'. Plus, with my cropped hair, army boots and charity-shop clothes I looked more like an advert alerting people to the dangers of alcohol abuse, than an ambassador who could bring shiny new folk to the 'brand'.

All I remember was that a van turned up at the beginning of term and it was full, and I mean *full*, of lager. At the back of the van was a small fridge, which I put in my room, then filled. With lager. I don't remember anything much for the next six months. By Christmas I had split up with Rob and was drinking heavily – you know, being a *grown-up*. I'd wake up on floors and try to piece together how I'd got there. I collapsed in the street. I drank like a pro until I got a stomach ulcer, by which time I had scraped through graduation and left the pressure cooker of college, so no longer needed the grog to hide my insecurities.

Considering how slapdash, hare-brained and ham-fisted we are, my double act with Mel had an extremely formal beginning. Shortly after we graduated I received a brief handwritten letter in the post.

> Dear Susan,
>   Would you like to be in a double act with me?
> Love Melanie

I believe I may have written back:

> Dear Melanie,
>   Yes I would.
> Love Susan

And so that was that.

Auld Reekie

Do you remember the Blair–Brown summit that famously took place in that Italian restaurant in north London? The power-transitioning pact made over meatballs, gnocchi and *affogato*? Well, I like to think Mel and I got there first, when in 1993, at the food court in Victoria station, on plastic chairs nestled between the warring outlets of Singapore Sam's and Spud-U-Like, we shook hands on a plan to take our first show to Edinburgh.

Mel and I had left it rather late to sort a venue for the festival, so after the highs of the Spud-U-Like summit we were forced to confront a more realistic reality. Come February, most venues are already fully booked, but we managed to get our friend Hartley, who was running the C Venue on Princess Street, to give us his last available slot, which happened to be at

10.05 a.m.

Yes, that holy grail of comedic timeslots, the hour of the day that *every* self-respecting performer wants to make their mark on. I can't imagine why there wasn't more of a clamour for the

10.05 a.m.

slot, since that's universally acknowledged to be *the most* fun time of day. What you might not know, is that at

10.05 a.m.

your body and mind are at their most receptive to sixty minutes of surrealist, stream-of-consciousness sketches performed by total unknowns in an airless box overlooking a busy thoroughfare. And if *that* isn't enough to convince you, the other *amazing* thing about the

10.05 a.m.

slot, is that it's not the more conventional

10.00 a.m.

slot, which is when all the competing shows start.

What can I say? We were way ahead of the curve.

And so, for our first Edinburgh Festival together, an event world renowned for its bacchanalian excess and hedonistic splendour, we had the

10.05 a.m.

slot, meaning we had to get up at

8.00 a.m.

EIGHT A.M. Just as our peers were going to bed after a night on the tiles, we would be getting up and bracing ourselves for the long walk to Princess Street from our student digs.

Putting on a show isn't cheap, so we scraped together what we could and borrowed money from our families on the understanding we'd try to turn a profit. Part of our crowd-luring strategy focused on the name of the show, *The Naked Brunch*. Great, eh? Eh? What do you mean, it's shit? You're obviously missing the hilarious subtext. It's a play on both William S. Burrough's seminal drug-vignette novel and the time of day we were performing. Brilliant, isn't it? And in no way obscure/ pretentious/doomed to failure.

I set off for this, our first Edinburgh Festival together, at around 8 p.m. one evening in August. I had a backpack and a large bin liner, which held my share of our vast array of props. Mum was having a dinner party, was elbow-deep in Marie Rose sauce and didn't even hear me say goodbye. I slipped out of the house. It felt exciting. I felt like Dick Whittington.

The plan was for me to take the direct train from Sanderstead to Victoria and meet Mel at the coach station. From there we'd get the all-night National Express to Scotland. It was a perfect plan, although if there was a flaw in it, that flaw would be called South East Trains.

I waited at the deserted platform for the 8.03 p.m. train. 8:03 p.m. came and went. No worries, I thought – I can still catch the 8.33 and be in plenty of time. 8.33 came and went. Still no train. Finally a bored adenoidal voice on the tannoy, 'South East Trains regrets to inform you that all trains have been cancelled due to a fault further up the line.' The whine of feedback. Then a deafening silence.

I went into a flat panic. *You can't do this*, I thought. *You can't have a fault on the line! Not now! Not today! I have to peddle my 'barely rehearsed'* form of sketch comedy at the Edinburgh Festival. I need to be there!*

I panicked. I didn't own a mobile, and the nearby payphone was so lacquered in acrid man-piss it had long since stopped working. There was only one thing to do. This was a bona-fide crisis, so it followed I'd need someone who could embrace that crisis. I needed to get Ann Perkins – Mega-Mum – involved.

I left the station and walked home, fast. The bag of props

---

* This was our first genuine review. You can't fault it for factual accuracy.

rattled in time with my footsteps. There was the rhythmic squeak of a plastic chicken and the rustle of a nylon Swedish-blonde-fantasy wig. From a distance it looked like I'd murdered Britt Ekland and kept her hair as some form of trophy.

I arrived home just after 9.15 p.m. Mum was half-cut,* in a velour playsuit, breadcrumbing the hell out of some Icelandic prawns. Dad was exchanging blue jokes with his best mate Mick and his wife Eve.

'What's happened?' said Mum, one eye on me, the other on a meringue nest.

'There are no trains, Mum. They're all cancelled. I'm going to miss my coach. I'm going to miss the festival.' And I was so tired and so exasperated, I might just have had a little cry.

There were two ways Mum could have gone. She could have pointed out that the festival runs for a whole month and therefore I would hardly miss a thing. OR she could join me in making a mountain out of a molehill. My mum's whole life has been about waiting and preparing for catastrophe to come knocking. And here it was. An actual catastrophe. And she wasn't about to look that shit-horse in the mouth.

'Right,' she said with a steeliness which was thrilling, 'I'm taking you. Call Victoria and be ready to leave in the next few minutes.'

I dragged down the enormous phone directory from the shelf and thumbed through its pages. Finally I arrived at the Customer Services number for Victoria Coach Station and dialled. Minutes later, someone answered.

* She'd had two sips of sherry. This is enough to get my mum hammered. Once she had a full glass of Cointreau and couldn't get out of bed the next day. 'My head and my body hurt,' she wailed. 'Is it Lyme's disease?' We had to explain gently to her that it was a hangover.

Woman: Hello. Victoria.

Me: Hello, Victoria. I'm Sue. I need you to do me a massive favour. I'm due to meet a friend of mine around about now and I am late. Very late. I need you to get a message to her. Can you do that?

Woman: Mmm. I don't know. We'd have to put it out on the tannoy. Is it an emergency?

I stared at the squeaky chicken in my bag. *Yes, of course!* I wanted to scream. *I'm young! EVERYTHING is an emergency!* 'It's very important I get in touch with her,' I replied, moderately but firmly. 'It's *urgent*.'

'OK,' she said. 'Who am I trying to contact?'

And then the full nightmare struck me. I was going to have to spell Mel's surname out to her. Over the years I'd come to realize that you have to set aside a good fifteen minutes to get that properly through to someone. I looked at my watch. It was 9.28 p.m.

'Mel,' I said desperately, hoping that would be sufficient.

'Mel who?' she replied.

DAMN!

Me: Won't 'Mel' do?

Woman: No, it won't. There might be lots of Mels. I'm afraid I'm going to need a surname.

I take a deep breath in preparation.

Me: Giedroyc.

Woman: [*slight pause*] Goodrich?

Me: Giedroyc.

Woman: Oh. Oh. OK. [*Another pause*] Say it again?

Me: [*slower this time*] Giedroyc.
Woman: And how do you spell that?

Trust me, that won't help, I think, but carry on nonetheless.

Me: G-I-E-D-R-O-Y-C.

I hear the endless scratch of her pen.

Woman: So that's Guy-ed-ro-ik?
Me: [*raising my voice in desperation*] It's pronounced Ged-roy-ch.
Woman: Gee-roy-cee.
Me: [*bellowing*] GED-ROY-CH.
Woman: Ged-royds?
Me: That'll do. Perfect. Thank you.

I gave her the message and put the phone down. It was now 9.31 p.m.

We ran down the front steps and hurled ourselves into the car. Then, of course, we had to negotiate the bloody garage.

'MIND THE SIDES!' shouted Mum. To herself.

It was now 9.35 p.m.

It's around nine miles from South Croydon to Victoria. I have never known anyone drive it in less than fifty minutes. Ann Perkins had just twenty-five.

'We're never going to make it. Everything's ruined,' I whined.

'Shut up,' she said. 'I'm concentrating.' We sat in silence. I imagined her dinner guests trying to make the best of their uncooked prawns and unfilled meringue nests and felt bad.

'Sorry, Mum.'

'Shut up.'

She gritted her teeth, the walnut of muscle in her cheek hardening. Ann was ready for business. She was heading for Victoria come what may. My heart was in my mouth as we sped through the leafy paradise of Thornton Heath and along the boulevards of Brixton.

Meanwhile, Mel had arrived on the bus station concourse and was waiting for me, oblivious to the drama taking place just a few miles south. She was loading her bin liner of props onto the coach when she heard the tannoy announcement.

You've never known true pain until you've heard a disincentivized transportation worker try to pronounce a Polish surname (before Poles were familiar visitors to our shores) over a public address system late at night. It was like someone firing vowels at a wall.

'Will Mel . . .

[*Her eyes taking it in*] 'Will Mel . . .

[*Plucking up courage*] 'Mel Gee . . .

[*Finally going for it*] 'Will Mel Gee-eye-ay-ee-dee-roo-ooo-eeck come to the information desk immediately.'

[*Pretty cocky now*] 'That's Miss Mel Gee-ee-der-ee-ooky-ck to the information desk.'

Finally, deducing that the only person on the concourse with a name even close to that being mangled was her, Mel approached the desk. The woman dutifully passed her a piece of paper with my succinct message on it. It read simply, 'HOLD THE COACH, Perks x'.

Back in south London, Mum was haring up the A23 in a trance state. It was as if fifty years of compliant behaviour was bubbling up inside her. Here was a woman whose entire life had consisted of behaving well, doing the right thing, doing what everyone else wanted. Here was a woman who could not and would not take it any more. *Screw you, authority! This is the real me. I've gone rogue!* I swear she ran a red light or two. She screeched into the coach station in what may or may not have been a handbrake turn. I kissed her on the cheek and flew out of the passenger door.

10.03 p.m.

Mel, meanwhile, was putting on one hell of a show, demonstrating pretty much all of the reasons she had been rejected from every drama school in Britain. She had assumed a starfish position in the doorway of the coach, effectively blocking it open, and was pretending to cry. The driver meanwhile was trying to close the pneumatic doors and get under way. I skidded across the concourse floor, heart in my mouth and yelled as I saw her. With that, I hurled myself, a squeaky chicken, Britt Ekland's hair and a load of miscellaneous junk into the bus, and the doors hissed shut behind us.

The coach was due to arrive at Edinburgh Waverley at 6 a.m. after an all-night potter up the M1. It transpired we were the only non-French-speaking people on the bus. Just Mel, myself and fifty-eight extremely shouty students from Paris. Our seats were in the shadow of the medicated toilet, which was continually in use – meaning that every time we tried to drift off, we'd be woken by a gust of something distinctly evocative of the second arrondissement.

Eight nostril-challenging hours later, we arrived.

There can be few less romantic starting points for any relationship than St Andrew's Square bus depot in Edinburgh, yet it was there I first fell in love with Scotland. Since then I've slept on the warm beaches of Arran in November, I've underwhelmed audiences from Cumbernauld to Aberdeen and back again, I've cried at the immaculate stillness of loch and mountain in Torridon, and I've tried skiing in Aviemore and lived to tell the tale. Scotland has been the crucible for my double act, the site of myriad memorable holidays and the settling point for my wanderlust brother, who married a girl from Perth and together created my brilliant wee nieces.

But it was the festival that started it all. I've spent every August since the age of fourteen at the foot of Edinburgh Castle, marching up and down the cobbles of the Royal Mile at festival time dressed as a milkmaid or bunny rabbit or zombie to advertise my latest hare-brained dramatic endeavour. It began when the Children's Music Theatre came to Croydon auditioning for their touring show. I managed to get a bit part and headed north for the summer with my oldest mate Gemma, who'd also bagged a role. It was the first time I'd been away from my parents. They saw it as a great artistic opportunity for their daughter; I saw it as a magical teenage sex workshop.

I went to the festival during my time at college too, taking part in execrable feminist reworkings and pretentious new writing. But it was that first show I did with Mel that truly sealed the city in my heart. The drunken ramblings on the cobbles of the Pleasance Courtyard. The late-night spicy haggis on the London Road. The thrill of seeing my peers Lee and Herring, Armstrong and Miller, the impeccable League of Gentlemen. My tribe, my new-found family. We lived on nothing but cold hot dogs and warm beer and the kindness of strangers chancing their hard-earned cash on our unique brand of utter silly. It's perhaps the closest I've ever been to truly, completely happy.

Our debut show at the Fringe, as I've already mentioned, was called *The Naked Brunch* – a little bit like a sketch show, a lot like being cornered by a couple of inmates from a psychiatric facility.

We got off the coach with everything we thought we needed: bags and bags of props, interminable voice-overs lovingly recorded to DAT, play-in music, costumes and publicity posters. What we didn't have, it turned out, was an end to the show. Somewhere along the line, due to laziness, forgetfulness or simple shame, we'd just not bothered to finish writing the thing.

The room we'd been assigned was a hot black sweat box on the top floor of the C Venue on Princess Street. It looked like somewhere you'd conduct an extraordinary rendition rather than pay to watch comedy. The heat was so extreme that later in the run, after numerous complaints, an enormous silver coil was put through the door to vent the steam and sweat. If it was hot at

10.05 a.m.

then I dread to think of the ambient temperature at 4 p.m. when the experimental troupe from Godalming began performing their production of *Equus*.

We treated the first show as a dress rehearsal. We hadn't meant to. It was just that no one turned up – and after all surely a performance is only a performance if there is someone there to watch it. Without that, it's just a thought experiment – or at best two nutters in a room shouting at each other in regional accents.

The second show was different. This time we had an audience, although 'audience' is a slightly grandiose term for a single person. This person came into the room wearing a large rucksack. Rather unusually, she didn't take it off as she sat down, and so sat perched forward at a forty-five-degree angle for the entirety of the show. At points during the performance she would take out a large street map of Edinburgh, which she would unfold and unfold and unfold until it covered almost her entire top half. Then, after examining it, she would fold and fold and fold it back into a neat concertina. At several points during the show I wondered if she'd perhaps mistaken the venue for Edinburgh Castle and found herself somewhat disappointed by the dimensions of the rooms.

The initial idea behind *The Naked Brunch* was to showcase sketch characters within an overriding narrative. This ended up being a rather shoddy conceit involving them all being trapped inside a computer game. The result was that it was meta without in any way being good. The characters included paramilitary Brown Owls, some Dutch VJs, a pair of US East Coast post-feminists and a couple of lovelorn Aussie PE teachers, who expressed their desire for one another exclusively through the medium of sport. That's one hell of a computer game, right there.

The problem was, the more we wrote, the bigger and more bizarre our characters became. And the bigger they became, the more constrictive and less credible the framework around them seemed. But, rather than ditching the whole thing and just delivering a simple sketch show, we persisted with the computer game theme, which petered out as the hour wore on. By the final sketch none of it, and I mean NONE OF IT, made any sense. So we did what so many young writers do when something isn't working. Nothing. We just left it and hoped the problem would go away all by itself.

It didn't.

Because there was no show-stopper ending, for some reason that has mercifully faded with time, we decided to end with our backs to the audience (singular) shining a torch on a croissant. Yep, shining a torch on a croissant. No dance numbers for us – no recapping, no show tunes – just a greasy baked semicircle caught in the thin beam of a cheap torch bought from Ali's Cave on the Lothian Road.

Don't ask me why. Even twenty-one years on. Don't ask me why.

When the show finally ground to a halt, the voice-over stopped and silence again prevailed, we burst through the fourth wall to have a chat with our lone punter.

Us: Hi!
Her: [*American*] Hi! [*Folding up her map again*]
Me: We're really sorry about that.
Her: About what?
Mel: The accent.
Her: What accent?
Me: The American accent . . . the American post-feminists.
Her: Oh. Really? American?
Mel: Yes. We're sorry.
Her: They were *Americans*?
Me: Yes.
Her: Oh. Oh, I didn't notice.

The run lasted for another three weeks.

Mel and I have been responsible for some truly disastrous performances over the years. Too many to mention. But let me give you my top four.

Auld Reekie

1. Stockton

In 1994/5 we embarked on a tour of small arts centres. If there was a tiny, dilapidated, endangered cultural space in the UK, we'd find it and half-fill it. One such space was in Stockton-on-Tees. Our manager, Ted, a fabulous pint-sized dynamo in double-denim, booked us in for a gig starting at 8 p.m. 'It'll be great,' he said. 'There's a do in there first and then a disco after, so there'll be a guaranteed crowd. It's all part of a package. It's going to be amazing. Amazing!'

When we arrived, bags of props in hand, we became aware of a group of women in the theatre, sat on chairs in a semicircle. There seemed to be an awful lot of crying and hugging.

Me: [*nervously*] What kind of 'do' is this?
Ted: Well . . . it's not so much a *do* . . . [*Suddenly sounding evasive*]
Mel: Why is everyone sobbing?
Ted: Well, the thing is . . .

Now I know we're in trouble – no sentence ends well that begins with 'The thing is . . .'

Ted: The thing is, it's not so much a 'do' as a support group.
Me: What do you mean 'support group'? What support group?

And then the truth emerged. We'd been booked to do our comedy show after a workshop for battered women organised by the charity Zero Tolerance. The audience was a mix of abused women and repentant, teary men. It couldn't get any worse.

It did.

Because after the support group, and just before we were due onstage, the organizers decided to put on a film. This hard-hitting documentary charted the emotional journeys of both perpetrators and victims of domestic abuse, and was punctuated by deep sobs emanating from the audience.

After a truly devastating thirty minutes, and just as a close-up of a bruised and swollen face faded into black, our cheesy 70s intro music began. As awkward emotional gear changes go, it was right up there with Phil and Holly on *This Morning* going from Syria to *Towie* and back again.

Mel: Shit! That's us!
Me: [*shouting to make myself heard over the keening*] Oh God . . .

And on we went, into the darkness. I never knew that bewilderment had a sound until that very moment. Now I know that it does.

After we finished the show (an hour-long affair that, it transpired, ran at only forty-three minutes without laughs) the disco began. No sooner had the smattering of applause died away than Gloria Gaynor's 'I Will Survive' kicked in, and the crying started again.

I ended up slow-dancing with a sixty-year-old woman from Macclesfield; Mel was locked into a deep sway with a former offender, and Ted, well Ted had been grabbed by a rather substantial woman and was now being rocked from side to side, his head trapped between her space-hopper breasts. We left him there, gently asphyxiating, as penance. He needed to know that when it came to being mis-sold a gig, we had zero tolerance.

2. Cambridge

Billed as a glorious homecoming by nobody except us, we returned to our old stomping ground, gigging at the Cambridge

University Playhouse as part of our tour in the autumn of 1995. In true Mel/Sue fashion, we had failed to book a lighting and sound operator for the show, hoping that local techie stalwart Liam would be available. I loved Liam – he was the stuff of legend. He was fuelled by two things: prawn cocktail crisps and an abject hatred of all performers. He also had the largest set of keys in East Anglia, which he hung from his belt, giving him his trademark limp. Liam huffed and eye-rolled his way through every piss-poor production I ever did at that theatre – and there were an awful lot of piss-poor productions – yet for some unknown reason he simply wasn't available when we came back that autumn.

At that time my brother was working as a manager of a foreign language school near Cambridge. The night before the gig he came over to visit, which set Mel thinking.

Mel: Maybe David could do the lights?

Me: David? What, my *brother*, David?

Mel: Yes. Why not?

Me: Have you actually met him?

Mel: Well of course I have . . .

Me: Then why are you even *asking*? He is the only person on the planet who is as technologically illiterate as I am.

Mel: He'll be fine. Plus I've always had a slight crush on him.

Me: He won't be fine. He's mildly dyspraxic and easily distracted, with a healthy dose of 'couldn't give a shit' thrown in for good measure.

Mel: I think it'll be hilarious. He doesn't even have to do much. Come on. It'll be fun!

The next night, the night of the performance, we received word from the front-of-house manager that the audience was seated and we were ready to go. Normally, when you get clearance, you make your way to the wings and get on with things as soon as possible, but our double act is a little different. It is *exactly* at that point, on the cusp of starting a show, that Mel's bowels swing into action.

Mel's GI tract is a source of wonderment to all those who know and love her. Or have sat on a bus near her. Or been in a room with her. Or a room after her. There is not one single event, emotion or situation that Mel's digestive system can't translate into instant and devastating flatus. And so, for decades, in those precious seconds before a performance – where you'd normally be riding the adrenalin rush, pacing, going through lines and focusing – I have had to endure the sights, sounds and aromas of Mel's malevolent wind. Or worse.

At the Edinburgh Festival of 1998 we took part in a gang show called *The Big Squeeze* with the brilliant Geraldine McNulty and our mega-mucker Emma Kennedy. Straight after our slot a friend, Penny, was performing her one-woman show at the venue. It was getting near the end of the run and we felt it was the comradely thing to do to stay on afterwards to cheer her on. As we were called backstage for our opening sketch, Mel, as always, heard the distant call of nature.

Mel: [*whispering*] I need a wee . . .

Me: Well why didn't you go thirty seconds ago? You remember thirty seconds ago? When we were downstairs? Next to a *toilet*.

Mel: It's not my fault! It's like a Pavlovian reaction. I get stressed.

Emma approaches, wearily.

Emma:	Is it Mel?
Me:	Yes.
Emma:	Does she need the toilet again?
Me:	*Of course* she needs the toilet . . .

Emma rolls her eyes and walks on.

Front-of-House Manager:	[*emerging from the shadows*] That's clearance.
Mel:	But I'm busting!
Gerry:	[*desperately trying to focus on the performance ahead*] Well go downstairs, for goodness' sake!

Opening music starts.

Mel:	Oh God! There's no time!
Me:	Oh for goodness' sake, Miggins, go in the bucket!

I point over to the black bucket in the wings that has been there since the beginning of the run. A paintbrush sits in a thin puddle of liquid at the bottom. Mel looks at it in desperation then parks herself above it. We look away. The sound of a zip. A deluge. The zip again. Then we all run onstage to do the show. Ah, showbiz.

Once done, we collected up the costumes and props littered at the side of stage and plonked ourselves in the auditorium in preparation for our mate's solo show. This turned out to be a marvellously involved affair with multiple characters and complex plots. We were lost in it – lost in it almost to the point of sleep – when suddenly Penny started talking in an Irish accent, transforming into the character of a raging fire-and-brimstone priest. There was a lot of vengeful Old Testament babbling and shouting at us, which roused us from unconsciousness. The character reached fever pitch, cursing us as sinners and telling us we needed to be bathed in the holy water of Christ the Redeemer. Whereupon she left the stage and reappeared a moment later . . .

. . . with the bucket.

Emma, Mel and myself sat suddenly upright, rigid with fear. Like animals on the plains who know instinctively that danger is coming.

Penny dipped the paintbrush into the bucket, then flung the liquid at the audience. The spray flew to the left and right of us. The audience laughed. 'Don't laugh!' I wanted to shout. 'You're being drenched in piss!' But I was stopped in my tracks by a frenzy of droplets raining down on my head. Mel refused to look, burying her face in her palms as the wee kept on coming and coming and coming.

That was the last time I went to an experimental theatre show. You don't get that with Shakespeare.

Anyhow, I've digressed. We're back in Cambridge, 1995, and my brother was in charge of operating the show. We'd been told to get to the wings and stand by, so we duly headed backstage and waited. And waited.

Finally, the intro music and voice-over began. Then stopped, abruptly. Then started again, this time at a deafening volume. We waited for the lights to dim in the auditorium. They didn't.

Mel: [*bellowing over the din*] Is that us? Should we just go on?
Me: I guess so . . .

The intro music suddenly stops. There is an all-encompassing silence.

Mel: [*pushing me forward, hissing*] Go on! Now! Now!

The moment we stepped onstage a strange thing happened: the house lights increased in intensity, thus illuminating the audience further, and the spotlights went down, thus plunging Mel and me into darkness. We were now in total silence and total blackout. It was a devastating comedic double whammy.

I looked up to the lighting booth and saw David staring at the script and shaking his head. It's not the sort of thing that inspires you to begin an eclectic offbeat hour of character comedy.

'I told you,' I hissed as another random piece of music exploded on the PA. 'He's a technological fucking *idiot* . . .'

A spotlight came on, stage left. *Finally!* We walked towards it. The moment we started to feel the heat of it, it flicked off again, only to reappear on the other side of the stage. So we turned around and walked across. The same thing happened. We began chasing visibility.

For the next hour we went on a voyage of audio-visual discovery. Sometimes we'd get a high-decibel burst of incongruous sound effect – a lion roaring, a juicy fart, some cicadas in the bush. Sometimes we would be squashed into a pinprick of light at the very back of the stage, desperate to be seen for at least a small percentage of the show. However, in the final ten minutes David appeared to find his mojo, opting for what became his signature lighting state – Guantanamo Bay. He decided to put every single light at his disposal on full – backstage, audience, side lights, spotlights – you name it. There was even a glitter ball going full pelt. He had also decided to alleviate some of the tension by stripping to the waist and donning a large Robin Hood hat that had obviously been lying around the booth.

The *Cambridge Evening News* review of that night said it all: '. . . it's hard to comment on the quality of the show, as the multiple technical failures rather overwhelmed proceedings. In fact, in all my decades as a theatre critic it's hard to bring to mind a more woeful display from a lighting and sound operator than the one witnessed last night.'

But hey, remember, ALL publicity is good publicity. Yes?

3. Brighton

The old Komedia in Brighton's Kemptown was one of my favourite venues ever – not least because its founders Colin, Marina and David were pretty much the only people who ever wanted to book us. It was like all great theatres – bijou and friendly, well loved by the locals, with good grub and a bit of jazz at the weekends.

It was 1996, and we were touring our third show, *Women in Uniform*. By now we had established a small (see also: negligible) posse of people who'd regularly turn out to see us – mainly sex workers, ex-offenders and those wrestling with their sexuality. Oh, and a man called Perv, who ran a nightclub nearby. I remember going to the Zap Bar with him one evening, and Mel had no idea it was gay night. At the end of the evening she merely said, 'It's nice that the women here are so *friendly*, isn't it?' I long for that naivety. Just for a second.

So, it's the opening night of a week-long run at the venue. We are in the dressing room getting ready when we suddenly get the all-clear to head to stage. This news, albeit entirely expected, causes Mel's digestive system, once again, to start firing on all cylinders.

'Sorry, mate, I'm desperate . . .'

Her limbic system has gone into high alert. This is fight-or-flight time. She needs to run, and in order to do that most effectively, she needs to get rid of anything extraneous that might inhibit her movement. And what she decides to get rid of is her microphone receiver pack. She summarily drops it into my hands and dashes for the toilet.

There's just one problem. The microphone equipment comes in two parts: firstly, the receiver, which I am now holding, and secondly, the microphone itself, which Mel is wearing on her lapel. Crucially, the two parts are connected by a metre-long cable. This expensive umbilical can't be disconnected at speed without risking damage, which means only one thing.

Where Mel goes, I go also.

I find myself standing next to her in a cramped bog, palms up, holding the receiver like it's the Holy Grail. She perches below making low moaning sounds. It begins like a distant rumble, like thunder. The hairs on my arm stand to attention. Then comes the noise. Like a thousand tins of beans being hurled against a wall. Then the toxic gust. I feel like Karen Silkwood: contaminated, angry, compelled to seek legal advice.

'Cheers, chum,' says Mel once the horror is over. 'Ooh, let me take that,' retrieving the receiver from my grasp and clipping it back on her belt. I say nothing.

Mel did the greatest gig of her life that night. She was light and springy and refreshed. I spent that hour dry-retching and trying to get enough oxygen in my lungs to say my lines.

As part of my rider,* we now have separate dressing rooms.

* This also includes five new-born puppies, a Clairol Foot Spa and a wheelie bin full of Reese's Pieces.

4. Leighton Buzzard

And so it came to pass, in the Year of Our Lord 1996, that we visited the Bedfordshire town of Leighton Buzzard. Sadly, it transpired that the residents were far from ready for our unique brand of poorly thought-out 'fun'. The venue we had been booked into was the council-run Library Theatre, which appeared on first impression to consist of an awful lot of library and not a lot of actual theatre.

There was a smattering of people in the audience, all of whom seemed furious before we'd even started. Well, if they were furious then, I don't have a descriptor for the hostile vibes we were getting a mere five minutes into proceedings. There is a profound telepathy at work in all close relationships – a shorthand, if you will. A flicker of the eyelid, a tilt or cock of the head, and you're both on the same page. Mel and I have that telepathy. As the atmosphere became increasingly toxic, we shot each other a glance. A glance that said, *Let's get this over with as quickly as possible.*

If we couldn't make them laugh, we could certainly get them home before they turned violent.

We increased the speed of our delivery, making snap cuts, overlapping one another's lines. We did not pause, because pausing is for laughter, and why wait for something that will never arrive? Under normal conditions our show ran for just over an hour. In Leighton Buzzard it lasted exactly thirty-six minutes, beating our previous record (Stockton-on-Tees) by a full seven minutes. We didn't bother coming back onstage for a bow; instead we used the closing music to cover the sound of our exit from the stage door. We sprinted for the station. Sprinted. Mercifully there was a London-bound train waiting on the platform as we arrived. As we hopped on, and the doors closed behind us, we saw a gang of young men running towards the carriage. To this day I have no idea whether they were members of our audience desperate to take us to the Old Mill and burn us or just regular Joes on a night out. But we've never gone back, just in case.

THREE

London

The Trouble with London

The essayist and lexicographer Dr Samuel Johnson famously once said, 'When a man is tired of London, he is tired of life.'

Well, Samuel, when a *woman* is tired of London, she usually tries to get away for the weekend – you know, get some perspective. She doesn't tend to think of it as a precursor for ending her existence. My advice would be: stop being so absolutist in your thinking. Think about changing it up. Failing that, some of the modern SSRIs are really very good.

I returned to London after college just as I was beginning my double act with Mel. I didn't have a bean and so made like Blanche duBois and depended on the kindness of strangers. I stayed, briefly, with Nicola's then boyfriend Seth, whose parents had a flat in a posh stucco square near Earl's Court. It was the model of elegance from the outside, but empty on the inside – 'all fur coat and no knickers' as my nan liked to say, just before they arrested her for soliciting.

Seth was a wiry, febrile genius who wanted to be a poet and ended up a venture capitalist. Life as Tennyson, it turns out, was a shrub short of the full hedge fund. Having said that, I wanted to be a novelist but was working on a direct sales marketing manual for Kleeneze. So much for *my* integrity.

Seth and I smoked, talked shit and ate fancy burgers from a place called Hollywood down the road. *Classy*. We listened to Radiohead and The The, read e e cummings and didn't use capitals for a year (which was both tough and compromising, since I was working as a copywriter at the time). We cried at

Anne Sexton and Louis MacNeice and Pablo Neruda and felt part of a tribe. Although had that tribe found out that we were living in a half-million-pound flat in the Sloane heartlands it might have been time for our membership to be rescinded. I slept on a sofa bed in a lounge with no furniture save a chicken-mesh sculpture of a woman who appeared to be giving the Hitler salute. I have no idea why she was there or how Seth, a devout Jew of Ashkenazi hue, felt about her. But there she stood, eight feet high, her outstretched arm suggesting a lazy *Lebensraum* in the vague direction of Fulham.

I loved Seth. He was an emotional soul. Once he took a bread knife and carved up his entire book collection. I thought that was kind of arty. Then he took a lighter and set fire to his eyebrows. I thought that was the right time to move out.

For the next few years I lived with Sarah and Nicola. We were the Three Graces in reverse – uncouth, grotty and lazy. Shortly after my stay at Seth's, his parents sold the Earl's Court flat and bought a disused office space at the end of a leafy cul-de-sac in Hampstead, north London. While they waited for planning permission to come through for their minimalist dream home, they kindly asked if we wanted to live there and keep the place occupied.

I had never, in all my life, seen such a beautiful part of town – a pristine village within the city. It had cobbled streets, and early-Victorian cottages with handmade dimpled-glass windows that moved like water when the sun caught them. Every front garden seemed to burst with flowers, and every house was studded with blue plaques that boasted of Constable, Blake and the like.

I'd never seen a plaque in Croydon, not one – I'm not sure the sort of thing that happens in Croydon would merit the attentions of English Heritage.

CAPTAIN SENSIBLE URINATED ON THIS CORNER

DIZZEE RASCAL STOPPED HERE TO ASK FOR DIRECTIONS

ADELE GOT WOLF-WHISTLED BY A ROOFER HERE

Our accommodation was basic, at best. In truth, our existence trod an extremely fine line between squatting and tenancy. The building itself was a frail white prefab with weeds growing through the concrete steps and looked at odds with the neighbouring mansions, with their exfoliated brickwork and Farrow & Ball facelifts.

Next door lived a man who owned an entire mobile phone network, in a house so tall we spent the first summer listening to the soundtrack of his lift being installed. He spent *his* first summer listening to a bunch of stoners rowing about Tory education policies and how best to fire flaming clods of horse shit at the Rt Hon. Michael Howard.

His daughter once knocked on our door and asked for a cardigan.

'I'd get my own, but I can't go back in the house,' she said.

'Why?' we asked, ignoring the look of horror on her face as she stared in at our accommodation.

'Oh,' she replied nonchalantly, 'it's on fire.'

It's on fire. That's the thing about the super-rich. Nothing, not even a domestic fireball, bothers them. Not even an inferno can dent their sense of entitlement.

I was unemployed, but hey, I had things to do. For starters, every other week Sarah and I would stroll down to the dole office on Finchley Road. Plus, since our building had no heating, much of our day was spent trying to get warm – like the Ancients did. Sarah devised an excellent thermal preservation technique whereby every morning we'd put our duvets on the floor, lie horizontally across them, then wrap ourselves up like albino sausage rolls. Finally, we'd stagger upright and take it in turns to run gaffer tape around each other to secure the wadding tight.

The whole day was spent like a game in *Jeux Sans Frontières*, hopping from one room to the next like giant Tampax, yelling, 'Who's got my lighter?'

We had no money for internal decoration, so we glued bits of newspaper to the wall like wallpaper – the Underclass Range from Cole and Son, Benefit Seekers by Osborne and Little. I say we had no money, we had a five-pound note, which was lovingly stuck to the wall. This was a special five-pound note – sacred no less – as it had been sent by Jilly Cooper to Nicola in response to a begging letter for money to fund her RADA tuition fees. We loved Jilly so much, we kept the fiver there in honour of her and her kindness, and there was never any privation, nor desperation deep or profound enough to incite any one of us to touch it.

There were no white goods in the flat, so every other day we would make something lovingly referred to as 'pants soup'. We'd gather our collective stash of underwear and dirty clothing, run a bath, chuck it all in with some cheap soda crystals and stir the resultant broth with a stick. Then we'd drain the bath, refill it a little to rinse, then hang the sodden items on a rail above the bath to drain. The soda had the same effect as Agent Orange – for the next twelve months I was puffy, red and horrendously, horrendously itchy.

I met a girl. Emma. She was a trainee lawyer who was a grown-up by day (she could cite precedents and article numbers and everything) and a total toddler by night. I know what you're thinking – *But Sue, you must have been inundated with women, what with you living in a squat with no washing facilities or heating* – well you'd be wrong. You'd be amazed how many girls are put off by the fact that a) you live inside a duvet and b) everything underneath that duvet is unwashed.

We met and seemed to bypass the normal parameters of friendship. There was no *Maybe let's meet next month for a coffee* or any of those boundaries. We met the next day, and very shortly afterwards, maybe even the day after that, we met again. Then we started meeting *every single day*, often sitting next to one another at my computer to play a Star Trek video game. This involved staring at a seemingly endless black screen and moving your mouse up and down, left and right in a vain attempt to find a Klingon. We never found a Klingon. It was forever dark in space. Although I did find that we were now sitting so close to one another that our legs were touching.

I became restless. I didn't sleep much at night and would catnap during the day. I stopped being interested in things. I sat daydreaming, waiting for Spock o'clock. Something felt wrong. Very wrong. I phoned my sister.

Me:	Gel, there's something wrong with me. I don't feel right. I can't sleep and I feel sick to my stomach. I just sit around . . .
Michelle:	Can I just stop you there?
Me:	Is it irritable bowel syndrome?
Michelle:	It's worse.
Me:	Oh God.
Michelle:	Yep.
Me:	Oh God. I'm in love, aren't I?
Michelle:	I am rather sorry to say, yes. Yes, you are.

Out and About

Every gay person in the world has an idealized notion of their coming-out in their head – a fantasy version which eases the anxiety about the inevitable horror to come. This was mine.

Mum is running her hands along the smooth clean lines of her kitchen, wondering if her obsession with minimalism isn't creating a rather austere living space. I come in just as she turns her attentions to the sofa.

Me: Mum, there's something you should know.

Mum: What is it, angel?

Me: I've been wanting to tell you for a while but couldn't find the right time.

Mum: [*plumping cushions*] Well, I think now is the perfect time. Sit! Can I get you a herbal tea?

Me: No, I'm fine.

Mum: Thank God. I don't have any mugs anyway. I got rid of them. You know I can't stand extraneous crockery. Anyway, go on.

Me: Well, the thing is . . . I'm gay, Mum.

A pause. Mum gets up wordlessly and walks to the window.

Me: Did you hear me, Mum? I'm gay.

Mum: [*muttering to herself*] Oh God.

Me: Mum?

Mum: Oh God, no . . .

Suddenly her legs seem to give way, and she collapses, grabbing at the damask curtains as she slides to the floor.

Mum: No! Not my little princess. Not my Susan. Oh God, I'm in shock. I'm going into shock. I can't believe it! I can't . . . I can't cope!

I walk over and offer her my hand.

Me: It is a shock?

Mum: It's a massive shock. I cannot think of anyone in the entire world less likely to be gay than you. You're so . . . un-gay.

Me: I know. Come on, Mum, please stop crying. Try and put into words your knee-jerk prejudices about something that is essentially nothing to do with you – merely a matter of personal choice that, due to bewildering social convention, I'm forced to share with blood relatives.

Mum: [*taking my hand, pulling herself up and resting against the sofa*] I guess, my initial worry is that now you're a lesbian –

Me: Yes . . .

Mum: – you'll have to spend the rest of your life in a fleece.

Me: We only wear fleeces 50 per cent of the time these days, Mum. Get with the programme. And there are so many advantages to me being a lesbian: I can perv over men without them noticing, and dress like a teenager well into my forties. Plus, you'll always be able to rely on me having spare wet-weather gear, should you need it.

Mum: But I assume, because you're such a maverick, that you will forgo the time-honoured lesbian obsession with cats?

Me: Yes. Yes, I will. Cats leave me cold. I shall have dogs. Many, many dogs.

Mum: You're so unique.

Me:	I know, Mum. I know.
Mum:	[*drying her tears*] You've totally changed my views on sexuality and gender politics. I'm going to tell everyone I know in the Croydon area, while making sure I credit you utterly and exclusively with this incredible transformation. Thank you.
Me:	You're welcome.
Mum:	I'm so proud of you, my darling.
Me:	Don't be silly. I'm just glad I've had such a powerful and positive impact on your life. Now go! Go tell everyone what you've learned here today.
Mum:	I shall.
Me:	And you'll credit me – remember?
Mum:	Of course. I love you so much.
Me:	I love you too. Now c'mon – get outta here. You're embarrassing me.

This is how it actually went.

Me:	[*on phone, strained voice*] Mum. Can I come home tomorrow?
Mum:	Yes. Why? Are you all right?
Me:	Yes. I just . . . I just want to talk to you about something.
Mum:	[*matter of factly while eating what sounds like toast*] Is it about you being gay?

Long, long pause.

Me:	Yes, it might be that.
Mum:	[*still munching*] *Is* it that?

Another long pause.

Me: It might be.

Mum: Fine. Well, just whenever you like. No rush. Lots of love,
        darling.

Click of the receiver.

And that's why I do what I do. You've got to get your drama
somewhere, haven't you?

Our next gaff was a flat on the fourth floor of a mansion block
in Abbey Road. By now Emma had moved in. In the basement
of this block lived John, the night porter, a waxy-faced man with
bad teeth who looked like the sort of thing Gunther von Hagens
had had a crack at plasticizing. John was a weapons-grade bore
who originally hailed from Sligo. Every night when we returned
home we'd run the gauntlet from the front door to the rickety
cage lift, desperate to avoid his hypnotic honeyed vowels. His
chat ammo of choice? The life and works of seventeenth-
century herbalist Nicholas Culpeper. It didn't matter what ail-
ment you had, John would let you know, in painstaking detail,
using his approximation of a Jacobean voice, what old Nicholas
would have done. (This invariably involved boiling onions . . .)
     Most nights, our arrival home went as follows.

*Open front door, clasp keys tightly to avoid jangling. Run to lift and press
button. The cabling sparks into life and the cage slowly descends. Suddenly
there is the sound of heavy footsteps ascending from the basement and the
noise of a key turning in a lock.*

Me: Shit . . . shit! [*Frantically jabbing at the lift button*]

The basement door swings open. The smell of boiled onions fills the lobby.

John: Well, hello, Susan.
Me: Hello, John. I was just –
John: Is that the sound of mucus in your passages?
Me: No.
John: I think it is. A little thickening of the membrane. I can hear
        it in your voice.

The cage drops into view. Salvation is at hand.

Me: No, I think it's just because . . . Well, you know, it's late. I'm
        tired . . .
John: The damp. Do you feel it in the flesh, the bones or the ven-
        tricles?
Me: Really . . .
John: Try thistles in wine. Culpeper says they 'expel superfluous
        melancholy from the body and make a man as merry as a
        cricket'. Will you do that?
Me: Yes. Yes, John. Absolutely.
John: Well, you're a feckin' liar as you can't get thistles this time of
        year. Honestly. They're ruled by Saturn and Mars, you
        know. Saturn and Mars!

*I rise in the iron cage, high above him, away from the smell of alliums and
the sound of silly oldy-worldy babble, back to the safety of the flat and a
double whisky.*

The strange thing about John was that, for all his guff about
late-medieval herbalism, he was a devout and unrepentant

chain-smoker. I don't know what Nicholas Culpeper said about tobacco, but we've had a few more credible physicians since who assert that it isn't the healthiest. More worrying, however, was John's insistence on carrying his air rifle with him wherever he went. Whether he was investigating a drains blockage or coming to collect the service charge, his trusty firearm would come with him.

'It's for the squirrels,' he'd insist as I backed away from him in the small kitchen in which we both found ourselves.

One morning, after we'd had to call upon his services to inspect some suspect cracks in the ceiling, I noticed him gazing intently out of the window. None of my attempts to lure him back on message were successful; he merely stared resolutely out until, in a flash, he raised his gun and popped a tree rodent out of the sky.

'Got the little bastard.'

During an impromptu birthday party, one of the more rowdy guests redecorated an entire wall with Cabernet Sauvignon. We did our best to conceal things from John, sneaking off to buy a tin of fresh paint, only to get collared at the last minute.

We turn the front door key and rush to the lift, stabbing at the button. The reflex of cabling as the iron box lowers towards us. We will it on. The sound of heavy footsteps heading upwards from the basement. The door opens. The stench of boiled onions.

John: How are ya, girls?

Me: Good, really good.

John: I see one of yous got mail from the hospital. Are you all right?

Sarah: It's mine, John. It's for me.

John: May I ask what's wrong wit ya? Only –

Sarah: It's nothing. Just a check-up.

John: Private, eh? Or is it your privates? Venereal disease, maybe?
           Well for that Culpeper would be recommending a poultice
           of stewed leeks – or wild pansies. It's not always the safest,
           but do you happen to have mercury in the house?

Sarah: No, John. It's not venereal disease.

John: Mmm. Shame.

The lift finally descends to the ground floor. Free at last.

Whereas Sarah spent the year dodging questions about her genitals, Nicola spent hers staging a John-and-Yoko-style bed-in with a gorgeous boy called Barney. They holed up in the box room overlooking the Abbey Road studios, surfacing occasionally to eat anything beige that might be lying around – bread, pasta, jacket potatoes . . .

Whatever gets you through the night.

After completing our twelve-month tenancy, we escaped John but went from the frying pan into the fire. We decided to move further north, to Golders Green, renting a ramshackle Edwardian house that had remained untouched since its first paint job. Our landlady was an extraordinary character named Rhoda, an indomitable South African in her early nineties. Half the time I had the sneaking suspicion she was being played by Barry Humphries.

Rhoda had never lived in the house but had a fixation with it that none of us could understand. Occasionally we'd hear mutterings that her son had lived there and had died in one of the rooms, but whatever her reason, she had instilled in the building a sort of Havisham's-by-proxy. The place remained as it had done for decades, and no amount of cajoling would get her to spend a penny on refurbishment. There was a small conservatory which had the rare distinction of being colder inside than out. Adjoining it was a small toilet which had been designated 'spider loo' in the first week after Emma sighted a huntsman suspended over the cistern. We never used it after that.

It was a strange relationship we enjoyed with Rhoda, with complex and ever-shifting boundaries. Sometimes we would be her surrogate children, then her friends, then strictly her tenants. The problem was, you never quite knew at what point on that continuum you were currently positioned. At the beginning of every week we'd do her food shopping and bring it round to her house. At the end of every week, by way of thanks, we'd receive a parcel from Fortnum & Mason containing one pack of sausages and two packs of ginger thins. The contents never changed. She had obviously taken one look at us and thought, *What those girls need are pigs and biscuits. Pigs and biscuits!*

Rhoda would also hold random, infrequent 'happenings'. Our attendance was mandatory. Invariably we would be stuck next to an old colonel or someone who had invented radiotherapy, but we were young, stupid and cocky, so were impervious to their stories and achievements.

On one such occasion we arrived on Rhoda's doorstep to be greeted by a beautiful black waiter. He seemed not to have a name but was merely part of the shadowy force known as 'the staff'. It was going to be one of those evenings. Rhoda was an unapologetic racist who had spent her formative years with no context other than apartheid, which meant you oscillated between hating her and feeling rather sorry for her. To be honest, on these evenings I felt sorry for everyone – suspended as we were in the aspic of class, power and money.

Rhoda's entry to these parties was the stuff of legend. There would be the sound of brass and the rumble of machinery as she wobbled into view, descending – on her Stannah stairlift – in fuschia dress and red velvet turban, blowing like billy-o on a hunting horn. We'd applaud awkwardly. The problem was on this particular night the stairlift got stuck mid-descent, so we were forced to carry on clapping for several minutes while the unnamed beautiful-black-man carried her down.

Finally she reached us. She stood, gathered herself, pulled the back of her dress from out of her large cotton pants and ushered us into the dining room.

'We're having cold soup!' she exclaimed cheerily. 'I asked *them* to make it,' gesturing to the staff. 'I asked them to make it with avocado. Never seen that before, and I thought it could be fun!'

Three vast tureens were brought in. The lids were lifted. A cumulus of fruit flies flew out of each. Inside sat a lurid green broth with thick skin on top. From where I was sitting, it looked like Kermit cellulite.

Well, I thought, *that is fun.*

A deep and profound silence set in over the guests after the very first mouthful, which had the consistency of petroleum. It was as if we had reached a common consensus that our energies were best spent focusing on getting the pea-coloured potage down our throats rather than attempting conversation.

'Get down, Blackie!' bellowed Rhoda at a sable Labrador bolting towards the table. Though even the Labrador, a breed famed for its untrammelled appetite, baulked at the contents of the tureen once he'd clapped eyes on it. There's a reason people don't make soup out of avocados. And that reason was now making itself incredibly clear to my colon.

That particular night I had been sat opposite Rhoda, while Emma was at the other end of the table next to a twinkly-eyed Polish octogenarian. He had been referred to vaguely as a 'war hero' – in fact, he may have referenced himself as such. Either way, we were careful to show maximum respect. That's why it felt particularly gauche that Emma should choose to pull faces at me for the entirety of the meal.

'What's up with you?' I hissed across the table as dessert arrived, which appeared to be cold rice pudding with an unidentifiable drizzle on the top. 'Why are you gurning at me?' Emma and I had just broken up and we were finding the transition into friends a little fraught.

'Him!' hissed Emma back. 'The guy next to me! He's had his hand on my knee all night!'

'What, the war veteran?'

'Veteran sex pest more like. What should I do?'

'I don't know. Has he crossed The Maginot Line?'

'Oh, piss off, Sue.'

It's dilemmas like this one we really need to see in *Debrett's*. Humans are tribal. We work through complex systems of affiliation which ebb and flow in individual importance. I am a human being, a woman, a daughter, a sibling, an agnostic, a feminist and a gay. Which of these important tribes I choose to affiliate with the most at any one point in time changes. So, what to do? Rumble him? Denounce him as a groper to the assembled diners and be true to ourselves as women and feminists? Or let him, a flaccid pensioner, keep his hand resting on Emma's leg and take the broader, human perspective.

It was an infernally difficult decision. In the end Emma decided to respect his service to our country in time of conflict by allowing his palm to rest for another hour on her thigh.

'It's my way of saying thank you,' she whispered.

Lest we forget.

Let Them Eat Lunch

A month after Rhoda's dinner party, in the spring of 1997, our agent asked Mel and me if we'd be prepared to audition for a Channel 4 live daytime show called *Light Lunch*. We were, it's fair to say, less than enamoured by the prospect. The daytime landscape was arid in those days, acres of dry *Kilroy*-ish terrain with the occasional Ricki Lake oasis. We turned up to the casting in our best 'smart' outfits – which in retrospect made us look like a supermarket security guard and GPO worker respectively. Despite repeated attempts by the channel and the production company to hire proper professionals, Nicky Campbell OBE and the like, we somehow managed to slip though the audition, through the pilot and on to the actual television. Up to that moment our combined media experience had been:

- dressing in full bridal outfits (brief movie review, the *Little Picture Show*)
- dressing up as bearded Highland crofters (non-speaking roles, *French and Saunders*)
- dressing up as Elizabeth Bennett and Unnamed Georgian Woman (non-speaking roles, *French and Saunders*)
- dressing up as Noel and Liam Gallagher (non-speaking roles in a thankfully un-broadcast pilot)

You can see from this extensive CV that we were, in so many ways, the ideal candidates for an hour-long live daily show.

Live television is the apotheosis of multi-tasking. It's like patting your head and rubbing your stomach at the same time. Add to that a shit-eating grin and you're pretty much there. Anything can happen and everything does – and that chaotic unpredictability is what I have always loved best, perhaps because it's the medium that closest matches the pinball tangentialism in my head. Whether or not *Light Lunch* was the show that Channel 4 actually wanted, I don't know – but it was a place where banality walked hand in hand with eccentricity, and I will always love it for that. Sometimes we got it right (I'm thinking of the unlikely but sublime pairing of Michael Bolton and John Inman) and sometimes, well, sometimes we got it wrong . . .

Mel and I had been obsessed with Kate O'Mara since we were kids – not only for her performance as the Rani, a power-dressing Time Lord in *Doctor Who*, but also for her mesmerizing turn in the epoch-defyingly abysmal *Triangle*. For those too young to remember *Triangle*, let me set the scene. It revolved around a ferry making its three-point journey from Felixstowe to Gothenburg to Amsterdam and back. I know – all the sexy places. Based on US show *The Love Boat*, the British version eschewed sun and fun, and instead gave us a soap opera on the choppy black waters of the North Sea. In one of the more memorable sequences Kate is forced to lie on deck, topless, sunbathing, while a punishing easterly wind necrotizes her nipples. Do watch it online and share her pain. For that sequence alone she will always be the stuff of legend.

I first crossed paths with Kate when I was on the Footlights tour in 1989 and we happened to converge at the Drum Theatre, Plymouth. I was in the studio space, in a wig, shouting; she was in the main house doing *Blithe Spirit* or something classy along those lines. I'd occasionally see her at the stage door, surrounded by adoring flunkies, beautiful and imperious, sporting cheekbones you could grate Parmesan on.

Connecting these two theatres was a public address system that fed into each and every dressing room. For a nineteen-year-old, it was just too much temptation. As part of a dare (I cannot, as you now know, resist any dare) I sneaked into the stage manager's lair, commandeered the microphone and bellowed into it, 'Kate O'Mara's pants to the laundry. Kate O'Mara's pants to the laundry, please.'

And then again, for good measure, just so *every single room* in the building could catch it, 'Kate O'Mara's pants to the laundry. Kate O'Mara's pants to the laundry, please.'

Then I went back to our green room, got on with our little show and thought no more of it. Time passed. Everything got lost in its midst.

Years later Kate O'Mara accepted an invitation to be a guest on *Light Lunch* and duly appeared, with fellow *Dynasty* actress Stephanie Beacham, on the show on 8 May 1997. We wanted to show these grandes dames full respect, and, erroneously believing that imitation was the sincerest form of flattery, we came to set with me dressed as Krystal Carrington (bouffant platinum hair, long fake nails, litres of lipgloss) and Mel as Alexis Carrington Colby (sharp black suit, shoulder pads, statement fascinator). Kate and Stephanie came dressed *as normal human beings.*

What started as something hilarious soon became one of the most painful interviews of my life. From the moment they came on set it became clear we had hugely misjudged the situation. It was, after all, like inviting Sir David Attenborough on and dressing up as a bonobo and a manatee respectively. The interview went from bad to worse when, in an ad break, Mel elected to ask Kate whether she remembered her pants being discussed on the tannoy system of a regional theatre nearly a decade previously. She didn't. But boy it must have been good for her to hear that story again.

By the time we came back live after the break, you could have not only cut the atmosphere with a knife, you could have portioned it up and served it to the assembled audience, who were now becoming aware there was 'a problem'. As the final question fell out of my mouth and languished in the ensuing silence I heard Stephanie mutter under her breath, 'You silly, silly girls.'

And do you know, she was absolutely right.

We were constantly putting our feet in it. When Patrick Duffy came on the show we sang an impromptu version of 'The Star-Spangled Banner' to welcome him and were most irked when he failed to stand to salute. It turns out we were actually singing *La Marseillaise*. Weeks later I found a woman wandering aimlessly around backstage and asked her if she wanted help in finding the audience seating. She was Susanne Vega. In the '*Star Wars* Reunion Special' Kenny Baker (R2D2) was accidentally dropped on the floor by our make-up supremo and mate 'Madame' JoJo. A *Robin's Nest* special, where we had finally learned our lesson and NOT dressed up, featured Tessa Wyatt and Richard O'Sullivan – neither of whom, it transpired, could remember a single bloody thing about the programme. And last but not least, my own personal favourite – the unholy alliance of Nookie Bear and Sooty. Yes, it was a puppet special. Aaah. Lovely puppets. Lovely, sweet, children's puppets. Lovely.

From the get-go it seemed that the personalities of Nookie and Sooty were not compatible. Or, perhaps more pertinently, the personalities of Roger de Courcey and Matthew Corbett were not compatible. Matthew was rolling with a benign kindergarten vibe, while Roger was going for something a little more late-night working men's club. The pair of them in combination was unsettling enough – and then we added the late Keith Harris and Orville to the mix.

The problems began when Nookie (Roger) picked on Sooty (Matthew), who brushed him off with characteristically silent insouciance. Then Nookie (Roger) picked on Orville (Keith), who bore it, literally, through gritted teeth. Desperate to calm an escalating situation, Sooty (Matthew) began gently stroking Nookie's (Roger's) arm, who responded by rolling his eyes and maniacally hissing, 'Go on, say something, Sooty.' Panicking, Orville (Keith) returned to his default mode, expressing a strong desire for flight. The painful hour ended with Nookie (Roger) hitting Sooty (Matthew). It was in essence Roger hitting Matthew, the puppet acting as a boxing glove with a face. In the post-Clarkson world we would have all got the sack as accessories to ABH, but this was 1998, so we simply tucked into a Summer Pudding and waited till the credits rolled.

In 1998, after 150 episodes, the show had reached its peak, before our tired capitulation led to *Light Lunch* becoming the less effective *Late Lunch*, and we walked away from it all in an optimistic, unfocused daze. The schedule of the show was such that real life had not only taken a back seat, it had ceased feeling like real life at all. We had become institutionalized, with little time for the important stuff happening outside the four walls of the studio – family, friends, relationships.

Over the last few years there had been occasional mentions of Dad feeling tired, but his mutterings were lost in the hullabaloo of work. There's always something, isn't there? Something

Spectacles

bright and shiny to take your gaze from where it should be. Change is often glacial. It happens under your nose, but so incrementally your eyes can't detect its movement. Dad's was a slow puncture. And I didn't notice there was something wrong until he was nearly pancake-flat.

I knew that he'd gone to the doctor's. I knew that he needed a scan. Then he had the scan and the next thing I knew was that it was cancer. On 23 December 1998 we found out Dad had cancer.

I arrived home on Christmas Eve and rang the doorbell. I'd lost my keys nearly a decade before but couldn't bear to tell Mum, lest she run wild with visions of homicidal maniacs wading their way through our luxuriantly tufted hall carpet with a beady eye on her knick-knacks.

She opened the door. Dad shuffled towards me from behind her and promptly burst into tears.

My dad. *Crying.*

I'd only seen him cry once before, when I was six and decided to run away from home. It wasn't much of a bid for freedom – in truth I'd talked a big game ('I'm going and I'm never coming back!'), but I'd only made it as far as the privet hedge in the garden. I snuggled into the shrubbery and ate a packet of salt and vinegar Chipsticks while my parents frantically screamed my name. Once the packet was empty, I made my triumphant entrance, expecting a fanfare as the Prodigal returned. In fact I got a clip around the ear and a tear-stained lecture from my dad. Turns out those few minutes, when they really thought they'd lost me, were enough to reduce him to rubble.

Dad was admitted to Mayday Hospital as soon as the Christmas holidays were over, in early January 1999. I remember the reassuring list of West Indian hips as my favourite nurse walked through the ward with the drinks trolley. I remember the kindness of an Australian man called Craig Backway, who, with a name like that was always destined for a colo-rectal unit some-where in the world. But most of all I remember trying not to think *anything*, not for a *second*, because thinking would lead to feeling, and feeling would lead me to the pressing reality that I might actually lose my dad.

I moved on. Kept busy. I was practical. It turns out that in a crisis I am 100 per cent my mother's daughter. I can do it. I can do anything. Just don't ask me to stop. I cannot, not for a *second*, stop.

Every night after work I would head down to sunny Thorn-ton Heath and joke around with everyone on the ward. *Look at me – I'm the life and soul – look at how much fun I am!* I have never brought my work home with me, but there I was, taking that exhausting, inflated version of myself out of hours, bouncing cheerily around the beds until visiting time was up and I could give way to silence.

I'd come home and cook dinner with my sister, who was still living at home and bearing the brunt of it all. We'd serve acres of lasagne, steaming colanders of fusilli and cheap tomato sauce that tasted faintly of metal. There were buckets of tea. Then we would laboriously wash and dry the dishes. We had a dishwasher. No matter. We wanted the extra work. We wanted something to do. When I finally gave in to tiredness, I'd sleep until dawn. At 5 a.m. it was time to get in the car and head north of the river to work. And repeat.

And repeat.

Dad's ward was like every NHS ward you've ever been in. The blue plastic sheeting, the beige plastic furniture, the tiny plastic cupboard where you keep the one or two things that mark you out as an individual human being. There are pipes and tubes and alarms. Trolleys rattle with packaged meds and blood-pressure monitors. The toilet signs take your gaze with a luminous yellow ferocity.

It was a men-only ward. Strong men. Fathers. They had been the axis on which their children plotted their burgeoning lives. And here they all were – brought down, levelled, lying there in hastily bought pyjamas and kept awake by each other's coughs, moans and excretions. Welcome to the grim camaraderie of cancer.

One by one they left. A bed would fall empty and then be filled again. Sometimes you would dare to ask whether they had managed to walk out of the ward themselves, or whether they had been pushed, on a trolley, to the silent chill of the basement below.

Dad had several friends on that ward, but in particular he bonded with a man called John. John was a good man. A good family man – like my dad. And his wife, Marian, was a good woman – like my mum. And their kids were good kids – like we hope we're good kids. John and Dad got diagnosed together (both tumours, graded C for 'Christ that's bad'), went through serial, brutal operations together and the endless ensuing blood tests, CT scans and radiotherapy. They even clicked their morphine pumps together, through the dead of night, in wordless synchronicity.

We shared a destiny. Their family and our family. Together.

As part of a randomized trial Dad wore a Hickman line for twelve months which pumped chemo through a capillary into the right atrium of his heart. I can still see my parents' fridge now, full to bursting with fruit, vegetables and fluorouracil 5FU. John, on the other hand, received his chemo once every month at the hospital. Random. Random. Random.

John didn't make it.

Dad did.

Dad 'beat' cancer. His mate didn't. Isn't that the definition of a pyrrhic victory?

I hate that phrase – 'beat cancer'. Cancer isn't a war or a fight that you win or lose. It's bad luck. It's bad genes. It's bad timing. It's a postcode lottery. Call it what you will, just don't call it a fight. Doing so makes all those who don't make it weak. Or losers. I hate that.

Surviving cancer is hard. It returns you to your home a different person. It changes you, changes your world view. Sometimes it changes you for the better – you're more resolved to squeeze the juice out of your remaining years. That at least is the trope we most often see in books and films. But sometimes it returns you scooped out and hollow – resentful that you've worked yourself to the bone for nearly fifty years and that what was supposed to be the glorious era of retirement has been scarred by disease and incapacitation.

That's the dad who came home to us. Silent. Sad. Reduced.

Dad's an empirical soul. He needs to see proof – evidence. And if you can't see it – if you can't pick through the mesh of your insides and see your guts free of taint for yourself – then how can you truly believe or trust that it is gone?

So yes, Dad survived cancer. But trust me, he didn't 'beat' it.

Sadness grew up around him like ivy. This man, the vital father who had worked hard and played harder, now sat in his chair, exhausted, for the best part of a decade. And as his world narrowed, so did Mum's. The two of them handcuffed together. For better, for worse. In sickness and ill health.

And perhaps that's why I rush at everything now with such intensity – because I know that maybe, one day, all that is coming for me. Maybe. But until then . . .

All clear.

Go on.

All clear.

A Gram of Gorilla

As my thirtieth birthday loomed, Mel went very quiet – possibly remembering her own thirtieth *two long years* before.

I had my suspicions she was organizing a surprise party.

I've never been any good at entertaining. Perhaps it comes from my mother's catastrophizing gene – 'Well I wouldn't want to cater. My friend Jean knows someone who got Cushing's from a mushroom vol-au-vent' – or perhaps it comes from my father's over-empathetic gene – 'Don't ask them. They won't want the imposition of being asked.' Either way, I fear holding a party. What if the people I know from school don't get on with the people I know from college? What if the people from college don't get on with my work colleagues? What if *any* of those people find out I'm not really an Olympic fencing champion?

It's made, as it turns out, for a rather compartmentalized life. And that's annoying and self-defeating. Silly me. Anyhow, I digress.

So, the story I'd been given was this. I was told to come to our local for 7.30 p.m. for a quiet meal with Mel and my closest mates. As I walked up to the main doors I could hear a throng of people shouting.

'I told you to get here at 7.30!'

'Shut up, Dan!'

'*You* shut up!'

'Shh, you bunch of twats – she's coming!'

I approached the door, and, even though I could imagine what lay the other side, I still felt sick with apprehension. As I pushed through, the place erupted.

SURPRISE!

I'll tell you what *was* a surprise – the fact that my parents were there. Why? Because it turns out their ability to keep a secret is second to none. They didn't tell me about the surprise party when I phoned to say I would come and see them for lunch on my birthday. They didn't tell me after I drove – for *two hours* in the pouring rain – the fifteen miles home to Croydon. They didn't tell me as I sat opposite them eating a metre of vegetarian lasagne. And they certainly didn't tell me as I turned round and drove – for another *two hours* – all the way back to north London.

'Careful when you brake!' said Mum as I pulled away. 'The roads are treacherous! And remember what I told you about that Yardie scam. If someone flashes their lights at you, don't flash back, else they'll carjack you and leave you for dead in Norbury.'

And with that she stood on the front step and waved until I disappeared into the distance.

Bastards. They must have got in their car and followed me as soon as I was out of sight. And so there they were, as I opened the door to the pub in Kensal Rise that very same evening.

'Surprise!' they shouted alongside everyone else.

'You utter pricks!' I shouted back into my mum and dad's faces, somewhat ungenerously.

I spent the evening getting very drunk. There were a few speeches, some mild indiscretions, some gift-giving. But as the night wore on, things took a sinister turn. At around 11 p.m. I became aware of a rather shifty-looking guy loitering at the margins, talking to Mel.

'Who's he?' I asked Emma. 'Do we know him?'

'I dunno. I mean, he's probably no one,' said Emma, unconvincingly.

I felt the cold hand of fear clamp around my throat.

Out of the corner of my eye I saw the man pull out of a bag what appeared to be a large Marigold studded with pubes. Next came a full body suit, similarly hairy, and a large *Planet of the Apes* face mask. I watched as Mel gave him a surreptitious thumbs up, and he disappeared into the toilets. I tried to carry on my conversation but found myself staring at the door, transfixed, waiting for the inevitable to appear.

I didn't have to wait long. The music suddenly changed. Leery music. Sexy music. The crowd moved back into a semi-circle leaving me isolated. Finally, emerging from the bogs, a figure resembling a bargain-basement silverback approached. I remember seeing an ex-boyfriend pre-emptively covering his face with his hands and hearing the sound of our mate Gareth, head flipped back like a Pez dispenser, laughing that room-filling boom of his.

What followed was so deeply traumatizing all I remember is a patchwork of images – fragments that come and go in no particular order:

Firstly, the man in the pube-suit lumbered towards me, arms outstretched. As he did so, his face mask slipped so that he could no longer see through the eyeholes. The lack of visibility meant he became less Gorilla in the Mist, more Gorilla's Slightly Pissed. His fingers made their first point of contact with me just around my nipples, whereupon he ground to a sudden halt.

In an instant he was frantically stripping. There was nothing erotic about it – it was simply mask off, suit off, job done. In fairness he did take his time struggling with one of the rubber gloves, which gave the performance a faint air of burlesque mystique. Other than that, he dispensed with his clothes with all the urgency of a contaminated chemist shedding a biohazard suit.

The man now stood before me wearing nothing but a pair of leopard-skin micro-pants and a furry gauntlet.

In a flash he had pushed me down to the floor and stood over me, gyrating. The PA kicked into Tight Fit's version of 'The Lion Sleeps Tonight', and I could see, as I lay there prostrate, Mr Gorilla's pelvis thrusting to the beat, and his ball sack following a second later, in joyous syncopation.

'Oh dear . . . Oh dear . . . No, that's . . . Oh. Oh dear . . .' said Mel weakly from the sidelines.

Mr Gorilla decided to take it up a notch. Without warning he spun round, squatted down onto all fours and started doing press-ups – ON ME – his body facing the other direction from mine. As his groin battered my nose, I got the unmistakable tang of unwashed fur fabric and sweaty seam. I gagged a little and tried to block out the fact that all the people I loved in the world were not only watching this horror unfold, but may actually have had an active role in planning it.

Added to which, I could hear him, each time his face descended towards my groin, moaning a name, rhythmically in time with his thrusts. It was indistinguishable at first, but gradually grew clearer.

'Mel . . .

'Oh, Mel . . .

'Yeah, that's right, Mel.

'Mel. You love it, Mel.

'You love it, don't you, Mel. Oh yeah . . .'

Let me tell you, there is only one thing worse than being cock-slammed by a man with questionable hygiene wearing a single poorly made gorilla glove in front of your family and friends. That is when the man with questionable hygiene wearing that single poorly made gorilla glove happens to be orgasmically groaning the name of your best mate.

The booking was made under the name of Mel. He thought I was Mel. Hell, everyone, even a bloody gorilla, thinks I'm Mel.

The atmosphere in the room had now changed. The laughter and cheering had subsided, and now there was just an uncomfortable silence. This was slowly turning into a primate re-versioning of *The Accused*.

'He was only supposed to read a poem,' said Mel despairingly, her voice now a mere whisper.

Mr Gorilla jumped up and pulled my limp body from off the floor. *It's over*, I thought. *Finally, it's over.*

It wasn't. He proceeded to lean me up against a wall and dry-hump me.

During the next five minute ordeal, I remember Mel approaching Mr Gorilla, proffering his other glove and gently encouraging, nay *pleading* with him to put his clothes back on. She then held up the suit, which now looked like a massive used condom that had been rolled on by a million Labradors. But no, he carried on, oblivious, until the final track had finished.

All I can say is this. Mel, you are fifty in a few years' time. On that day I will find you – and I will be bringing Cheetah with me.

Births, Deaths, Marriages

Melanie Giedroyc, who is nearly two years older than I am, could have chosen any outfit she wanted to dress me in for her wedding, and boy, she really thought about it. *She's my maid of honour, after all*, she mused, *so I could legitimately put her in a peach meringue with puffball sleeves. Or something bias-cut, in ivory. She'd love that. Mmm . . . But what would cause maximum damage? What would cause maximum damage to Sue's already fragile psyche?*

She finally found the ideal sartorial weapon, in the form of a pair of acid-pink silk pyjamas with a Mao collar. It was November. I looked like a Chinese Jane from Rod, Jane and Freddy – but colder.

I turned up late to Mel's wedding, like I do to all weddings. You see, I have form when it comes to public splicings. I was so late for my friend Catherine Hood's nuptials that she was already at the door of the church when I arrived. As I wandered down the aisle, desperate to find a seat, the organist started 'Here Comes the Bride' – which caused quite a stir, I can tell you. 'Gosh, we didn't think it was *that* sort of marriage. Why on earth didn't she *say* . . .?'

I went one better for my brother's wedding. I nearly didn't turn up at all.

It took place in Perth in Scotland over a long and very drunken weekend. I arrived heartbroken and skinny (which is the best kind of heartbroken) and spent the night before the ceremony ruefully reflecting on yet another failed relationship. The next morning I saw my family for a full Scottish breakfast, after which we all went to our respective rooms to get ready. The plan was we'd rendezvous at 11 a.m. and the minibus would take us all from there. Simple. What could possibly go wrong?

OK, so I was a little late. Maybe five minutes – ten, tops. Quarter of an hour at the most. I may or may not have been watching a World Cup match, which might have gone to penalties. Plus I had to do my hair. I have the hair of a baby – fine and flyaway – and it takes tubs of goop to make it do anything or go anywhere. In the end I was forced to grease it into a shape thereafter rather unkindly known as the 'wonky cockerel'. I put on my suit, a rather flamboyant affair in a rich Lenten purple which with hindsight made me look like a Laurence Llewelyn-Bowen impersonator. Finally, after twenty minutes – max – I headed down to reception.

The hotel was silent. No one was there. Not in the entrance hall or the bar or the dining room. The panic was immediate. There is no way my anxious mother and equally anxious sister would not have been on time. They would, if they had been allowed, have camped out all night outside the church with sandwiches and a Thermos. I approached the woman on the front desk.

Me: Scuse me. Do you know whether the minibus for the wedding party has arrived?
Woman: Oh aye, that's away now.
Me: What do you mean away?
Woman: They've been away up the church – ooh – about ten minutes ago. Hang on – let me check . . .
Me: No, it's fine . . .
Woman: It's nae bother. I'll check for you.

She proceeds to ring each and every room. I desperately try to interject . . .

Me:	Listen . . .
Woman:	Och, I'm not getting an answer from your mum and dad.
Me:	It's really OK.
Woman:	Let me try your sister's room.
Me:	Please.
Woman:	It's ringing!

Five whole minutes pass as I watch this sweet, kindly woman help me. For a moment I long for the unhelpful churlishness of a London receptionist. If nothing else, impoliteness is a time-saver.

Woman:	Nope. All gone!

Now I could have just *rung* my mum, but this was 2001. Mobile phones were the size of house bricks and the price of unicorns. I did own one, but as usual I hadn't bothered charging it.

You need to know this about me. In almost all situations I have no charge on my mobile phone, plus:

b. little or no idea of where I am
c. little or no cash
d. no credit card
e. an extremely, *extremely* limited well of personal resourcefulness

So, the facts were these. My brother, my beloved brother, was getting married in twenty minutes. My family had all left without me in the minibus provided. I had lost the invite months ago and had no idea which church they were getting married in. Desperate, I turned again to the kindly receptionist.

Me: Sorry, would you be able to call me a cab? As soon as possible?
Woman: Of course, dear. Let me ring my pal Sammy, up at the station. He's the best driver round this way.
Me: Thank you.

The phone rings. I hear a man answer.

Woman: Is that you, Sammy? Halloo, it's only Moira up the hill. How are you?

The man rumbles a response.

Woman: I'm very glad to hear it. Will you be wanting your tea again tonight, only it's no bother for me to fix it . . .

More rumbling.

Woman: I can do you soup and a roll?

Monosyllabic bark.

Woman: Will you be needing something more substantial?

Miscellaneous jibber-jabber.

Me: Seriously, I should be getting on . . .
Woman: How's Jacky? His hip still giving him bother? Ach, poor lamb . . .

I wonder how long it might take. How long my instant-gratification city-honed demanding personality can take. The answer is thirty seconds.

Me: [*shouting maniacally over her*] I need a cab now! Now!
             NOW!

Five minutes later a smiley-faced octogenarian with grey mutton chops pulls up at the hotel entrance.

Cabbie: Right, where can I take you?
Me: To a church. Any church. All the churches. NOW!

I had turned into everyone's worst nightmare of a Londoner. Rude, pushy and with wonky cockerel hair.

Perth has at least fourteen churches. I know because I visited them all, one after another. I had no idea which denomination the building I was supposed to be in was, so the cabbie and I did a whistle-stop tour of two Methodists, one Presbyterian, a Church of Scotland, Free Church of Scotland and the distinctly happy-clappy Evangelical Church of the Nazarene.

I had all but given up hope when suddenly a long, sleek black limo came into view. It was a fifty-fifty chance – either wedding or funeral cortège. I took that chance.

'Follow that car!' I bellowed at the minicab driver while secretly wondering whether, if I had indeed chosen wrongly, I could rock my purple Regency-fop look at a crematorium.

We followed the car until it came to a halt at yet another of Perth's churches. I held my breath to see whether a cadaver or my sister-in-law-to-be would emerge from the vehicle. I can still feel the relief as she got out – radiant, nervous and beautiful.

'STOP THE CAR,' I screamed, 'and have soup and a roll on me!' I shoved a twenty-quid note into the driver's lap.

I will always remember Lynne's face as I sprinted past her. The organ started up. *Not again*, I was thinking. *Don't go down the aisle to 'Here Comes the Bride' again.* I pelted through the church door and past the pews until I found my family, at the front. Michelle was sobbing. Dad was fiddling with the stop-watch setting on his wristwatch. Mum was rocking anxiously and threw her hands in the air as I dropped into the seat next to her.

Mum: Oh gosh, Susan! I'm so sorry – we forgot all about you!

Me: [*hissing*] There are only three of us! And one of us is busy getting married! So really you only had *two of us* to remember. You forgot about 50 per cent, 0.05 of your available children!

My sister carries on sobbing, clinging on to me like a taffeta barnacle.

Mum: [*wailing*] You're right! I'm a terrible mother!

Me: Oh Christ, here we go again . . .

Dad: [*bellowing*] What's going on with you?

Me: What do you mean?

Dad: Is that deliberate?

Me: Is what deliberate?

Dad: You. You look like Laurence Llewelyn-Bowen.

And then the bride walked up the aisle. I will never forget the face of my sister-in-law-to-be as she walked past our assembled family: two keening women, a man holding a digital watch timing how long it was taking her to get to the altar, and a tardy, dishelleved lesbian dressed like Beau

Brummell. It was a face that said, *Is it too late for me to pull out?*

Welcome. Welcome to Clan Perkins, love.

But back to Mel's wedding – Mel, who is nearly two years older than me. The groom was (and still is) a wonderful man called Ben, who is six foot five inches worth of utter magnificence. Their ceremony was a perfectly beautiful, simple affair at the local church, followed by a reception at the village hall. I don't think I'm breaking any confidences by revealing that Mel was four months pregnant when she walked down the aisle. As a result, she was having alterations to her dress every single week in the run-up to the actual day. Forty-eight hours before the event the seamstress finally gave up on any attempt at finesse and simply installed a couple of giant side panels which made room for last-minute expansion. Even so, on the morning of the ceremony the bridesmaids were frantically unpicking seams to make way for a little extra baby spread.

So, I was the maid of honour – a maid in psychedelic jim-jams thanks to Mel. This job carried with it responsibilities. (I know, have the people closest to me learned *nothing* by now? If there are responsibilities to be dished out, give them to *responsible people,* not the distracted moon child in the dirty glasses.)

My prescribed role was to give a speech celebrating the bride. After Gorillagate? I don't think so. Truthfully, it felt strange. Public speaking was something I did for work. I didn't want this to feel like work; I wanted it to be real and raw and heartfelt. So I decided not to prepare anything. When the time came, I got up, stood in front of the assembled crowd and immediately realized I'd made a huge mistake.

As I began speaking, there was this sudden tightening in my throat. My breathing became shallow. *I must be going down with something*, I thought and carried on. The tightness persisted, moving deep into my chest.

I'd never actually been called upon to describe my relationship with Mel before; I'd only ever spoken about it in terms of what it *wasn't* . . .

Are you best friends? No.

Like sisters? No.

Twins? No.

Just work colleagues? No.

Are you lovers? GET OUT OF TOWN – THAT'S GROSS!

Yet here I was, finally, having to define it. Having to stand there and give my account of what she meant to me, this other strand of my double helix. The more I spoke, the more I started to connect with what I was really feeling.

Loss.

I know, I really am an A-grade arsehole. There I am, putting myself and my emotions in the centre of my mate's BIG DAY. I felt all the joy of the occasion, for sure, but it was accompanied by a profound sense of something being over. It felt like a death. I was a mourner, as well as a celebrant, at the wedding.

I was so overcome that I spent the next three hours clinging to the bride like a luminescent koala. So much so that in every photo it looks like it was Mel and I getting hitched. The three hours after that I spent clinging to the groom so it looked like Ben and I were getting hitched. As a result there's not one single photo of that day where the newly-weds are actually pic-tured *next to each other* – photo-bombed as they were by me, the Girl in the Pink Pyjamas.

When Mel went into labour I paced up and down my front room like a laboratory animal. Occasionally she was able to get word out from the hospital: she'd had a curry, she'd been induced, she'd been induced again. For three days she wan-dered the corridors of the hospital hooked to a drip, desperate for some cervical reaction. Something. Anything. Then everything went quiet.

Radio silence.

Those hours felt the longest of my life. We're never, ever not in touch. Finally the phone rang. There was a weak voice at the end of the phone – familiar but battered. An old friend. A new mother.

Breaking into a hospital is very hard to do. Trust me, that night I tried. I busted through fire doors and circumvented matrons; I even managed to make it as far as the inner sanctum of the maternity unit. Sadly, my progress ended there. There were even alarms going off. Bloody security. Storm in a teacup, I'm telling you. There really was no need for that armlock and all that shouting.

The next day I opted to go through more-official channels and turn up at visiting hours. I was shocked by how tired Mel looked. But radiant too. How could she manage that? How you could look ruined and complete at the same time?

Once mother and baby were back at home later that night, I

dropped round. We lay on the bed on a bedspread made by my mum for Mel's thirtieth. We'd lain there a million times – laughing and gossiping – but this time, instead of talking, we were silent, in a kind of awe at the little thing she had created. Mel bent her head forward and lightly touched her daughter's nose with her own, and I watched her watching her child.

She's done it, I thought, *this friend of mine. She's crossed the Rubicon. She's gone somewhere I can never go, somewhere beyond the reach of my understanding or experience. We've gone everywhere hand in hand together. But I can't go here. Not here. I can't go here with you and share it.* It was one of the most beautiful and painful experiences of my life, that hour on the bed with my darling mate and her hours-old child. I could feel that love, that transcendent love, but as if through glass. I could see it, but I couldn't get at it.

I think that night was perhaps the first time I had to contend with the painful reality of being a grown-up – that messy, unarticulated feelings stay with you for ever without finding resolution. You just live with this unnamed weird stuff. We all do. So I did what I'd seen proper grown-ups do – I swallowed it down, all of it, took a deep breath and moved on.

Over the ten years we had gigged together we had gone from performing to no one to performing to thousands and back, in 2003, to performing to just a few disinterested people again. Our final ever tour date was at the famous Haymarket Theatre in Leicester. There were fewer than a hundred people dotted around the stalls and circle. That night we said the words in the right order but there was no joy behind them. We simply couldn't inhabit the fun any more. There was no work on the horizon and there was no interest in us any more. We knew it was over. Our double act was done.

Until our own little cake-baby arrived some seven years later.

When it comes to Mel and me, I genuinely forget where her experiences end and mine begin. Writing this book, I was about to recount an anecdote from school involving a pair of pants and a discus, and then realized it wasn't my anecdote at all. It wasn't my life, but hers. Such is the hive mind, the collective consciousness we have become over the years.

Sometimes when we're drunk we'll try and articulate all that stuff – that awkward stuff that sits at the margins of love and friendship. But mainly we leave it alone, leave it all unsaid and carry on regardless in a thoroughly British fashion. What I do know is that this kinship will always remain. It is constant. It is a love that cannot be weathered, not by time, not by circumstance.

Nothing can alter it.

Unless, of course, UKIP get into power and has her sent back to Eastern Europe.

FOUR
Cornwall

The Ballad of Pickle and Parker, or How I Fell in Love

They say a dog is a man's best friend. Well, Nicola, Sarah, Emma, Mel, Neil, Gemma and Andy are my best friends, and what's more they don't shit on the carpet and whine outside my bedroom door for food at 5.30 a.m.*

It was all Emma's fault. She started it. She got a beagle called Poppy, and there was something so intoxicating about the constant exhaustion, commitment and inability to have a second to oneself that it made me want one of my own.

I'm nothing if not impulsive, so the following week my sister and I duly headed to the same breeder in Cheshire – a redoubtable woman called Janet, all flush-faced and tweedy. She was the sort of woman who displayed rosettes on the wall rather than family photos, and who just might have kept a Shetland pony in her living room. I suspect she would have found even a no-nonsense approach a little frilly for her tastes.

I had barely set foot through Janet's door when I was greeted with the now-familiar gust of wet dog and Dettol. Suddenly, out of nowhere, a miniature pinscher thundered towards me and began making breakfast of my trouser leg.

Janet: You all right?
Me: Yes, thank you.
Janet: Well shut t' bloody door then.

* OK, Mel did once, but it was a long time ago now.

Me: Oh yes, sorry.

She sizes me up for a few seconds while the dog yaps incessantly at my heels.

Janet: Will you BE QUIET, Jasper! [*To me*] See there, over t' way?

She motions across the street with her free hand, the other attempting to wrestle the dog's jaws from my ankle.

Me: Yes . . .
Janet: Little bastard over there, hangs himself from the beams every night, watching me.
Me: Really? Your neighbour . . . *hangs* himself?
Janet: Auto-erotic something. I don't know. Dirty bugger. I just shut me curtains. Out of sight and all that. Do what he likes then. I don't mind. Anyway, come and meet Prunella.
Me: Prunella?
Janet: The bitch. Now mind yourself down t' stairs – they've gone to shit.

I wander into a field behind the house, towards a large enclosure. I honestly have no clue what I'm looking for. I've never had a dog before, so the idea of looking for something more than just the standard four legs, tail and face, is totally new to me.

Janet: Right. Pups are only couple weeks old, so don't go near 'em. You can have a peak through int' kennel, but more than that and I'll give you what for.

I peer through the wooden slats and the effect is instant. My skin slackens, my eyes widen and what feels like the distillation of a million Disney films starts working simultaneously on my heartstrings. Even the usually pragmatic Michelle stands there for half an hour with her hand over her mouth, entranced.

Janet: They've all gone, been sold – bar t' little one. Runt. We've had to bottle-feed her, but she's right as rain now. You want me to put tha name down or what?

Me: Yes.

I speak without thinking. It's not a conscious response. All rationality has left the building. In fact, from that point on rationality never returns.

Janet: Right. Back in a month then. I'll show you t' door. I said MIND T' STEPS!

When I returned four weeks later I was once again led to the field outside, to the wooden hut where I'd first seen the litter.

I waited in silence with Janet, even though I had no idea what I was waiting for. It would have made for the most tedious episode of *Springwatch* ever recorded, that's for certain. Finally, after many minutes, a single pup emerged, stretching and yawning as she hit the daylight.

'Ooh, here she comes. She knows she's for you all right. Come here, girl.'

With one motion, she scooped up the dog, who was so small she fitted on her outstretched hand. She stayed there, surfing Janet's palm, legs wobbling to the sides and outsize ears flapping in the breeze, giving the horizon that bored thousand-mile stare that I would come to know and love.

'Right, here you are . . .'

Whereupon Janet transferred her into my hands, this little warm thing that smelled of milk and sawdust. Eight weeks old. 2.26 kilos.

The exact weight of love.

Janet, meanwhile, had taken a large pair of what looked like bolt cutters and was trimming the dog's nails as she wriggled in my arms. I had no idea what on earth to do next. It was a singularly odd sensation. I'd never been in love and not known what to do about it.

Me: What . . . what do I do?
Janet: Don't look at her, touch her, do owt for her – she's a dog – not a human. Be strict with the little bugger.

She turns to the dog.

Janet: Right you, don't give me that look. I'm glad to be shot of you. Needy, you were, terribly needy. Go on and piss off, and don't be a pain. Don't give her grief, like you're wont to. Go on.

As she turns away from us, I see a single silvery tear making its way down her cheek.

I put Pickle, as she was to be known, in the car, in a crate like I'd been told, and instantly knew I'd done wrong. She gave me a look – the sort of look that Damian gave his nanny in *The Omen* just before she hangs herself from the light fitting. I know now this was Pickle's first attempt at mind control. She became much more effective at it over the eleven years she allowed me to live with her. Within a minute I'd buckled. She was out of the crate and in my sister's arms, and from that moment on it didn't matter what grate or luggage rack or obstacle blocked her way – she would always find a way to barge through from the boot onto the passenger seat. That was *her* seat. *She* was the co-pilot.

Once home, I tried to give her boundaries – NO to the sofa, NO to the bed, NO to my entire dinner – but within a week of arriving at my house she merely had to flash me one of her celebrated withering looks before I'd be racing for the treats jar or rushing over to adjust the contours of her bedding for greater comfort. It wasn't just *mi casa su casa*. It was my bed your bed, my food your food, my life your life. I would go to sleep with her curled at my feet and would wake to find her head on the pillow next to mine, paw over my shoulder, staring at me intently. She was the only creature I've ever met that was as wilful, stubborn and downright odd as I am.

Pickle redefined contrary. She would have broken Cesar Millan in a heartbeat. If there was something a dog was supposed to do, she refrained from doing it. It wasn't that she overtly refused; she just found the request itself nonsensical. She didn't come back when called or run for balls or play with other dogs. Why on earth would you want to do *that*? She would just sniff things, wee on them, then run off in the opposite direction everyone else was heading in.

If she was bored (heaven forbid), she would systematically destroy anything and everything I was fond of. If I watched too much telly, she'd eat her way through the cables. Problem solved. If I headed for the door without her, she would eye up the CD rack, and one by one would crunch the plastic cases between her jaws. Let me tell you from experience – Led Zeppelin and PJ Harvey sound exactly the same once a six-month-old hound has been at them.

Now I had a dog, I had to do the one thing I had avoided all of my life – exercise. I began walking on Hampstead Heath every day, and for the first time I got it. I got how beautiful it all was, you know – *outside*. I grew to appreciate the subtle shifting of colours and textures as one season greeted another. I started to love the reddy slush of autumn, the reassuring suck of December mud, the white winter sun struggling for definition in the white winter sky. And then I'd look forward to the fat spring grass and the paths slowly turning to powder in the heat of whatever summer we had.

It was a love affair. A love affair between me and my dog. And then it became a love affair between me and my dog and the Great Outdoors. And then, just when I thought I couldn't feel any more goddam love, there came the biggest love of all.

And with her came another bloody beagle.

Parker.

I met Kate in the summer of 2003. We would occasionally bump into one other, and as we had friends in common we'd share the odd wander until our paths home diverged. That year there was an Indian summer, and I remember the sun stretching out across endless balmy evenings. The grass was high, and lovers, drunk on cheap fizzy plonk, rolled around on the margins of the meadows. By autumn we had started to arrange to meet, rather than relying on haphazardly finding one another. Once a week. Then twice. Then more. For an hour. Then two. Then more. By November we were walking four hours a day, seven days a week. Even the dogs were exhausted.

Something felt wrong. Very wrong. I phoned Michelle.

Me: Gel, there's something wrong with me. I don't feel right. I can't sleep and I feel sick to my stomach. I just sit around . . .

The Ballad of Pickle and Parker, or How I Fell in Love

Michelle:	Can I stop you there?
Me:	Is it gout?
Michelle:	It's worse.
Me:	I'm in love, aren't I?
Michelle:	I am rather sorry to say, yes, you are.

Two weeks later Kate turned up at my door with a plastic bag containing a toothbrush and her purse, and Parker on a lead. Nothing more. It was all we needed. It was perfect.

Parker was a rather different beast to Pickle. Whereas Pickle was mercurial and charismatic, Parker was lumbering and distinctly on the spectrum. Added to which her breath was a cross between closing time at Billingsgate and the mother alien in *Aliens*. If she licked you, you had to wash it off pronto, lest it burn your skin to the bone. But I loved her from the outset.

We all just loved each other from the outset.

A Shock to the System

As you may have gathered by now, I'm not someone who understands halves, let alone how to do things by them. I probably wouldn't recognize a half if it came up and punched me, though I'd remember the punch itself as a bit, well, half-arsed.

In 2007 I started experiencing severe stabbing pains in the centre of my chest. I would become dizzy and then occasionally collapse. Once, after a gig in Darlington, I spent half an hour on all fours crawling down a hotel corridor trying to get to my room. In retrospect, this would probably be in the top three distressing half-hours on all fours I've had, and, trust me, that's a very long list. There would be days when I'd find it hard even to walk up a single flight of stairs without my head getting foggy and my legs giving way.

One morning after a really acute attack, I was panicked enough to head down to the A&E department of my local hospital. I was admitted to triage pretty sharpish and was duly weighed and measured before sitting down for a blood pressure test. There was a hiss of air as the armband deflated, whereupon the nurse looked quizzical.

Nurse: Are you all right?
Me: Well, no. Not really. That's why, you know, I've come here, you know, to a *hospital* . . .
Nurse: Mmm . . . [*A long and confused silence*] Are you an Olympic athlete by any chance?

I am going to pause for a brief while, just to illustrate how *ludicrous* that question was.

I loved school, mainly because I loved wearing a uniform. In uniform we were all the same, Stepford Kids in navy-blue pleats and nylon shirts. In uniform you couldn't tell who was cool, or whose parents had money, or who was hitting puberty first or last. But in gym kit – that was another story. There is nowhere to hide in an Aertex shirt and granny pants. Trust me, I tried. In PE we were exposed and vulnerable. And I hated it.

I knew from an early age I wasn't cut out for sport. I successfully managed the carb loading, so I was 50 per cent of the way there, but the bit after that, the running and jumping bit, just bored the tits off me. Added to which, I'm lazy. Oh, and weak.

My first memory of running was as a six-year-old at Catholic school playing kiss chase. I was finally collared under the vast statue of the Virgin Mary. Yes, my very first kiss took place under the baleful eye of the mother of Christ. Pathologize *that*, O therapists of London town . . .

In my teens, at a school sports day, I ran the 100 metres. I didn't finish it. You don't see that very often, do you – a runner stopping before the finishing line in a sprint race. Mind you, there were mitigating circumstances. Midway, I was overtaken by my friend Karen Flanders, who was under five feet tall and heavily asthmatic, and the sight of her wheezing next to and then past me made me wee a little. That's another reason I'm no good at physical activity – I have a singularly lame pelvic floor, and it's liable to give way, like old plasterboard, at any given minute.

Much of my antipathy towards sport stems from a genuine failure to understand the point of it. After all, time outside kicking things and throwing things takes you away from a song on the piano or a good book or film. Don't get me wrong – if you throw a ball at me, I will catch it. It's a reflex. I respond a little like Robert De Niro's character in *Awakenings*. Job done. But if you throw the ball and I have to *run* for it – well, as far as I'm concerned that means you've not thrown the ball accurately enough, so why should I reward your incompetence with a return? You're effectively asking me to patronize you, and hey, little lady, I won't do it.

I am as boundaried with all physical activities. I have rules. I *will* swim a little in the sea, as long as there is no one within five miles of the beach to catch sight of me in my cossie. As a result I have not swum since December 1976. As for swimming baths, forget it.

'Hi there, stranger! Mind if I join you in that Petri dish of piss and bacteria? And hey, why don't I strip down to my bra and pants so you can see what I look like with virtually no clothes on!'

I did once go horse riding, but I actually like my vagina so refused to do it again. However, if you're unhappy with your pudenda, why not hop on a pony and batter your genitals into a totally new shape! Plus, the relentless pounding motion provides its own anaesthesia so you won't feel a thing until it's too late!

My dad had been sporty in his youth – although (and this is crucial) not *talented* and sporty. He expended an awful lot of energy, but to no real avail. He was goalkeeper for his local football team as a lad, and his claim to fame was that he dislocated every single one of his fingers while diving to make a save. If only one of those precious fingers had touched the actual ball, he could have been a legend.

In his forties he took up golf because it was an excellent way, as he put it, 'to get away from all you women'. I remembered this, and so in my thirties, when keen to 'get away from all you women' I gave it a go. MISTAKE. It turns out that the golf course is like a living-history documentary, where men dress up in diamond-patterned jumpers and adopt the gender posturings of the 1970s.

I have set foot on links twice and both times have resulted in explosive arguments. The second time, I was following a friend around a course when some twonk in plus fours made a 'hilarious' comment about us having a hole in one, or some such. Needless to say, the red mist came down and I ended up chasing him in a golf buggy until I was overcome with laughter. It's amazing how quickly a high-tensile situation can be defused by a ride in an open-sided electric vehicle.

Throughout most of my adolescence until my mid-thirties, I evaluated all sporting activities according to how likely it was I'd be able to smoke while doing them. I first took up smoking when I was sixteen and was immediately in love with it. It remains one of the very few things I was ever any good at. For this reason, I was a huge fan of rounders. I would always be picked last for the team, and would march delightedly to the outfield. While everyone else slugged away with ball and bat in the centre of things, I'd spark up a Marlboro and find out what base my fellow fielders had got to at the weekend.

I am digressing. You get my point. *I don't do sport.* And so, with that in mind, let's return to the A&E department and the triage nurse's question.

Nurse: Are you an Olympic athlete by any chance?

I slowly survey my sprawling midriff.

Me: No. No, I'm not.
Nurse: You're sure you're not in training?

Me: Absolutely sure.

Nurse: Gosh. Well, in that case you're technically dead. I'm flum-
          moxed. I've never seen a reading like that. Let me get
          someone . . .

Less than five minutes later I was wheeled into the resuscita-
tion unit. By now I felt woozy and confused. Next to me lay a
fifty-something man out for the count, getting his pinstriped
suit cut from his body with a pair of surgical shears. There was
the squirt of gel as lubricant was applied to the paddles followed by the mandatory holler of 'Stand clear!'

The patient spasmed for a second, then was still, then suddenly sat bolt upright.

'I'M AN ESTATE AGENT!' he bellowed, before collapsing
back down again.

The estate agent was deemed drunk and given some IV flu-
ids, but he remained an estate agent, for which, sadly, there is
still no cure. I, however, proved a somewhat more mysterious
case and so was kept in overnight for observation.

Kate arrived to find me rigged up to drips and nebulizers
and lay in the bed with me until the staff finally chucked her
out at around midnight.

The next morning when she phoned, I immediately knew
something was wrong. I pushed her and pushed her to tell me
what was up, and she finally gave way. She had come home
from the hospital, put the dogs to bed and was just getting
ready to go to sleep herself when there was an almighty crash
at the front window. She ran to the front of the flat to find a
man in motorbike leathers and full-face visor smashing his way
through the lounge. His two accomplices were revving their
scooters outside.

Kate didn't get to the end of the story before I was unclipping my oxygen monitors and peeling the electrodes from my chest. It didn't matter what the doctors wanted or what tests they had planned, I was going home. I arrived to find shards of window glass littering the flat. The dogs were still shaking from the ordeal. Kate was doing her best to appear stoical, but I could see the upset beneath.

I know what it is like to feel unsafe. I have been in a nasty relationship and know what it is like for the ground to feel unpredictable and volatile. All I wanted was to get her away. Perhaps to get me away too. To get us away.

What might you have done after a burglary? What pragmatic steps might you have taken? Fixed another lock on the door? Joined the Neighbourhood Watch?

We sold up and moved to a farm in Cornwall.

The Nuts End Up at the Bottom

The track to the house was long and unmade. A tombola of gravel churned against the underside of the car as we bumped along. The estate agent had told us to take a look ourselves – it was so far out of town that she couldn't be bothered to attend the viewing.

We had only got halfway down the track when I knew I wanted to live there. By the time the house itself came into view, I was phoning to make an offer. It was a futile gesture as that part of the world has never had, and will never have, mobile reception. In fact, in that part of the world it's widely believed that electricity comes in buckets from the Magic Well.

The ridge of the slate roof undulated like a wave and the guttering below clung to it for dear life. Inside it stank of damp, the staircase was rotten and most of the downstairs had been pine clad then painted in a deep-orange stain. No matter. I loved it. It wormed its way into my heart and it has never left. As the conveyancing rumbled on, I sat at my desk in London and made plans. Kate would paint, and I would . . . I would . . . well, I'd have a vegetable garden and keep chickens. I could make artisanal chutney! Bespoke jams! Unusual pestos!

It was going to be heaven.

The day we arrived the entire neighbourhood came to say hello, including several artists, a semi-professional water diviner and a white witch. I'm a fan of white witches. After telling me my aura was pink, she winked and said, 'You're in the right place. The South West is like a Christmas stocking –

all the nuts end up at the bottom.' And with those words of wisdom, she turned on her ruby slippers and left.

That afternoon, as a spectacular sea mist rolled in, we headed to the local shop to get firelighters. On returning we found a brace of partridge nailed to the front door, with a long trail of blood dripping down the paintwork. I remain unclear as to whether it was a neighbour's way of saying hello or the Cornish mafia's version of the horse's head in the bed.

I had imagined heaven, and indeed it was. It was heaven for exactly four days. Because the week I moved there the work phone started ringing again.

Music, Maestra, Please

As a child I believed that piano lessons, like everything else related to education and self-improvement, were to be endured. I knew what suffering was; after all I was brought up a Catholic. I'd read *Foxe's Book of Martyrs* and so knew how to accept my lot with a silent and resolute dignity. Playing the piano was simply something I 'should do' – another unexamined, unemotional achievement on the way to adulthood.

Once a week, every week, I would get out of the car, leather satchel flapping in the wind, and wander down the path to Mrs Green's house. The door would open, there would be a gust of boiled cabbage, and a kindly, frail old woman with a single Nanny McPhee tooth would usher me into her lounge. I'd sit at the piano, place my hands in the grooves of yellowed ivory, invent an ever-more elaborate illness which had impeded my practice that week, then inflict an hour's worth of broken scales, faltering arpeggios and syncopated Mozart on her. Poor, poor Mrs Green.

I passed all my grades by the time I was fourteen, due, quite frankly, to my teacher's persistence rather than any real talent on my part. And yet, despite those certificates, I couldn't do the one thing any decent musician would want to do – play a tune. Outside the rigours of the Associated Board syllabus, the three-minute exercises in technique to which I had become accustomed, I was utterly stuck.

Then along came Michiyo Onoue, beautiful, bright and talented – just the sort of lovely girl that other girls love to hate.

Aged just fifteen, she sat down at the rickety piano at school assembly – a spot previously ruled by me – and played Chopin's *Fantaisie-Impromptu*. Perfectly. Musically. It was as if she had exposed me for the faker I was. I never played the piano again. I never played anything again.

So, it's 2008. I am in Cornwall. The work phone is ringing.* I am deep in a raised bed, using a tape measure to make sure my borlotti bean seedlings are planted exactly twenty-five centimetres apart. I am nothing if not my father's daughter.

The job on offer was a show called *Maestro*, a music commission for BBC2 in which eight people compete to learn the basics of conducting an orchestra. I said no. My turning down interesting jobs on successful shows will become a motif, as you shall see.† Thankfully, my amazing friend/agent Debi Allen persuaded me to change my mind by repeatedly shouting 'You're wrong' at various hours of the day and night. A few weeks later I left Cornwall early one morning to begin filming.

I turned up in Britain's sexiest town – Watford – in what I now, with hindsight, see was a DISGUSTING shirt. There was a crowd assembling outside the concert hall, including my fellow contestants:

- King of the swing, the adorable Peter Snow

* I don't have a separate phone for work. Separate phones are for criminals, billionaires and Batman.
† And yet I readily agreed to be the voice of cluster-fuck omni-flop *Don't Scare the Hare*. I really am a proper cretin.

- Suave and sophisticated Katie Derham
- Evergreen beauty, actress and cake mogul Jane Asher
- Man-explosion Goldie
- Gentleman and clown extraordinaire Bradley Walsh
- Eternal Hutch David Soul
- Handsome cheese-botherer Alex James

Inside the hall there was the sound of the orchestra warming up: a wheeze of horns, the bubbling of clarinets, the knife-edge finessing of strings. It's a sound that immediately heightens my senses. It's a sound that says, *Something amazing is about to happen.*

We were each handed sheet music for a famous piece. The tunes were universally known, so it wasn't too onerous for those unfamiliar with scores. Five of us knew how to read music. The remaining three, who happened to be the professional musicians of the group, didn't. I got Johann Strauss's waltz, 'The Blue Danube' – you know, the one that's always on when you inadvertently come across Classic FM. It's a majestic piece of writing, but we've oversung and overplayed it into little more than a cliché. Now it sounds like something that might have been dreamed up to advertise a Kia Picanto.

We barely had a moment to collect our thoughts before we were herded one by one into the concert hall like Brahms to the slaughter. Peter was first. He had been given the tune from Prokofiev's *Romeo and Juliet*, more commonly known as 'Music for Lord Sugar to sack people to'. Bradley and I glued our ears to the door to listen. Surely the Human Swingometer would be a genius conductor, yet the noise within sounded less like star-crossed lovers and more like a fight in a squeezebox museum.

Then it was my turn. There was a suck from the weighted

door as I pushed it open, puncturing the seal on the assembled musicians inside. The orchestra. I'd never seen one up close. The nearest I'd been was the darkest reaches of the dress circle in the Fairfield Halls when Arthur Davison's Family Concerts came to Croydon when I was a kid. I remember an old man standing in a crucifix shape at the head of a bunch of monochromatic dervishes, all blowing, bowing and bashing the hell out of their instruments. It was exhilarating. *So* exhilarating that the combination of too much excitement and a face-full of ice lollies meant I was fast asleep within the first five minutes.

I walked over, past the violins, to the podium. It felt distinctly odd. Instead of following my instinct to face the audience, I had to stand with my arse towards them, staring instead at the semicircle of strangers below. It was then I got a sense of how truly out of my depth I was. I made a joke. It was lame. There was silence. After all, words aren't what turn musicians on.

The orchestra had been charged with following our beat exactly. Whatever moves we busted, whatever time we set, they would follow. I took a deep breath. My shoulders instantly rose to my cheeks with fear. *Come on! This is easy. It's just waving. I know the piece is in three, and I know how to beat three, so I'm laughing.*

The traditional way to beat three is to make a triangle shape, first going down from your head to your chest, then horizontally away from your body, then up to the original starting point around about your head. I put my hand down for the first beat. Some of the band started. Some followed a beat later. The musicians fell, one by one, like dominos, into a puddle of sound. If Les Dawson did strings, this was exactly the noise he would have made.

I was confused. *I'm making triangles*, I thought. *Why aren't they playing along to my triangles?* The orchestra appeared to be looking in my general direction, but just in case some of them had missed me, I started making larger, more emphatic, triangles. The sound dragged still further. *What's going on? WHY CAN'T YOU FOLLOW MY TRIANGLES?* I carried on. By now I looked like Bruce Willis in *Die Hard 2* when he's on the runway frantically waving at the doomed and rapidly descending plane.

After nearly three minutes of manic, incomprehensible semaphore, I was shattered. My face was red. My arm hurt. The piece didn't so much end as gradually disappear – with more of a whimper than a bang.

One by one we lined up to receive this punishment. Our embarrassments were nothing short of genius, a televisual *coup de grâce* – the death blow to those who believe that the conductor doesn't *do* anything. They patently do, because you can see me on screen *not doing it*.

Conductors are deeply enigmatic figures, their profession shrouded in mystery. 'What does a conductor do?' is the second most iterated question on the planet after 'What do lesbians do in bed?' (God forbid, I'd now be tasked with answering both.)

Although a few international conductors are venerated, most stick wavers are, at best, merely tolerated by the band. There's probably a maestro joke for every orchestra in the world, but the one I heard most often was:

Q: What's the difference between a bull and an orchestra?
A: With a bull, the horns are at the front and the shit up the back.

My personal favourite (when enquiring who is in charge of the baton for the night) was the fabulous line, 'Who's doing the carving?'

After the humiliation of Baton Camp, it was time to learn

what 'doing the carving' actually entailed. We spent the next few months studying and rehearsing at the Trinity Music College at Greenwich, a cluster of impeccable Regency buildings in south-east London. My mentor was the charming Jason Lai, who had the face of an angel and the terrifying intensity of Mussolini. That time, out of the sight of the camera, studying scores, developing my instinct, physicality and confidence, turned out to be one of the most profound periods of my life.

Everything I am about to say about my experiences as a conductor I say as a rank amateur. It may seem – especially if you, Dear Reader, are a professional musician – childish, naive or misguided. To you, the professional, I will most likely seem as much of an advert for musicianship as Maria Schneider is for butter. But this is what the experience felt like to inhabit, so forgive what are inevitable simplifications and gaps in my knowledge.

To make something as discernible as sound, you begin with silence. Silence is the essential canvas onto which everything else is laid. A piece starts and ends with silence, and into that calm, still space, before a single note is struck, the conductor must give what is known as the upbeat. This is the upward motion that announces that the first beat of the piece is coming. It is a signpost. It prepares. With it you are flagging your intent, you are gathering the energy of the group in order to unleash it upon the auditorium. The upbeat will carry messages about the tone, the feeling of the music and sometimes, although not always, its speed. I have seen some conductors give an upbeat as if they are gathering the air towards them like unruly children. Some simply waggle their fingers. Others expand their chests, raise their heads and violently push to the heavens. Each upbeat for each piece is different, and each conductor will give it in their own inimitable fashion.

(At this point, now I'm getting into this, I can't tell you *how much easier* it is to answer the question 'What do lesbians do in bed?')

In basic terms, your lead hand sets the speed, or tempo. It's responsible for 'distributing music on the axis of time' as the New York Philharmonic's Esa-Pekka Salonen rather beautifully describes it. More often than not, a conductor holds a baton in their lead hand (in my case the left, as I am left-handed) – a white pointy stick which amplifies your hand movements, making them easier to see from the back of the orchestra.

Your *other* hand is tasked with providing notes on expression and timbre. What is important? Which line do you want to shine in that moment? With what kind of sound? What colours and textures do you want to show? It's a kind of 'emotional ventriloquism', as Justin Davidson of *New York* magazine puts it. It's feeling by proxy. You calibrate the mood, then ask the musicians to physically create it for you.

You can tell a lot from the way someone holds their baton. (Oh, stop it.) It's a pretty good indication, I think, of how someone approaches power in general. Do you grab at it? Do you bully or do you cajole? Or does it bounce, all loose and fanciful? I've never felt very comfortable with a baton in my hand (I said *stop it*) perhaps because I feel, inherently, I don't deserve to brandish one. I'm much more comfortable with a pencil or a biro. Once I even used a toothbrush for a concert. However you hold it, I'm afraid I don't agree with the loaded notion of the maestro, i.e. the conductor as boss. For me, the conductor is the moderator of a million exciting artistic conversations happening simultaneously – a graphic equalizer, a sculptor of sound.

OK, now to the beat. The beat is always a downstroke. Place your hand in front of you, palm up. Then bring your lead hand down to clap it. Clap it rhythmically for a while. Then remove your bottom hand. When you create a beat for the orchestra, you are essentially replicating hitting a surface somewhere in front of you.

Of course, it's not just about the beat but about everything between it too, which would explain why, during my 'Blue Danube', the orchestra got progressively slower the larger my triangles became. The space between the beat got larger, and so the beat itself slowed down. Also, I was marking time with stiff, rigid lines, so the music sounded stiff and rigid too. If you flow, they flow. And if you manically score a giant Dairylea in the sky, then your 'Danube' will sound truly, truly shite.

The hardest thing about conducting is that you cannot wholeheartedly listen to the orchestra. You have to be a fraction ahead, leading the beat. If you get lost in the music they are making, you are already slowing down. You must be simultaneously in the now and the next, creating a feedback loop, a charmed circle, a beating heart with you at the centre of it.

That's the idea. The reality, as I discovered, proved to be somewhat harder.

The first live show on *Maestro* featured music from film and TV and I struck gold with *The Simpsons*. I loved it. It had a chaotic, wonky intensity with everyone, especially brass and percussion, at full tilt. I started to learn how to echo the textures of the piece with my physicality. This was hard, as I have very poor posture and don't love the way I look. I may have sloughed off a slight stammer, but hints of chronic shyness remain in my lolloping walk, dropped head and sloping shoulders. It took a team of mentors to get me to stand straight, and to look the orchestra in the eye. So much of the work of the conductor is in the eyes. You gaze at strangers with the intimacy of a lover, glare at them with the visceral hatred of a rival. It is not for the shy, it is not for the weak, it is certainly, as I was to discover, not for the emotionally closed.

Opera week arrived, and I was given the famous aria 'O mio babbino caro' from Puccini's *Gianni Schicchi* to carve to. It's a song that speaks of yearning and desire, as a daughter tells her father of her love for her boyfriend. It's searing, soaring, open-hearted stuff.

And I couldn't do it.

This was the first time I'd had to conduct slow music, and I immediately felt myself resisting. It made me uncomfortable – the delicacy, the poignancy, the messy emotional intrusion of it all. Quite simply it was asking something of me I didn't want to give.

Like many families, the Perkinses aren't given to grand displays of affection. We don't say, 'I love you.' We *think* it, but we don't *say* it. That sort of thing would be far too continental and embarrassing. Love, in my family, is generally assumed rather than iterated. *I wouldn't want to force it down your throat*, I can imagine my mum and dad saying, like it would be an unbearable burden they'd be saddling me with. My parents never heard it from their parents, so they weren't accustomed to saying it in return. You pass on what you get, don't you? The family baton of hopes and dreams and happiness and screw-ups. You pass it down the line like a relay across time and space.

I say 'I love you' all the time. I say it to partners* and friends. I write it on Post-it notes and scribble it on chalkboards. I sign

---

* One at a time. I am too tired to be polyamorous.

off emails with it and whisper it down the phone. I like saying it as often as I can. But in my family it remains resolutely unsaid. Which isn't to say that my folks didn't love me. I always felt loved. Always. I just didn't have it *confirmed* to me in the way you see in movies and on TV.

This is what you need to know. I am an appalling, appalling softie. But somehow, somewhere along the line, I've learned how to hide it. Hide that sentimentality and vulnerability. Control the emotions beneath. My dad does it using data. My mum does it by catastrophizing, so that reality always turns out better than her imaginings. I do it with words. Bluster. It fortifies me against the outside world.

Take away the words, and I am lost.

Music asks questions that your head will attempt to answer, but only your heart can truly understand. If you try to hide your heart, then you are not a musician. The one thing I had never given music, in all the years at Mrs Green's, hacking at the ivories, was my vulnerability. My passion. My soul – whatever *that* is. It's a big ask for a weirdo like me who has spent her life concealing her vulnerability with fake, polysyllabic bravado.

The final was between me and Goldie. I love Goldie. He's an explosive keg of raw energy and ideas. He's fun. He looked the part too, all handsome in his spanking tux.

It meant more than I thought it might to win – because, while it's utterly true to say that the experience itself was reward enough, the previous years had been so very dispiriting. I hadn't worked for as long as I could remember. I'd left the familiarity of London and the job I loved, but, more importantly, I'd lost every trace of self-belief. And that night, the night when the result came in, was the start of my rebuilding myself from scratch.

When I allowed myself to think about conducting in Hyde Park at the Last Night of the Proms, many images sprang to mind. None of them included a horde of menopausal women throwing knickers onto the stage, shouting 'We love you, Terry Wogan' while I drove my hands to the beat of 'Pomp and Circumstance'. There wasn't a lot of pomp, and as for the circumstance, well someone's large frilly camisole was now draped across my left foot.

While the Proms was a strange come-down from the show, the most extraordinary night of my life was gifted to me by conducting. Comic Relief took command of the Albert Hall one night in May 2011, in an effort to break the Guinness world record for the most kazoo players playing simultaneously. The place was packed. It was a fabulous bill – Julian Lloyd Webber, Nicola Benedetti, Tim Vine and the gorgeous BBC Concert Orchestra.

I had the honour of conducting two pieces with the band. Firstly, 'Mambo' from Leonard Bernstein's *West Side Story*. It's hard for a stolid northern European like me to conjure the spirit of Cuba. 'Mambo' is fast and vertical, with jagged offbeats, dizzying virtuoso brass and whirlwind percussion. There's a riot of bongos, timbales and cowbells. It is jumping. It screams life from the top of its lungs. If you want to see the Albert Hall being ripped apart by the sheer joyous force of it, then check out Gustavo Dudamel leading the Simon Bolivar Orchestra at the Proms on YouTube and prepare to SOAR, baby.

I wasn't particularly worried about 'Mambo'. It's frenetic and has its own momentum, as with *The Simpsons*. Most importantly, it asks nothing complicated from you emotionally; it merely requires the maximum amount of joy you can throw at it. If an amateur like me can just start it off right, then if things go off the rails, the tuned percussion will glue themselves to the beat so everyone can hang off them if needs be.

At the end of the night came my personal nemesis, Elgar's 'Nimrod'. It is one of those pieces often deemed hackneyed, and yet, when you hear it, I challenge you not to be flooded with sentiment. It's in our DNA that piece, whether we like it or not. It has an ancestral vibration that reaches out from the past and pulls you to it. It is for us what Barber's 'Adagio for Strings' is for the Americans, a wordless evocation of the soul of a nation.

Go on, get it down from your shelf if you have it. If not, download it now. I like Sir Colin Davis's version, but there are millions to choose from. Get it and put it on – loud. Let it wash over you, as each bar gradually increases in intensity. Like a clenched fist gently unfurling and then reaching for the heavens . . .

'Nimrod' is however an utter nightmare to conduct. On the page it looks relatively simple. It's in three – yes, that old chestnut – but such a *slow* three. With 'Nimrod' and other slow burners it isn't so much about what you do with the beat, it's what you do *between* it – how you sculpt the space within the notes so that it flows and builds to its ultimate crescendo. And Jesus, it's tiring. Try drawing your hand across your body in long, smooth lines for four minutes or so. It becomes agony after a while.

What I wasn't expecting, though, was how I'd *feel*. Nothing prepared me for that.

I put down a beat for the violins and watched as their bows skimmed across the strings. So far, so good. At bar three I turned to the violas, and they expanded the line with an incredible sweetness. And then it happened. A mere five or six bars in I started to lose myself in the music. Just a little at first. But then, slowly and inexorably, it began to eat me up. My hand started to droop. So much so I couldn't hold the baton. I dropped it on the stand and carried on with just my hands, fingers dragging as if hanging off a boat and dangling in the water beneath. The sound began to lag.

I wasn't leading. I wasn't following either. I was inside it, inside the guts of it, and I couldn't get out. My chest vibrated with the sound. My head flooded with a million sudden thoughts and feelings – snapshots, sounds, smells. My past. My family. Love and the loss that walks so closely behind it. My hand was now so heavy I could barely drag it across my body.

The music was either too big for me, or I was too small for it. Either way, I will never forget being so utterly overwhelmed. In that moment I understood something profound – that words would only distort should I choose them to describe it. I learned about performance, connection, intimacy, sadness. I learned about me. Every part of myself I tried to hide, it came looking for – ripping me open like a tin can.

All of which made for a bloody *terrible* 'Nimrod', so I'm sorry if you were listening.

The next day I obsessed about the fact that I'd had the opportunity of conducting one of the greatest pieces of music ever written in one of the greatest concert halls in the world, and I'd blown it. It was too slow. It was too leaden. All day long it hung over me – the shame, the shame of getting it wrong.

I arrived home the next night to have dinner with my parents. As usual, I hadn't told them I was doing a gig. After we'd eaten, I went into the kitchen to help Mum with the washing-up. Minutes passed with nothing but the squeak of dishcloth on glass as our soundtrack.

Then Mum piped up, 'I heard your concert on Radio 3 last night.'

'Really?' I had completely forgotten it had been a live broadcast. There was a pause. 'It was terrible. Sorry, Mum. It was too bloody slow.'

I reached for the tea towel in embarrassment. Mum turned to face me. 'No, Susan, it was yours. And it was perfect.'

There was that silence again.

I love you, I thought.

I thought but didn't say.

I love you.

Oh No, I Can't

By now I was travelling up and down the country so frequently I could recite the whole of the First Great Western London-to-Penzance timetable from memory. It was an utterly pointless skill to have, of course, since First Great Western rarely stuck to it. For them the timetable appeared to be more of a suggestion than a schedule. Still, the trains themselves were always a pleasant surprise when they arrived.

I was happy in Cornwall. I learned how to build a drystone wall (well, I watched Kate do it); I was twitching ('Look, there's a magpie! And another! And another!'), and I was growing heritage seed vegetables (I had some of the most bulbous 'Chioggia' in West Penwith). Then I'd leave my rural idyll, get on a train, and six hours later find myself spewed forth into the madness and filth of Paddington. At home I was quiet and still. At work I was manic and displaced. Slowly I became happy in neither state. The grass was always greener. I lived on the road, between here and there, in perpetual motion. Slowly my mind became as fragmented and split as my time.

After *Maestro* I started doing piecemeal bits of television. I dressed as an elf for an insert on *Countryfile*. I contributed to various talking-heads shows, *I Love The Eighties*, *Britain's Best Wasps*, *My Top Ten Favourite Lists* – that sort of thing. Then came the blink-and-you'll-miss-it *Never Mind the Full Stops*, a BBC4 panel show about grammar. That's right. Grammar. You know – colons, parentheses, ellipsis – the natural springboard for comedic badinage.

The show was hosted by Julian Fellowes before he was Mr Downton. Back then he was just Nice Posh Man in Salmon-Coloured Chinos. Julian was utterly convinced that I'd been one of the presenters on *Loose Women*. No matter how many times I tried to disabuse him of this notion, he resolutely clung to it.

Julian: And on the panel to my right we have . . .
Me: Sue.
Julian: Yes! Hello, Sue.
Me: Hello.
Julian: Now you did that show at lunchtime . . .
Me: *Light Lunch.*
Julian: *Loose Women*, that's right. There were a few of you – around a table. You'd talk about repatriating ethnic minorities and menstruation, that sort of thing . . .
Me: You're thinking of Jane McDonald . . .
Julian: No, definitely you. Anyway, lovely to have you on the show. Can you start by telling us what a demonstrative pronoun is?

Five minutes later.

Julian: That's right, David – one point to your team! The answer was indeed epanadiplosis. Now Sue, over to you . . . Now I don't suppose you get many of these on *Loose Women*, but what's a dangling modifier?

While taping one of these episodes I encountered the tele-visual legend that is Daisy Goodwin. Daisy has a Silicon Valley mainframe for a brain and an extraordinary capacity for fusing the clever and the populist. Some of the greatest shows of the last twenty years have had her manicured hands on them. A few months later she recommended me for a one-off gastronomic history documentary called *Edwardian Supersize Me*.

My co-presenter was the gorgeous choleric writer and columnist Giles Coren. I loved him from the get-go. I'd already had the honour of working with his dad, Alan, and his sister, Victoria, and meeting him merely proved there's no such thing as a mediocre Coren. There was a weird chemistry between me and Giles – an immediate closeness that sometimes veered towards the sibling and occasionally towards the sexual. I do believe we may have snogged under a table at some point during the seventeenth century. If so, then I was a very lucky Hanoverian.

The general gist of *Edwardian Supersizers* was that we dressed up in period costume and ate what posh people would eat in the early 1900s. Every day for ten days I scoffed over 5,000 calories. For breakfast there were mutton chops, devilled kidneys and eggs, followed by platters of game birds – widgeon, teal and snipe. For lunch I would stagger under the weight of roast beef and towering puddings. At dinner there would be endless bottles of plonk and the ferric tang of duck cooked in its own blood. I ate all of this while encased in an unyielding whalebone corset. My waist maintained its rigid twenty-one inches, but all that food had to go somewhere. By the end of each night a vast uni-tit of lard would form around my décolletage, on which I could rest my head as I became more and more hammered.

Supersizers ended up running for a couple of series, with a few spin-off shows thereafter. What started off as a history documentary soon became a drinking competition with a few Wiki facts thrown in. Giles truly channelled George IV and passed out in a grate after getting hitched to my Caroline of Brunswick. I collapsed in a French chateau dressed as Marie

Antoinette and had to be dragged down three flights of stairs by my ankles. Giles pissed in a bucket by his chair during a Samuel Pepys feast, and I fell face down into the lap of a respected historian and stayed there, snoring, while he told me about coffee-drinking in the Restoration period.

That show remains one of my favourite things, extemporaneous, unpredictable and new. The only thing I didn't like about it was the medical. For such a free-form show, it felt odd to have this heavy-handed formatting bookend. We were required to have blood tests at the beginning and end of every week to see whether or not our metabolisms had been affected by the onslaught of booze and offal we had subjected them to.

In Victorian week the show had more of a female slant. This was the era that saw the rise of anorexia, drug addiction (laudanum) and the early stirrings of feminism, after all. Giles was delighted that his arm was not required for pin-cushion services (he is prick-averse), so I gamely rolled up my sleeves alone. My blood was duly taken; I was whisked to west London and spent a week in a farthingale, retching over a sheep's head and drunkenly snogging a bunch of elderly contributors who'd only turned up to talk about turkey production in nineteenth-century Norfolk.

As Giles wrapped for the week, lucky bastard, I got sent to the clinic to discover how my body chemistry had shifted over the last seven days. The doctor, formerly upbeat and open, had seemed shifty during filming. We completed the shoot whereupon she asked if she could have a word in private. It turned out one of my readings was off. Like off-the-chart off. Prolactin. Bloody prolactin. You make it when you're stressed. If you're really stressed you can show readings of up to 23 or so. If you're pregnant (the hormone is produced during pregnancy) it can get up to nearly 400.

My reading was 3200.

I explained that I wasn't stressed. I explained that I wasn't pregnant.

Then she explained I had a brain tumour.

The littlest things freak me out – arriving late for a meeting, not having the right pen to hand, being mistaken for a *Loose Women* presenter. But when life gets properly hardcore, I have the strangest ability to relax. Maybe I enjoy the fact that finally, *finally* something is out of my control.

And so I was perfectly calm as I walked into the deserted nuclear medicine unit at my local hospital. Calm while they scanned my bones. Calmer still as the magnets clanged and clanked around my ears as my body lay strapped to a table. I was even calm, six weeks later, when the time came for me to see the consultant to get my results.

The best way to tell a woman she can't have children

Consultant:	Hi. Are you Susan?
Me:	Yes.
Consultant:	It's lovely to meet you. I'm Mr X and I'm the endocrinology consultant here. Now, do step inside and have a seat. OK, well, I imagine you have an awful lot of questions, and I'm happy to answer all of them as fully and comprehensively as I can. Let me tell you what we *do* know first of all. You OK?
Me:	Yes. Yes. It's just a little weird.
Consultant:	Of course. Hospitals are deeply scary places if you're not familiar with them. Try not to worry because you're in very safe hands. Now we have the results of your blood tests and scans. You have a micro-prolactinoma, which is a tumour of your

pituitary gland. Now the great news is that it is benign, and that it won't require surgery. The only issues that arise from this tumour are that you are more susceptible to osteoporosis and that it causes fertility issues . . .

Fade to black.

NOT the best way to tell a woman she can't have children

Consultant: Hi, right. Let's have a look at your scans. So, there's your pituitary there, right in the middle of your head. And see that lump? That's a tumour. Don't need to take it out; we can keep an eye on it by looking at your bloods and monitoring you regularly. Now, you married?

Me: No.

Consultant: Boyfriend?

Me: No. I'm gay.

Consultant: Oh, OK. Well that makes it easier. You're most likely infertile. You can't have kids.

Fade to black.

That's how I found out.

I was fine for about twenty minutes. Fine to rebook another appointment, head down the stairs to the exit and greet the late-spring sunshine. Fine to buy a grande latte from a tax-avoiding multinational and walk, sipping it, up the hill home. I was fine right up to the point my flat came into view, then I slumped down on my front step, shaking. I rang Kate.

'I don't know why I'm upset,' I sobbed. 'It's not like it was on my mind to have kids. I wasn't planning it. It wasn't on my horizon. It's just so brutal though – the reality that there's nothing more than me. I'm it. I'm the end of the line . . .'

She listened. Occasionally she interjected. But mainly she listened.

I cried myself hoarse till my eyes ran on empty. Then I hung up, opened the front door and let Pickle lick the tears from my face.

All Cats Are Grey

It's a summer's morning, 11 June 2008 to be precise, and I'm driving through wide, faceless south London streets. The radio is on, a phone-in show, and an adenoidal presenter with too much jolly in his genes is wittering down the microphone. It's the usual fare, a dollop of banality, a splash of whimsy and a heavy dose of censorious middle-aged morality.

'What would *you* do if you woke up and it was 2049?'

'Water – good thing or bad thing? Let us know. Call 0207 . . .'

'What *is* the point of cats? You know the number – 0207 . . .'

I am making the trip to see my grandmother, Granny Smith – who, like her fruit namesake, is crisp and bitter but a firm favourite nonetheless. She has just turned one hundred years old, and my entire family is congregating at her old people's home. This may or may not be the thing that finally pushes her over the edge.

The radio is still blaring: 'So our topic this morning – what's the most unusual thing you've done for love?'

I switch it off as I pull up outside the residential home – a loveless, anonymous red-brick on the edge of Kent.

Inside, there is the smell of overcooked greens and a million heavy exhalations. Snooker blares from the television. A dozen eyes gaze in a myopic haze in the general direction of the screen. In the distance I can hear the sound of a bewildered man refusing to take his meds.

I am met in the hall by a sprightly lady called Judy.

'You here to see Lil?'

'Yes,' I reply.

'She's a slouch that one – only a hundred. I did that last year. It's a breeze! I'll go see if I can root out the little darling.'

This is the first time I have heard my grandmother referred to as a 'little darling'. Granny Smith is a redoubtable bag of paper-thin skin full of bile and piss and grit, who has sloughed off war (twice), cancer (twice) and the death of her beloved husband Stan (once, obviously) to get to this point. Whatever she is, she is certainly *not* a little darling . . .

Judy bounces around the communal lounge like a new-born gazelle, enquiring about Grandma's whereabouts. I watch her dart here and there, sharp as a tack and bright as a button.

She returns.

'They've found her. They've wheeled her outside to get some air. Shall I show you through?'

Grandma is indeed outside, in the garden, where she sits surrounded by my family in her wheelchair. I am late. I am always late. She winks at me as I bend to kiss her, and as I do I breathe in the familiar top note of lily of the valley mixed with cheap carbolic, a scent that takes me back to a time and place before words came and got in the way of everything.

She looks older – it's only been a few months since I last saw her, but she looks older. From the side you can see the milky sheen of developing cataracts, and a wobble of goitrous chin that makes me grin. *That's coming for me one day*, I think, and then I stop grinning.

We crowd around her chair and have our photo taken. There's me, David, Lynne, Michelle and Mum. Gran is holding something and beaming proudly. It's a card from the Queen.

'What's this?' I say, staring at the cheap paper. 'Is that it?'

I'm genuinely shocked. Her Majesty's signature is photo-copied – the whole thing mass-produced and impersonal. It's a far cry from the romantic notions you have of the 'telegram'.

'Well that's not worth waiting a hundred years for,' I scoff, almost offended on her behalf.

But Grandma isn't laughing. Grandma isn't joining in. In fact she is totally silent.

And then I realize that this isn't just a card to her.

Grandma's father hailed from Leipzig, her mum from Moscow, and she was born (one of eight children) in Riga, Latvia. The family fled from the pogroms, and for a while her dad was interned in the Isle of Wight. During the war a Quaker couple took her and her sister on holiday to the seaside but, on finding out they had German blood, deliberately starved them. It scarred her for life and taught her to conceal her identity, her ethnicity. It was wrong to be foreign, it was wrong to be Ashkenazi. Right up until her death she would staunchly deny she was Jewish, though when drunk (which was most of the time, courtesy of Harvey's Bristol Cream) she would launch into snatches of Yiddish.

So it isn't just a card; it's so much more than that. For her, an immigrant, it is everything – validation, acceptance, authentication. It says, *I belong. I belong because the Queen, the head of state, says so. And here's the proof.*

Gran moved into the home in 1994, just after Granddad died, and it quickly became clear she wasn't built for communal living. Firstly she was a racist and secondly she was hard of hearing, which meant that every time she felt like giving her views on benefit claimants or Labour's 'open door' policy, she did so in the LOUDEST VOICE IMAGINABLE. She was that particular breed of immigrant who felt, with absolute conviction, that the UK government should have left the gates open just long enough for *her* to enter the country, and then shut and bolted them immediately behind her so that no one else could come in.

And I mean *no one* else. The best thing you could say about her attitude to foreigners was that she was an equal-opportunities hater, meaning no particular group was singled out more than the other. Having said that, there was something particularly painful about the way she described and referred to any nurses of colour.

'Get me the nurse,' she'd demand, annoyed, as I wheeled her around.

'Do you mean May?' I'd enquire.

'Is she the chocolate one?'

I'd remain silent for a while, gritting my teeth, remembering something from Sunday school way back, something about hating the sin, not the sinner.

'Grandma, she's from–'

'Milk chocolate? That one? No, not that one – the Bourne-ville one.'

As she carried on, yelling her way through the various cocoa-solid options, I would let loose my grip on her wheel-chair, and off she would drift, away from me. Sometimes, in these situations, the best way to get an errant pensioner to behave is to just roll them down a ramp into the sun room, where they can bake under the hermetically sealed uPVC win-dows until penitent.

Coming out to a grandparent is one of the most toe-curling, awful experiences of one's life. Having to shout one's sexual proclivities into the impaired ear of a nonagenarian surely ranks in anyone's list of top-ten worst moments. Now imagine that same pensioner is losing her memory . . .

Towards the end of her hundredth year Granny Smith started to become more and more forgetful. I'm reluctant to use the word dementia, as she could still recall with pinpoint accuracy the price of a pair of mules she bought in Colchester in 1968. But the past, and the people who inhabited it, was becoming increasingly hazy, blurred and vignetted by age. This meant that *every time* I saw her, I had to come out to her in a process I liked to call

GROUNDHOG GAY.

Every time I made the pilgrimage to her bedside, it was the same painful routine.

Me:	Hi, Gran.
Gran:	Oh hello. Who are you?
Me:	I'm Susan, I'm your eldest grandchild.
Gran:	Oh. [*Pause*] Are you married?
Me:	No, Gran.
Gran:	Why not?
Me:	[*long sigh*] I'm gay.
Gran:	Oh. Oh dear.

A month or so later I'm back. I enter the room and settle next to her chair.

Me:	Hi, Gran.
Gran:	Oh hello. Who are you?
Me:	I'm Susan, I'm your eldest grandchild.
Gran:	Oh. [*Pause*] Are you married?
Me:	No, Gran.
Gran:	Why not?

Me: [*long sigh*] I'm gay.
Gran: Oh. Oh dear.

The last time I saw Granny Smith was that day of her centenary. When the heat of the midday sun became too much I wheeled her back inside while my family went in search of a hundred candles for the cake. Her room was dark and embraced her with a silence you could almost touch. I went up to her and held her hand, a jumble of bones and rope veins wrapped in translucent skin.

Me: Hi, Gran.
Gran: Oh, hello. Who are you?
Me: I'm Susan, I'm your eldest grandchild.
Gran: Oh. [*Pause*] Are you married?

The silence grows heavy.

Me: Yes. Yes, I am. I'm married to a lovely man called . . . Simon. And we have . . . three kids. You remember?
Gran: Oh yes. Lovely. Well done.

I walked away from the home and got in the car, my face streaming with tears. I knew it was the last time I'd ever see her. I turned the key in the ignition and the radio blared once more. The phone-in was still running, and for the first time ever I wanted to ring in. I wanted to ring in and tell them about the most unusual thing I'd done for love.

One hundred-plus years on the planet, a million rich and varied life experiences, and the one, single thing that Grandma Smith chose to share with subsequent generations was this pearl of wisdom she gave my mum. When I was around sixteen, my mum duly shared it with me. Here goes.

All cats are grey.

Yes, that's it. That's what she gave us. No family heirlooms, no jewellery or photos. Just that phrase.

All cats are grey.

This pithy little saying originates from John Heywood's book of proverbs, published in 1546: 'When all candles be out, all cats be grey.'

From which we can deduce two things:

1. John is implying that, in the dark, physical appearance is irrelevant.
2. John obviously spoke in a thick West Country accent straight out of Central Casting. Think of him as a kind of sixteenth-century Jethro.

This saying is now generally attributed to Benjamin Franklin, who used it when arguing why one should not necessarily dismiss an older woman. In other words, they may not look like much, but they become more appealing a prospect in the pitch black. Charming.

Have you seen a picture of Benjamin Franklin? He looks like a Scotch egg in a wind tunnel. No wonder he was advocating a world where we should dismiss a person's physical attributes. You would need a written guarantee of zero light pollution before you laid a finger on him, and even then you'd need a promise of no kissing. And even then ... well, there's still all your OTHER senses ... You'd be able to taste and smell and touch him and . . . Oh no, he'd just feel like a blood-temperature landslide. Not for me, thanks.

What's even odder is that the man who reminded us that we all look the same when the lights are out spent most of his spare time trying to illuminate the skies with either electricity or his own invention, the lightning rod. That's one hell of a mixed message right there.

I often wonder why Grandma chose to hand down this particular phrase. Perhaps it was her polite way of saying, *You Perkinses are none of you lookers but, don't worry, in a power cut you'll really come in to your own.* Or was it just aimed at me? Was she saying, *Susan, always date in dim lighting?*

Of course, if I were *only* judged on physical appearance I would have never got very far, which isn't to say that looks aren't important. Visual attraction is the portal that leads to the really great stuff, like how people like their tea, whether they mind burned toast, what they think of Cy Twombly and Carol Ann Duffy and if can they stomach West End musicals.

All of which goes to say, *Grandma, that's great, but all you've done is confused Mum and then confused me and then confused Michelle. I think, on reflection, in terms of a legacy, we'd have preferred jewellery. Don't need the diamonds – the paste stuff would do. Whatever's in the bottom of your cupboards. Just a token. Thanks.*

The End of the Line

Pickle first had cancer at two years old, a hard lump that ulcerated as soon as the vet's needle touched it. It was a mast cell tumour; nothing much on the outside, malignant as hell on the inside. It was a vicious op – the wide margin of tissue they needed to cut away meant her skin was stretched as tight as a drum around her back, with thick steel stitches holding it all together at her chest.

That night was the first and last time I ever heard her cry.

'Keep her lead-walked for a fortnight; she'll want to rest,' said the nurse as Kate and I arrived to pick her up.

Two days later she slipped her collar on a walk and went hunting in the woods for an hour and a half. Impossible, impossible beast.

Less than a year later Pickle developed a limp. I took her to see the vet, Joshua, a brilliant man with a look of mild exasperation etched permanently on his forehead. I guess I would too, were I to spend my days listening to people with too much money asking whether Chianti the bichon frise needs her teeth whitening or Sally the Burmese needs leg warmers now the nights are drawing in.

Joshua felt round Pickle's back legs. Pickle endured it as per because she had already eyed up her prize – a jar of treats on the side cabinet. He then asked me to take her for a walk up and down the street so he could examine her gait. We pounded the pavement. Nothing. Much as I tried to get her to limp she seemed sound again – until the fourth lap, when her back left started failing again.

Josh: Ah, I see it. It's probably a strain.
Me: But what if it isn't?
Josh: [*a pause, then that exasperated face*] It *is* probably a strain.
Me: Shouldn't she have an X-ray?
Josh: I don't think that's necessary. Take her home and keep an eye on her. And then, if it persists and you're worried, bring her back and we can look into getting some diagnostic work done.
Me: I am. I am worried. I'm already worried . . .

There is a loud crash from inside the surgery. Pickle has finally claimed her biscuits. Joshua says nothing but raises his eyes to the heavens.

For the next two weeks I watched Pickle like a hawk. The limp would come and go, but it seemed to increase in severity each time. I phoned Mum. That was the worst thing I could have done.

Me: I've looked in the medical encyclopedia. It could be rickets. And . . . and do dogs get deep vein thrombosis?

After a month I returned to the surgery. A new jar of treats sat on the side.

Me: Josh, it's got worse.
Josh: Really? OK, well, let's have a look at her.

Pickle once again endured an examination and the endless walking outside. Nothing. In the end Josh agreed to perform an X-ray. I arrived at 4 p.m. to pick her up.

Me: How is she? What did it show?
Josh: It was inconclusive.
Me: What does that mean?

Josh: It could be a repetitive strain or cartilage issues or something not showing up on the slides. Just try not to worry.

Lindsay the nurse: She'll be very tired. Just lead-walk her for a few days.

There is a loud crash from inside the consulting room. Pickle, high on meds, has just found the new jar of treats.

Two weeks later and I was frantic. I headed back to the surgery.

Me: [*wailing*] What else can we do?

Josh: [*by now a broken man*] Well, there is a specific orthopaedic hospital near Bedford, but I really don't think–

Me: Yes! Let's do that!

And so I drove Pickle to Hertfordshire for further examination. The team there kept her in overnight for observation (£400), and the next day she was taken, in a private human ambulance (£250), for an MRI at the neighbouring hospital (£400). After another overnight stay (£400) I picked her up and waited for Joshua to get the results. I was terrified. Finally, I got the call.

Josh: OK, so I've got the results of all the MRIs and bone scans. And –

Me: Oh God.

Josh: I don't know how to say this . . .

Me: Oh God.

Josh: There's –

Me: What?

Josh: There's –

Me: I can't live without her!

Josh: There's nothing wrong with her.

Me: Sorry?

Josh: Nothing. Not a thing.

Me: I don't understand.

Josh: I've reviewed everything and spoken to my colleagues at the hospital, and . . . well, the truth is –

Me: Oh no . . .

Josh: She's doing it for attention.

Me: What?

Josh: She wants your attention. That's why she's doing it.

Me: You mean . . . you mean she's *putting it on*?

Josh: Yes.

Me: You're telling me I've got a dog with Munchausen's?

Josh: Yes, if you put it like that.

Me: Three THOUSAND pounds, and she just wants my attention?

Josh: Yes.

There is a pause. In the background a fully operational Pickle is desperately launching herself in the direction of the treats jar. I march over to her until I loom large.

Me: You want my attention do you, little Pickle?

She sneezes on my foot, then looks up.

Me: WELL YOU'VE GOT IT NOW.

We didn't make it, Kate and I. Not in the end. My schedule, my stupidity, my thoughtlessness made an ex of her. We could have got through it. She could be sitting here as I write, shaking her tousled head at my silly puns and childish efforts to make you love me, but that's hindsight for you. I made the worst mistake of my life. And then she made the worst of hers. You see, it turns out that my capacity for total self-destruction was matched only by her own – compatible to the last.

We didn't speak for a while and got on with our lives, meeting new people and forging new paths. Her absence became the right side of bearable. Just. When Pickle was diagnosed with terminal cancer last year, I sat at my computer and emailed her. She had the right to say goodbye. I asked her if she would like to be there at the end. She replied that yes, she would.

And so we met on the Heath and walked together – all of us. Then we went back to my flat to prepare for the unthinkable.*

When Joshua had left with Pickle's body and all had fallen quiet, Kate and I sat beside one another on the sofa. We drank tumblers of whisky, hands shaking, in total shock that we'd just killed our little girl – that we had just lost part of our family. As we talked, I could feel our ties weakening, one by one, and realized that soon I would have nothing left to moor me to her. I would just be cast adrift on an ocean of memory and regret.

After a while Kate got up to leave, and I joined her, with Parker ambling behind, seemingly untroubled by the loss and in dire need of a piss. She walked round the block with me, arm linked in mine, the years forgotten.

Then she got in her car and left.

---

* Later that night I wrote a letter to my dog. It is here, at the end of this chapter, exactly as I wrote it.

It turns out that I had been in SUCH shock during the euthanasia procedure that I had forgotten to fill out the requisite paperwork. So when I phoned the surgery a few weeks later to pick up Pickle's ashes there was a slightly awkward encounter with the receptionist.

Me: Hi. I'm just ringing to see when I can pick up my dog.
Woman: Ah. OK.
Me: Is there a problem?
Woman: Well . . . she's still with us.
Me: What do you mean – still with you?

An uncomfortable pause.

Woman: We've been . . . waiting on your instructions.

Finally, it dawned on me. She was in their fridge-freezer. She'd been in it for six weeks. I thought I'd sorted the cremation out but in reality hadn't handed over the correct forms or money or anything. I felt awful, truly awful, though I was momentarily cheered by a friend reminding me that Pickle had spent the majority of her life trying to get into fridges, and therefore it was fitting, in death, that she had finally got her wish.

I didn't pick up Pickle until 10 March, a warm spring day. The waiting room was empty. I had a lump in my throat, but tried to style it out and pass it off as typhoid.

It was the weight that got me – the sheer weight. I don't know. I thought that the ashes would be light, like grey candy-

244

floss, that I would take the bag and swing it into the air, and she
and I would go walking into the fresh spring morning together,
united once more. No one tells you how heavy the urn is going
to be or how much dust you'll have to spread. No one tells you
how to deal with someone handing you something you adored
in a carrier bag in front of a waiting room full of hacking cats
and three-legged dogs. It's hard to be nonchalant in that situation. It's hard to pretend that being handed a plastic sack full of
something you love is an everyday occurrence.

The urn weighed one kilogram. The exact weight of loss.

I'd like to say that we sprinkled the ashes together, Kate and I,
in the fields of Cornwall a few months later – that our eyes
locked in that moment, as the wind took the hard grey dust
and spirited it away into the sky. And that all the pain of those
awful yesterdays went with it, blown to nothing, leaving only
the purest concentrate of love behind.

Wouldn't that have been wonderful? A perfect, full circle,
the sort of thing writers write about.

And I guess I am a writer now, and I could write that – I
could write the perfect ending. I'd love to, you know. More
than anything, I'd love to.

But it didn't happen. Why would it? Life doesn't give you the
neatly tied ends of a romcom. The world would be insufferably
saccharine if it did, plus we're so contrary as a species, we'd only
sit around longing for the tragedy and agony of unrequited love.

And yet, in all the loss, something of the family remains –
Parker, our arthritic darling, now with blue discs for eyes and

pegs for legs – and my beloved Heath, which holds the memories of yesterday in its boughs and meadows.

This is the tree where you first kissed me. Sometimes it is full of leaf and fills the sky, sometimes it is thin and stark, like it is now. This is the tumulus where we cried that final time. Here is the path where you first held my hand. Here is the wood we made our own. Here are the secret short cuts, the magnolia with one flower, the mournful benches, the familiar pooches. Here they all are.

We occasionally bump into each other, never arranged, always haphazard. And we walk a little, until our paths home diverge. Look at the emotional palindrome we have become.

And my feet marching this ground, day after day, tell the tale of

You and I, you and I, you and I, and trees and sky and always and for ever but

Gone.

A Letter to Pickle

My darling girl,

First, a confession: I had you killed. I planned it and everything; asked the vet round and a nurse in a green uniform with white piping – all with the express intention of ending your life. Yes, I know. I know you had no idea, because I had been practising for weeks how to keep it from you, and how – when that time came – I could stop my chest from bursting with the fear and horror and unbearable, unbearable pain of it all.

I sat there, in your kitchen (it was always your kitchen), numb, and filled in a form about what to do with your remains. I ticked boxes as you lay wheezing in your sleep on the bed next door. I made a series of informed, clinical decisions on the whys and wherefores of that beautiful, familiar body that had started to so badly let you down. Then, once the formalities were over, I came in and did what I've done so many days and nights over so many months and years. I lay behind you, left arm wrapped round your battle-scarred chest and whispered into your ear.

I love you.

So that was my secret. And I kept it from you until your ribs stopped their heaving and your legs went limp and your head fell as heavy as grief itself in my arms. Then, when I knew you were no longer listening, I let it out – that raging, raging river of loss. I cried until my skin felt burned and my ears grew tired from the sound of it all.

It wasn't pretty.

OK. Confession over.

Now what you also need to know is that this is NOT a eulogy. Quite frankly, Pickle, you don't deserve one, because, as you are well aware, your behaviour from birth, right up to the bitter end, was unequivocally terrible.

As a pup, you crunched every CD cover in the house for fun. You chewed through electrical cable and telephone wires. You ripped shoes and gobbled plastic. You dived into bins, rolled in shit and licked piss off of pavements. You ate my bedposts.

As an adult you graduated to raiding fridges and picnics, you stole ice cream from the mouths of infants, you jumped onto Christmas tables laden with pudding and cake and blithely walked through them all, inhaling everything in your wake.

You puked on everything decent I ever owned. You never came when called, never followed a path, never observed the Green Cross Code and only sat on command when you could see either a cube of cheese or chicken in my hand (organic, or free range at a push).

And last, but not least, you shat in my bed (yes, I know they were dry and discreet little shits, but they were still shits, you shit).

Here's another thing, while I'm at it. I'm angry. Why? Because you, madam, are a liar. You made me think you were OK. You allowed me to drop you off at our mate Scarlett's farm and leave you there for weeks while I went away working thinking that all was well. Yet it wasn't, was it? The cancer fire was already lit, sweeping through your body, laying waste to it while my back was turned.

I look back at photos sent to me while I was away from you, and I can see it now – that faint dimming of the eyes, the gentle slackening of muscle. The tiniest, tiniest changes in that cashmere fur of yours. It haunts me still. Had I been there, I would have noticed, would I not? Me, your anxious guardian and keeper of eleven and a half years.

I found out about the lump the day I landed. Scarlett rang me with the news as I boarded a train for Willesden Junction. The most

*momentous moments can come at the most banal. It had just
appeared, out of nowhere, as surprising and fast as you, on your
neck. You never did anything by halves, and there it was, the size of
a lemon, wrapped round your lymph.*

*I took you home the next day, to Cornwall, the place that we love
best, and you allowed me, for a while at least, to believe that nothing
was wrong. We rose at sunset, in the light of those Disney-pink
skies, and walked the ancient tracks together – before you got bored
and veered off, full tilt, in search of the latest scent.*

*But your lies could only carry you so far before your body gave
you away. I saw your chest starting to heave when you took a breath
at night. Your bark became hoarse. You no longer tore around the
house causing havoc. You were biddable (you were never biddable),
you ate slowly (oh, don't be ridiculous).*

*Yet still, the denial. Forgive me for that. After all, we'd beaten it
before, you and I. Twice. Even when the vet told me your lungs were
hung with cancerous cobwebs and there was nothing more to be
done, I went out and started doing. I sped to the health food store
and returned with tinctures and unguents and capsules. And there
you were having to eat your precious last dinners covered in the
dusty yellow pall of turmeric and a slick of Omega 3s. So silly. So
silly, in retrospect. I should have let you eat cake and biscuits and
toast and porridge. But I thought I could save you. I really thought I
could.*

*I didn't ever believe that something as alive as you could ever
succumb to something as ordinary as death.*

*After all, how could you be sick when you ran and jumped and
played, day after day after day?*

*And then, I got it. You were doing it all for me. You were dragging
yourself into the light, every morning, for me. All of it. For me.*

*And as fierce and possessive as my love was, I couldn't let you do
that any more.*

Spectacles

You were eighty years old, by human reckoning. You were eighty years old and you still flew into the boot of the car without assistance (assistance is for old dogs, you didn't know how to be an old dog), you still strode the Heath with that graceful, lupine lope of yours. You skidded round corners, you sniffed and barked and hectored and lived to life's outer margins. On the day you died, you pottered for over an hour in the meadows with the sun on your back, without a care in the world. I am so very grateful for that.

When someone once took a punch at me, you leaped in the air and took it. When I discovered I couldn't have children, you let me use your neck as a hankie. You were my longest relationship, although I think any decent psychologist would have deemed us irredeemably co-dependent. You were the engine of my life, the metronome of my day. You set the pulse and everything and everyone moved to it. What a skill. I woke to your gentle scratch on the door (it wasn't gentle, it was horrific and you have destroyed every door in every house we have lived in – I am just trying to make you sound nice), and the last sound at night was the sound of you crawling under your blanket and giving that big, deep, satisfied sigh.

I have said I love you to many people over many years: friends, family, lovers. Some you liked, some you didn't. But my love for you was different. It filled those spaces that words can't reach.

You were the peg on which I hung all the baggage that couldn't be named. You were the pure, innocent joy of grass and sky and wind and sun. It was a love beyond the limits of patience and sense and commensuration. It was as nonsensical as it was boundless. You alchemist. You nightmare.

Thank you for walking alongside me* during the hardest,

---

* I say alongside, you're a beagle. More like 400 yards to the right. In a thicket.

weirdest, most extreme times of my life, and never loving me less for the poor choices I made and the ridiculous roads I took us down.

Thank you, little Pickle. I love you.

From the four-eyed one who shouted at you, held you, laughed at you, fed you and, for some reason utterly unbeknownst to you, put all your shit in bags.

X

Pickle Perkins
Born: 20-08-02
Skipped to next destination: 14-01-14

Back to Black

In the autumn of 2009, as I turned forty, my life as I knew it ended. I will never know to what extent I pushed it to change and to what extent I was simply a lemming senselessly trundling over that midlife-crisis cliff. I lost my love, my future and my bearings. Completely.

The house in Cornwall was a wreck. I could neither bear to live in it, nor get rid of it. I simply locked it up and left it – out of sight, out of mind. It became like a museum – the past, preserved in aspic. As each month went on, the place got danker. Blue mould blossomed on the sofas and crept up the walls. Thick boughs of cobwebs hung from the ceiling. I remember driving down, intending to spend the weekend there and clear everything out. I walked into the bedroom and saw Kate's book still on the bed, upturned, where she had left it. I burst into tears, walked out the door and drove straight back to London.

I rented a tiny one-bedroom flat on an alleyway down to the Hampstead Ponds. The flat itself was about as soulless a thing as I have ever encountered, but the beagles liked it, and therefore I made do.

It has such a stagnant feel, that passageway down to the water. The ponds reek of sadness. The fishermen sit there in the autumn and try to catch something other than rusty bikes and gym shoes. People stand by the water watching the ducks and wonder whether to throw bread, or themselves, into the murk. A very famous photograph of Nick Drake was taken right by the little side door that led to my garden. He is mid-lollop, back to the camera, his dog Gus alongside him. I was that close to the great man. I wondered if the sadness he felt and the sadness I felt were a contagion – a plague that ravaged the area. A sadness that not even our faithful hounds could alleviate.

Every mood should have a soundtrack, and this soundtrack's name was Brad. Brad was my next-door neighbour, who I was secretly fond of, but he kept even more antisocial hours than I did. At around 2 a.m. he would put on some deeply drearsome 1940s crooner, and the depressing waft would seep through the walls and up the chimney until dawn. I would hammer on his door until it stopped. I'd post expletive-strewn A4 rants through his letter box. Brad would reply on a postcard of Christopher Marlowe or the Earl of Rochester. He had style and class, that one. It seemed almost a shame to report someone of his *noblesse* to Camden Council for noise pollution.

Despite the posh postcode, it felt like an unsafe place. Occasionally I'd wake, and a burly fisherman would be in my garden trying to drag his rod out of the water beyond. I had another horrific break-in which still haunts me. After that, after the safety seal was broken, the energy changed, my luck ran out, and everything and everyone seemed to find the flat fair game. Including the local wildlife.

One night there was the sound of crashing and scuttling in the kitchen. I came out to look in a state of total panic. Pickle and Parker, characteristically, did nothing dogs are supposed to do and merely lay in their baskets, snoring. Minutes passed. Nothing. Not a sound. I was about to return to bed when I noticed something sticking out from beneath the fridge. That something turned out to be a tail. A foot-long tail that could only belong to

a rat. A dirty rat.

At which point, I did what any normal human lady would do.

I moved out.

Luckily, I had some friends over the road – Jenny and Ewan. She was a fabulous Welsh earth mother, he a slightly deranged but affable stoner. I rang their doorbell.

Jenny: Hey, love, you all right?
Me: No. I'm sorry. No.
Jenny: Jesus, you look as white as a sheet. Come in, come in!

I scuttle in, still shaking with shock.

Ewan: What is it? Do you need me to sort someone out?
Jenny: Ewan, stop being a prick.
Ewan: What?
Jenny: Come on, love. You tell us what it is. Come on, have a seat.
Ewan: Honestly, though, I'm not that pissed. I can go and sort them out.
Jenny: Ewan! Now what is it?
Me: There's a rat in my kitchen

You can imagine how the next five minutes panned out.

Me: There's a rat in my kitchen.
Jenny/Ewan: What are you gonna do?
Me: There's a rat in my kitchen.
Jenny/Ewan: What are you gonna do?
Me: I'm gonna fix that rat, that's what I'm going to do.

After we'd wrung the life out of that joke (and several minutes beyond), Jenny and I started making up the spare room. Ewan got busy rolling a forty-seven-paper spliff, whilst regaling us with his own personal rat stories.

Ewan: I'll go kill it if you want. I've done it before.

Jenny: Have you fuck. You've never killed a thing.

Ewan: Yep, I have. I've killed one. I have!

Me: How?

Ewan: I was round my mate's – on the lash – and I see it scut-tling along the skirting. And I just reacted, quick as a flash . . .

Jenny: You're so spaced you can't react to shit.

Ewan: We had a massive ghetto blaster –

Jenny: Ewan! You can't call it that! Sue, can you call it that now?

Me: I don't think so. No.

Ewan: Massive thing – twin speakers, the lot. And I kicked it against the rat and it kind of pinned him against the wall so he was trapped. Then I grabbed a CD, threw it, and – BOOM – it decapitated him. Head clean off.

A pronounced pause.

Jenny: Ewan, you telling me the rat was killed by a flying CD?

Ewan: Yep.

Another silence.

Ewan: *Ballbreaker*. AC/DC. Love that album.

I moved out a week later.

It takes me substantially longer to learn life's lessons than most. I'm stubborn, I'm a creature of habit, and, for all that I'm addicted to experience, I dislike change. So what did I do? I stayed in the same area, and moved around the corner to yet another basement flat.

My first morning there I was woken by the doors bouncing on their hinges. Above me the ceiling vibrated so intensely that I thought it would cave in. It was rhythmic and heavy. I feared the worst. Sex slavers, porn makers, Grindr addicts . . .

I ran upstairs in my Union Jack onesie and pair of Crocs – because I'm classy like that and I like to make a good first impression. I expected to find an orgy going on – swingers in full swing – instead I was greeted by a breezy whip-thin German woman called Jolanda with a pronounced speech impediment.

Jolanda: Hello, I'm Jolanda.
Me: I'm Sue.
Jolanda: Are you calling about the noise?
Me: Yes, it's horrendous.
Jolanda: Oh. Well, I'm wee-bounding.
Me: Wee-bounding?
Jolanda: Yes. Wee-bounding.
Me: Wee-bounding. Right. Mmm. I'm sorry, forgive me – I've got no idea what that is.
Jolanda: You know. Wee-bounding. Like twampolining.
Me: Oh. *Wee*-bounding! I see!
Jolanda: It's gweat for the lymphatic system. You should twy it.
Me: Well, I might. It's just that the bouncing is . . . well, it's terrifying.
Jolanda: Should I wee-bound later?
Me: Yes, you do that.

Jolanda was true to her word, and the rebounding moved to around 10 a.m. for a week.

Week two, I was woken at 6 a.m. by the sound of something resembling the running of the Pamplona bulls. I put on my Crocs and ran upstairs. Then ran down again because I'd forgotten my onesie. I ran up for the second time, now clothed, and hammered on the door. Jolanda popped her head out of the window and greeted me joyfully.

Jolanda:	Hi, Sue!
Me:	Hi, Jolanda.
Jolanda:	You're up early!
Me:	Yes. Strange that.

Hostile pause.

Jolanda:	I'm not wee-bounding, Sue.
Me:	No. What *are* you doing?
Jolanda:	Bikwam.
Me:	Bikwam? I'm sorry, I've no idea what that is.
Jolanda:	You know. Bikwam.
Me:	Bikwam. Nope. Still no idea.
Jolanda:	Bikwam yoga.
Me:	Oh! Yes! I see!
Jolanda:	Should I Bikwam later?
Me:	Yes, perhaps sometime between the wee-bounding and the indoor Lacwosse.

I moved out four months later.

The Cock and the Car

I was wandering back from work one afternoon when I noticed my car had been vandalized. There were deep key marks down the length of one side, right down to the metal. It wasn't a posh car, just a dusty, knackered old Mark 4 Golf ('rides like a Thai prostitute!' – *Top Gear Magazine*) but I loved it. As I wandered around to the front, it became clear that the damage wasn't just limited to a cursory keying – this was full-on vandalism. There, on the bonnet of the car, scratched deep, was a cock.

A cock. I couldn't believe it. A cock. On *my car*. A lovingly drawn shaft and helmet scored for all time into my beloved jalopy.

I went inside. My younger girlfriend was sat, dressed like Cinderella's Buttons, listening to white noise with a lady yodelling on top. Young people, honestly.

'What's up, honey?' she called.

'It's my car. Someone's defaced my car. They've drawn a cock on it.'

'It's London, babe,' she said, breezily, swaying her head in time to the static.

Well, people might draw genitals on cars where you live, you crrrazy hipster, but here they don't, I thought but didn't say.

I was a pressure cooker for the next hour. A cock on my car. Why? How? Mainly *why*? I decided to call Emma. She used to be a lawyer, after all. She, at least, would be a voice of reason in all of this. After three failed attempts she finally answered.

Em: I told you not to call me again.

Me: Hilarious. Listen, you're not going to believe this. Some little shit has scratched a cock on my car!

I didn't get the opportunity to finish the story, as there followed ten minutes of raucous laughter and mockery, some of which was extremely unkind. Emma was patently going to be useless, so I put the phone down on her, mid-roar, and called Nicola.

Nic: What's up? You split up with someone again?

Me: No. Not yet.

Nic: Oh. So what's up?

Me: Well, someone's scratched a cock on my car.

Nic: What – keyed it?

Me: Yes.

Nic: Wow. Shit. [*Pause*] That's a hate crime.

Me: Is it?

Nic: Yep.

Me: Really?

Nic: Yep. Classic.

Me: *Classic?*

Nic: Yeah.

Me: Yes. Yes, it is, isn't it? That's what I thought. It's a classic hate crime.

Nic: You shouldn't let them get away with it. Call the police. I would. I think they have a unit for that sort of thing.

Me: Do they?

Nic: Expect so. That's abuse, plain and simple. It's homophobic abuse.

Nicola is an amazing actor and has played a lot of detectives in her time, so when she says something about law enforcement,

I believe her. In the same way I'd believe Martin Shaw if he talked about open-heart surgery, or Robert Powell if he disclosed what *really* happened at the Last Supper.

Buoyed by our conversation, I put the phone down and immediately called the nearest police station, who duly transferred me to the relevant unit. Within five seconds of calling and explaining my situation, I could hear a wheezing noise that may or may not have been laughter in the background. In my mind I chose to rebrand it as an asthma attack.

To the credit of the local crime team, a mere hour later a young man in uniform appeared, clutching a Moleskine, the notebook of Hemingway and trainee coppers.

Policeman: So . . . what's happened?
Me: My car has been the victim of a homophobic attack.
Policeman: Your car?
Me: Yes.
Policeman: OK. Is your car gay?
Me: No! I mean . . . I don't know – I haven't asked.
Policeman: Right . . .
Me: What I mean is that I'm gay and I've been targeted. There's a cock keyed on the bonnet. Look!

I gesture in the vague direction of the bell-end. The copper moves to the front of the car to study it more closely.

Me: See it?
Him: Yes.
Me: See the cock?!

There is a long pause. What's he playing at? I think. Finally, he breaks the silence.

Him: The *cock*?

Me: Yes.

Him: Oh.

Me: What?

Him: Looks like a smiley face to me.

Everything goes very quiet. Silence except for the thumping of my pulse. I go around to join him.

Him: Look. See? Two eyes and a smile.

As he said it the image in front of me transformed. Suddenly the shallow shaft wasn't a shaft at all – it was two downward strokes representing eyes. The helmet – that expansive semi-circle – wasn't a helmet but a broad, beaming grin. The vandal's scratches had gone from angry penis to Cheshire Cat in a heartbeat.

There was a long pause, finally punctuated by the policeman clearing his throat. I guess they learn that at Hendon – how to cut through awkward moments with a classic copper's cough.

Then horror dawned on me, the horror of what he must be thinking. Either it had been so long since I'd seen a cock that I no longer knew what one looked like (or at least couldn't distinguish between one and a smiley face) OR I am so obsessed with cocks that I see them *everywhere*, even on the bonnets of cars. I'm like that character in *The Sixth Sense* – I see penises. ALL THE TIME.

We wandered down the street towards his panda car. I tried to make small talk. It failed. It was then we noticed that all the other cars had been defaced. They too had smiley faces and scarred sides. I hadn't been singled out. I hadn't been targeted.

There was no penis. There was no homophobic hate crime. In fact there was nothing but a lingering sense of humiliation that still makes itself felt every time I think back.

The Moleskine shut, the key turned in the panda's ignition and the policeman drove away. In a fit of humiliation and despair I scratched a pair of tits on my girlfriend's bike.

That's London for you.

Getting It Wrong

When you agree to take part in a panel show, you do so with the tacit understanding that there will be little or no prep required – that you can turn up an hour beforehand and 'riff' or 'banter' your way through it. This means that if and when you are goddam awful, you can defend yourself by saying that it was all spur-of-the-moment, off-the-cuff-type stuff. If that doesn't work, you can claim you were:

a. on new meds
b. experiencing a break-up
c. under the illusion you were appearing on *Question Time*, and the first you realized it was a panel show was when one of the male comics started talking about wanking.

Some shows, however, particularly those with more of a chat-show bent, require my least-favourite thing in the world – the Briefing Chat. A briefing chat is a prearranged phone call that you have completely forgotten about. It is so boring a thing, it disappears from the mind almost as soon as it has been mentioned. A briefing chat is usually scheduled for first thing in the morning, invariably after a night on the sauce, and because you have erased it from your memory is always a surprise. On the other end of the phone is an exhausted, underpaid researcher asking a series of complex and detailed questions you're ill equipped to answer at that ungodly hour. These questions had, of course, been emailed to you days before, but you studiously refused to engage with them.

The resultant interview is a cluster bomb of mistakes, apologies and knee-jerk decision-making.

Researcher: What do you think about the rise of fascism?
Me: [*wiping sleep from my eyes*] Not nice.
Researcher: What is your favourite kind of horse?
Me: A brown one.
Researcher: Describe yourself in three words.
Me: Tired. Sorry. [*Pause*] Did I say sorry? OK. Tired.
Researcher: Do you like sausages?
Me: No.
Researcher: Shame. We were thinking of doing an item about sausages. Never mind. How about rivers? Like them?
Me: Well . . .
Researcher: What would you do if you had scissors for feet?
Me: Oh . . . Errr . . .
Researcher: Who would be your ideal dinner party guests? Name any sixteen from history.
Me: Sixteen? Oh God, I don't think I have enough cutlery . . .
Researcher: One last thing. We're going to end with a song. Do you mind dressing up as a wizard and joining in?

It was during one such briefing chat that I properly, properly shamed myself. I had been booked to appear on *The Matt Lucas Awards*, unsurprisingly presented by the lovely Matt Lucas. The rough premise of the show was that three guests would compete to win awards for 'Best' or 'Worst' in different categories.

'Sooooooooo . . .' said the researcher at the end of the

phone, with the elastic vowels of the truly bored, 'our first category is "Worst Holiday Destination".'

Fabulous! I had been waiting all my adult life for that question, and here it was, all teed up and ready to go.

'That's easy! Torremolinos! Next!'

I paused, expecting him to say 'Right answer!' and move on to the next question. (It's a known fact that Torremolinos is the definitive answer to 'Where is the worst place you've ever been?' no matter how extensively you've travelled.)

'Great!' said the researcher, in a tone that screamed *NOT GREAT!* 'Thing is . . . we want something a little more . . .'

But it's about ME! MY worst destination! Surely I am best, some would say uniquely, *placed to answer questions about my own likes and dislikes,* I screamed. Inside my head.

Me:	But Torremolinos really is hellish! Or at least, it was. I don't know what it's like now, but back then, in the early 80s, it was full of British Bulldog bars and lager louts and high-rises, and no one spoke Spanish. In fact, it was about as authentically Spanish as Nigel Farage in a Real Madrid strip enjoying a Pata Negra toastie . . .
Researcher:	Mmm . . . Thing is, we've got Richard Madeley on the show, and he's saying Benidorm, so we want something a little bit more . . .
Me:	Un-Spanish?
Researcher:	Yes.
Me:	So it can't be Spain?
Researcher:	We'd rather not.
Me:	I can't choose anything from Spain?
Researcher:	No.
Me:	Even if it was, genuinely, the most hellish place I've

	been.
Researcher:	No.
Me:	OK. [*Pause*] So the most hellish place I've been can't be the answer to the question 'Where's the most hellish place you've been?'
Researcher:	No.
Me:	I get it.
Reseacher:	Soooooooooo . . . anything else?

I froze. I didn't want to let on that I'd barely seen anything of the world. I cast my mind back to the pebbles and crosswinds of the South Coast, the Costa del Sol, the East Coast of America. Nothing much to play with there. But then I remembered a trip I'd made with Mel and her family to the Isle of Skye – that beautiful, craggy wilderness to the north-west of Glasgow. I got a couple of random pictures at first – a wild and windy day, rain scoring across the Cuillin, the igneous black peaks barely decipherable in the gloom – then, slowly, fragments of memory started to form around the snapshots.

We'd gone walking and got caught in the rain. We'd decided to find an indoor attraction. We'd taken Mel's niece and nephews to the Serpentarium . . .

The researcher was becoming impatient. 'Anything?'

I was being rushed. I panicked. I forced the jigsaw to piece itself together. Emotions came in to fill the cracks; sounds, smells, sensations.

'The Serpentarium on the Isle of Skye!' I blurted without thinking.

'OK, that sounds good . . .'

Before I continue, let me tell you, as honestly as I can, what I really remember of that day.

Mel, her brother and his kids, Emma and myself were staying with lovely Lady Claire McDonald at Kinloch Lodge, the family seat of the McDonald clan. We'd had warm scones and kippers for breakfast (note how my memory so perfectly records food) and browsed through the numerous oil paintings of previous McDonalds that hung on the wall. We'd particularly enjoyed the portrait of Lord Ronald McDonald although were sad he was without his trademark red wig and large yellow shoes. It was raining. A gale was blowing. We enquired as to what might be a fun thing to do with the kids if the weather stayed inclement, and Lady Claire recommended the nearby reptile sanctuary. So off we went.

Memories are slippery bastards – bring them into the light, handle them too often, they'll bend, change colour. Keep them in the dark and they'll slowly retreat to a place you can't find them. In truth, I could only recall the very basics of that trip:

- We approached an unprepossessing low-rise.
- A large sign outside proclaimed something along the lines of WELCOME TO THE MOST EXCITING EXPERIENCE ON EARTH. We took a photo of the two of us outside it.
- A kindly woman welcomed us in.
- Jan, Mel's nephew, was frightened of snakes, but the aforementioned kindly women got a wee albino corn snake out of his tank and let him hold it. At first Jan was loath to touch it, but slowly he became transfixed by how smooth it was, how strong. By the end he didn't want to leave, his phobia totally cured.
- We went back to Kinloch Lodge for high tea by the

roaring fire. I can remember the EXACT contents of
the tea, but I won't bore you with the details.

And that's it. That's the sum total of my real memories.
    And so back to the briefing chat.

Me: The Serpentarium on the Isle of Skye!
Man: OK, that sounds good . . .

*I hear the sound of sticky biro on paper as the researcher jots down 'Serpen-
tarium'. I wonder if he spells it correctly, an indictment of both the skills
shortage in television and my own inveterate snobbishness. There is an
expectant pause.*

Man: So the Serpentarium is your worst holiday destination.

*So, just like that, my trip has been rebranded 'the world's worst'. Suddenly
it's become a fact.*

Man: Why was it hell? What was so hellish about it?

It was sealed. Now I had to find something negative, even if it
was barely there – blow it out of all proportion and bend it so
it was funny. Fill it with stuff that would make it entertaining.
Neatly tie off experiences with an exhilarating, upbeat flour-
ish. So my imagination set to work, rounding off the rough
edges, adding detail, quirks, shaping it into a perfect narrative.
To sell. To sell to the crowd, whoever they might be.
    Which is what I did.
    And so the yarn began. Into all those blank spaces little silly
details got poured. Into the silences went 'funny' dialogue.
That quiet, sweet visitor centre became a dark dungeon with

sticky walls. The bucket that had been in the corner became the snakes' repository. The snakes themselves were things of horror. On and on I went, like a dancing bear, until I felt the researcher was happy. And every adornment, whether big or small, went down as fact. FACT. How tragic that I'd rather invent an experience than admit the simple truth:

a. I hadn't had many *real* experiences.
b. I have a terrible memory for anything outside of comestibles.

And then I went one step further by going on national television and saying it all out loud, in public. And the more detail I threw in about how dreadful it was, the more people laughed, and the more people laughed, the more I embellished the detail.

Even as I did it, I felt something was wrong. It felt personal. It wasn't like I was slating Benidorm – a burned tract of land filled with drunk people (there, I have slated it) – this felt way too singular and personal a target.

But I did it. I complied. I did my bit. I made myself look good by making some strangers look worse. And then I got into a nice car and got whisked home.

For the next twenty-four hours I felt uncomfortable but wrote it off as general post-performance malaise. Then I returned to normal, went about my daily business – everything was fine. The show aired. I didn't see it because recording a television show then tuning in to watch it is like a dog returning to its own vomit. Plus, there's always this annoying speccy girl in my shows who irritates the living hell out of me.

About a week after airing I was checking my Twitter feed

when I noticed a message from a man who seemed hurt and angry. It's rare that a negative post has adverbs in it, so it stuck out from the usual crowd of trolls and click-baiters. I read on. The man, it transpired, was the son of the couple who owned the Serpentarium. Understandably, he wanted to know why, instead of all the corporate holiday behemoths out there, I had chosen to focus my limp comedic ire on his parents' tiny rescue centre.

Oh. Didn't I mention that bit? Yes, it's a wildlife sanctuary. It's a CHARITY. It's a NON-PROFIT ORGANIZATION.

I did what I always do when confronted by a calm, rational adult with a genuine point to make – I became a terrified, whiny child. I immediately followed him back so we could continue the conversation privately on direct message.

It became clear, pretty quickly, that my comments had had an impact on the island. Folk had rallied round the couple, who were well loved and respected. There was outrage that I could have picked so small and innocent a target. I think there might have even been an article or two in the local press.

I privately messaged their son who, even though protected by the anonymity of social media, opted to be a gentleman and was dignified throughout. Our exchange went something like this:

Me: I am so so so sorry. What would you like me to do?
Son: Why did you do it?
Me: I don't know. I really feel awful about it. What can I do to make it better?
Son: I don't know. That's up to you. Personally, I think you should call them.
Me: Oh.

My worst nightmare is unfolding. I am going to actually have to take responsibility. For myself. I carry on typing.

Me: Would that . . . help?
Son: Well, it might. You should ring them.

Their number follows. The digits of doom. Then we say goodbye.

I sat on the number for a day, working up the courage to call. Eventually I took a deep breath and dialled.

'Hello,' came a gentle voice at the other end. It was a voice I remembered, the voice of the kindly woman who had cured Jan of his snake phobia.

Me: Hello. My name is Sue.
Woman: Hello!
Me: Sue Perkins.
Woman: Oh.

There is squirmy moment during which my arse makes buttons.

Woman: Well, I am surprised to hear from you. We didn't think
                you'd ring.
Me: I am so, so sorry.
Woman: OK . . .
Me: Really, I am.
Woman: The thing is, we don't mind that you didn't like our Ser-
                pentarium, but we did mind that you implied we don't
                treat the snakes well. Because, well . . . the thing is, we
                love those snakes and we're the only hope they've got.
                There's no one else doing the work we're doing. And we
                don't get paid for it; we just do it because we want to help.

Another pause – just long enough for me to fully inhabit what a monumental twat I've been.

Me: I'm sorry – it just came out.

Her response is simple, measured.

Woman: Really? *Really?*

Of course it didn't just slip out. I chose to do it. Not because I wanted to hurt a lovely couple on the beautiful Isle of Skye, but because I was too lazy to commit to a better option. It wasn't anyone's fault but mine. Not the researcher or the producer or the programme or the BBC. It was me, just me. I did it.

I've done lots of things I shouldn't. I have behaved in loutish and cavalier ways. I have hurt those I loved. But there's something about that still, small voice I keep coming back to, that small, still voice that remains in my head every time I give an interview, or tell a story, or embellish an anecdote. That still, small voice that peeps through for a tiny moment, just to catch me before I fall – that makes me stop and think, *Who does it hurt? Why am I choosing that target? Can they fight back?* That still, small voice that simply says:

  'Really?

  'Really?'

The Power of Trance

At last, I'm happy again. The dust I kicked up around me aged forty is finally, finally settling. I have moved to a top-floor flat, so there is no zealous German above me performing esoteric crack-of-dawn exercises. There are no rats. No rogue fishermen. I do, however, live above the north London legend that is Sylv, a septuagenarian peroxide and perma-tanned powerhouse who spends nine months of the year in a boob tube.

Sylv's modus operandi is to greet you with a threat.

'I'm going to rip your fucking head off if you don't take them bins out . . . Morning, darling!'

'If you don't wipe your boots when you come in I'll carve off your ear 'oles and fucking post 'em to you. Now where you been? I've missed ya . . .'

I love Sylv. We keep an eye out for each other. I find her cheap antibiotics on the Internet and she power-hoses journal-ists off the top step. It's a perfect symbiotic relationship.

I am now with my new partner, Anna. There's that old adage: you don't know how long you've been contending with the gloom until someone turns the lights on. Well Anna didn't just turn the lights on; she brought several spotlights, a couple of flares and a glitter ball for good measure.

She has balls of steel, a heart of gold and a pancreas of pew-ter (though she's having an op for that). If you want to know what kind of a person she is, then consider that this is the woman who organized a full-on thirty-strong rounders match in the park, just so I, aged forty-five, could finally know what it's like to be picked for a team. I'll always love her for that.

Anna is not only excellent at her television job, she's also training to be a cognitive hypnotherapist. On the one hand, this is wonderful – I now have a first-hand resource when life is difficult. On the other, it's a total and utter nightmare. Now every time we have a row, I find myself put in a trance-like daze with my subconscious self being informed that it is a total and utter arsehole. A lot like my conscious self.

After one such row Anna suggested (see also: demanded) I might want to do some timeline regression, a process which involves going back to a difficult past event, amending it, then leaving it well and truly behind. I say she suggested; in truth, I no longer know whether I have anything approaching free will or if everything I do is being subliminally influenced (see also: demanded) by her. Maybe I've just become her mind-bitch.

I like hypnotherapy – it works for me. It helped me quit smoking, dulled my tinnitus and calmed my PTSD (gifted to me by that second break-in). These were, however, sessions conducted by qualified healthcare professionals in a dispassionate environment. It's an entirely different ball game when that professional is

a. your girlfriend
b. has an agenda
c. not yet a professional.

Much as Anna has the makings of an incredible practitioner, she is only halfway through her diploma. At the moment her technique consists of lots of swearing and flicking through manuals, the flow of the therapeutic process slightly jarred by the constant, exasperated, 'Oh wait, I haven't done that bit yet.'

Would you let a trainee hairdresser loose on your fringe? Maybe.

Would you let a hobbyist accountant loose on your VAT return? Possibly.

Would you let an unqualified hypnotherapist tinker with the darkest recesses of your mind after doing only half of the required reading? I did.

As part of her studies Anna needed a guinea pig to practise on. And apparently I was it. Our first few sessions together were something of a mixed bag, although they started well enough. It's fair to say Anna had mastered the art of getting me *into* a trance state, but was less confident about getting me *out* of one. In the first session Anna suggested (see also: demanded) that I should examine the feelings I still had for an ex and our excruciatingly painful break-up through a technique known as visual squash.

We settled down on the sofa – me lying prostrate, Anna sitting by my side. As I feel shattered most of the time, the induction bit was easy.

Anna: You are feeling sleeeeeepy . . .
Me: Yes, I am . . .
Anna: You are feeling nice and relaaaaaaxed . . .
Me: Why are you doing that weird voice?

It has suddenly become soft and silky. And more than a little bit posh.

Anna: Shuuuuuut uuuuuup.

And off I went, down an imaginary flight of steps, each tread sending me deeper and deeper into trance.

I listened to her voice, felt my muscles relax and my bones

melt. My body felt like warm syrup in a drawstring bag. If you've not experienced it, the hypnotic state is hard to describe – in that moment you are both a particle and a wave, resisting and complying, acquiescing and questioning. A dance between the self you live with and know and the one behind the scenes, pulling the strings, that you don't.

Anna asked me to imagine the break-up as an object. Immediately I felt my left hand sag with the weight of a large spiky metal ball. She carried on talking. The weight in my arm grew more intense. She carried on talking. I could feel the prickles of the ball digging into my palm. She carried on talking.

And then she stopped.

Anna: Shit!
Me: [*struggling to speak*] What's going on?

I am still in a dream state but slowly become aware of the frantic flicking of pages in the background.

Anna: Oh God, I think I've done it wrong . . .

My consciousness scrambles to attention. I sit up, suddenly taut with anxiety, my eyes still closed.

Me: What do you mean 'done it wrong'?
Anna: I can't remember what you do after that.
Me: What are you talking about!? What . . . What am I going to do with this?! [*I moan, struggling to raise my leaden arm*]
Anna: I don't know. We haven't got to that bit yet.

The imaginary ball feels heavy and cold in my hand.

Me: Does that mean I am going to have to just carry her around
         with me?
Anna: For God's sake! Yes! Probably!

Since then I've been a weekly guinea pig. Every Sunday night
I've had sessions in metaphor therapy, positive and negative
hallucination, future pacing – all in an effort to stop me, and
these are Anna's words, from being a 'massive dick'. It got to
the stage where I became frightened of the sound of her key in
the lock. Until she hypnotized me out of that.

One particular Sunday night Anna came back, the familiar
textbook a little more thumbed and nearly completed. This
week, I was informed, it was time for the *Time Tunnel*.

I assumed the position.

Anna: Right, so what would you like to achieve?
Me: I'd like . . . Gosh, that's a big one. Well, I'd like to be more
         free. More creative. Confident. Socially adept. I'd like a
         house, if I'm honest. I like the flat, but I'd love a house. I'd
         like not to be blocked. I'd –
Anna: Right, Sue – do you want to pick just *one*?

[It really is impossible to underestimate how annoying she finds me.]

Me: OK. I'd like to be more creatively free.

We established that my life's timeline was above me, running
from left to right, like a zip wire. I'm a fairly visual person, so I
could see it clearly and it was easy to hop on board. Using this
zip wire I could scoot along to points in my past and look down
from a position of safety.

Anna: Right, Sue, if you'd like to travel back to a point in time when you feel you are being blocked.

There's a nagging itch in my big toe. I can't move to assuage it. I am too busy, too busy travelling down my own personal zip wire to the past.
    And I am there.

Anna: Where are you?
Me: I'm over my bedroom.
Anna: How old are you?
Me: I'm eight.
Anna: Who's in the bedroom with you?
Me: My mum.
Anna: OK, do you want to go down into the room . . .
Me: I'm in the room.
Anna: Right . . .
Me: She's SO annoying . . .

My hands move to my hips and my jaw juts out like a chicken. I am the very model of petulance.

Anna: And what are you talking about?
Me: I've done a project. On the Romans.
Anna: Right . . .
Me: I could do a project on anything I wanted. That's what the teacher said. So I've done it on Roman food. I've done a bunch of papier mâché grapes and a papier mâché dormouse.

There is the sound of a snigger. Both levels of my consciousness choose to ignore it.

Me: Mum's saying that it isn't right. That the perspective isn't right and that the dormouse is way too big.

Anna: OK, Sue, listen to my voice. Now let's try to turn the colour down on the scene . . .

Me: Shut up! I'm busy talking to my mum. I am SO angry. I can do a project on anything I want and I want to do it on Roman food and it doesn't matter that the dormouse is three times the size of a bunch of grapes because I have been told I can do anything I want . . .

Fifteen minutes later I am hoarse, arguing with a mother in a tight perm and pink jogging suit who hasn't existed for thirty-five years. Anna's interventions are now becoming desperate.

Anna: And now let's move upwards, can you do that?

Me: Yes.

Anna: OK then, let's go upwards – back to your safe place, and look down on the scene from above. Does that seem better?

Me: Yes.

Anna: [*palpable relief in her voice*] Thank God.

Me: Oh, hang on – no.

Anna: Christ! [*Now despair*] Do you want to go back down?

Me: Yes.

And I'm in my childhood bedroom again. Hands on hips, locked in an eternal battle of wills with Ann Perkins.

Me: It doesn't matter that the grapes are blue! I can do anything I want! I can do anything I want! The teacher said! The grapes could be orange or red or white . . .

Another ten minutes pass. I am exhausted and grow quiet. Anna leads me back onto the zip wire and I look down at myself and my mum. I feel calm. Resolved.

Anna: OK, now let's move along the years.
Me: Stop!

We've barely moved six months or so.

Anna: [*muttering*] Give me strength . . . What is it? How old are you?
Me: I'm eight and a half.
Anna: What's happened?
Me: I've done a project on drums. I can do anything I want, and I've chosen drums. She's saying the snare drum's too big . . .

We never did timeline regression again. Shortly after that Anna stopped using me as a guinea pig and started practising on her friend Lesley. Now she is fully qualified and will be the most amazing therapist. Even better, I no longer have to be the trial-and-error brain she practises on. These days, when we row, I don't have to spend hours in a trance state – I can just be like everyone else. I can storm off to the pub, have a drink and crawl back later full of regret.

But every so often I get the strangest feeling, like a ball of heavy metal in my left hand, weighing me down.

It's All Over the Front Page

I have 'issues' with driving.* When everyone else at school turned seventeen, they seemed to absorb the Highway Code through osmosis and instantly understand the multitasking of mirror, signal and manoeuvre. They'd sail through their parallel parks and three-point-turns and were, in a heartbeat, racing to exotic places like Woldingham, Westerham and West Wickham. *I want to go to West Wickham!* I'd think while sitting red-faced atop my rusty Chopper, chain-smoking and contemplating the slight incline home.

The only compensation for being a non-driver was that I could drink myself unconscious every night of the week and rely on my boyfriend Rob for transportation home. Rob owned a diarrhoea-coloured Datsun Cherry, the only vehicle on earth that could make the idea of walking preferable to a teenager. You'd hear it before you could see it. Hell, you could *smell* it before you could see it. His arrival was heralded by the roar of ripped clutch and the reek of a benzo-cloud of horror hydrocarbons.

'Yes, everyone!' I'd shout to bystanders. 'This is MY BOYFRIEND! He drives the car of a Latin-teaching MOT-failing sex offender! Deal with it!'

* According to every DVLA examiner I came across 1986–99.

I am in denial about how many times I failed my driving test. It may be as few as three, it may be as many as six. I care not. It's like your A levels. Nobody asks you about the results until you're in court.

If the test had been purely academic, I'd have passed with flying colours. Annoyingly there's this practical section, where you actually have to get in a car. All my tests *started* well enough. I managed to get into the correct side of the vehicle, the side by the steering wheel, and turn the key in the ignition. But after that it all went downhill. As did I – usually during the hill-start portion of the exam. There would be the inevitable squelch of tyre against kerb, the nudge of bumper on bollard, the crack of examiner's head against windscreen – those tell-tale signs that my vehicular dreams were over and that once again I'd be getting the night bus home.

One reason for my consistent failure may have been my eye-sight. My right eye has the vision of a sparrowhawk; my left, however, is a mess. I had an accident as a kid, and it's now a short-sighted ball of jelly with peripheral double vision. I'm not sure if they do something as basic as this now, but the first part of the driving test used to be a bit like an eye exam. You had to read the number plate on the car in front of you, just so they could check you had eyes that worked. It's a fairly com-monsensical starting point for a test in my opinion, but one I had to try and get around. I was in denial and too vain to get a pair of glasses, so my eyes had bewilderingly different depths of focus. In order to get a crisp image, I had to cup my left eye so that the sparrowhawk side of me could go about its busi-ness. However, it proved quite hard to do this without alerting the attention of the examiner. On my first test I overdid it and looked like a budget pirate. The sight of me, Cyclops, palm over one eye, did nothing to instil confidence in him. Next time I was more subtle – pretending I was scratching my eyebrow. The third I pretended to be winking at a passing builder while recording the plate details.

I finally passed my test at the age of twenty-nine and a bit. By which I mean thirty. Mel and I sat our exams in the same week, and it is still a bone of contention between us that I scored one mark higher than her in the written test. (I knew the depth of tread that tyres need, she didn't. It doesn't matter.*)

Just because I'm not *good* at driving, doesn't mean I don't *like* driving. My love of motoring stems from when I was seven years old. Our road was on a small incline, and our house sat at the very top. Our car, as you know, was always parked half-in and half-out of the garage, due to the construction issues outlined earlier. Having said that, even if the garage *had* been built to the correct dimensions, and the car *could* have fitted inside, I still believe Mum would have parked the car where she could see it. There are two possible explanations for this.

a. Mum adheres to the now outdated Copenhagen intepretation of quantum mechanics, which posits that an object exists in simultaneous states until observed. Thus, if the car was parked *inside* the garage, it could be both safe *and* stolen. By observing the car half-out of the garage, Mum can maintain the knowledge the car is safe.

b. Mum is nuts.

I'm digressing. So, I'm seven. My mum is taking my brother and me somewhere – judo, ballet or some combination of the two – but she has forgotten something and rushes back to

* It really, really does.

the house. I climb into the driver's seat. My brother climbs into the passenger seat next to me.

'We're going to do driving,' I say, leaning right into his face.

'OK,' he says, playing along as always.

I have been studying my parents for years. I know what to do. It takes all my strength, and both hands, to lift the handbrake and let it fall again. But I manage. Slowly the wheels turn, gaining momentum as we reverse.

'We're doing driving,' I tell David.

'OK', he says, head pressed back into the seat.

I see Mum coming down the steps of the house. Then I see her seeing us. Her mouth widens into a scream. It all goes a bit slo-mo from there.

I still remember the thrill of it. The acceleration. The slow turn of the steering wheel. The bump as we crash into the neighbour's wall, the crumble of brick against metal until we finally come to a halt. The screaming. The terrible screaming. It's a series of sensations I've relived several times since then – although the thrill is somewhat lessened when you're the one who has to pay the bill.

So, at the tender age of twenty-nine, I was officially allowed on the roads. To celebrate the occasion I bought an ex-boy-friend's car – a turd-green Spanish ringer which he, for some reason, appeared very keen to get rid of.

The week after my test I thought I'd take my baby for a spin, so I hopped in and turned the key in the ignition. Radio 1 blared from the speakers so loudly I couldn't hear myself think. Perfect. I put the car into reverse, floored the clutch and pumped the accelerator. Nothing. I pumped again – couldn't hear a sausage. So I lifted the handbrake and put the pedal to the metal. Still nothing. Something must be wrong. I lifted the clutch a tad, and that was when it happened. The car lurched back with such force I was in danger of severing my head with my own jowls. I smashed into the car behind, then, panicking, removed both feet from the pedals and promptly stalled.

The car behind belonged to my wonderful mate Neil, who had heard the roar of an engine and the thump of heavy house music and come to take a look just in time to see a cloud of smoke billowing from my exhaust as I hurtled backwards at breakneck speed. I don't know exactly what happens when you reverse at full speed into a stationary car. But I do know how much it costs.

£1,200

Every year since then I have managed to put on a similarly cretinous display. I have reversed into fork-lift trucks, boulders and gates. For me the bumpers of a car exist solely to provide a handy first-hand indicator of just how close you are to an object.

But this year I excelled myself. I didn't just stick to *my* car.

Poo-etry in motion

One Friday night I planned to collect my surviving dog, Parker, from the farm where she stayed when I was working. The idea was then for Anna and myself to carry on and have a weekend away in the West Country. There was just one slight problem.

Me: Sweetie . . .
Anna: You never call me sweetie. What do you want?
Me: Can we take *your* car this weekend?
Anna: Why can't we take yours?
Me: It's in the garage getting serviced, and I can't be bothered to pick it up. Pleeeease . . .

Spectacles

Anna: [*loud and forceful exhalation*] I've just had it valeted. I love
         Parker, but she smells.
Me: No she doesn't!*
Anna: She really does . . .
Me: Listen, she'll be on her blanket buckled up on the back seat.
         You won't even know she's there . . .

We arrived at the farm and Parker seemed her usual self,
namely emotionally disconnected and food-obsessed. I clipped
her into her seat belt on the back seat and we all got under
way.

Half an hour into the onward journey I became aware of
the dog circling on the back seat and pulling on her lead. Then
came a wave of heavy stink – gastric, fecal – all the smells you
never want to smell in a confined space.

Anna: Your dog has just thrown up.
Me: [*instantly defensive*] Oh, FFS!
Anna: [*peering round*] It's all over her blanket.
Me: [*even more defensive*] Right. Right! Well I'll pull into the ser-
         vice station and sort it out then. Jesus!

Bridgwater Services

is my least favourite service station on the M5. It has an air of
menace that not even the finest Greggs Baked Bean Lattice can
alleviate. Whereas most service-area car parks are open to the
air and spacious, this is cramped and concrete. The parking is
free, as is the overpowering stench of piss that greets you upon
leaving your vehicle.

* She does.

288

I pulled in, whipped Parker's puke-sodden blanket out of the car and popped it in a bin. Thankfully Anna's upholstery was untouched. Phew. I went off to grab us some sandwiches, which we ate in an uncomfortable silence in the front seat. I was a ticking time bomb of rage. I love my dog. I wanted Anna to love my dog. Why, therefore, had my dog decided to vomit in her car? Did she *want* Anna to hate her?

After wolfing down something that claimed to be a crayfish bap, we bickered about where to recycle the leftovers. I was a dick. The bicker quickly developed into a full-blown row – so full-blown that we didn't notice the dog panting in the back.

We got under way again and managed around ten or so miles before we noticed Parker's heavy breathing – gusts of stale stomach air pumping onto the back of our necks. Before long, that wave of sick/shit was back.

Anna: She's done it again.
Me: Fuck!

I turn round to see a bile-coated turd nestled into the seat, sticky brown liquid oozing into the fabric.

Anna: Keep your eyes on the road, Sue!
Me: Fuck's SAKE!
Anna: Just concentrate on driving!
Me: Jesus Christ, that bloody dog!
Anna: Is her arse supposed to be blue?

Taunton Deane Services

is a civilized bijou outlet – a series of dark low-rise buildings accessible through a cobbled entranceway lined with picnic benches for the discerning outdoors eater. By the time I pulled in, Parker was standing in her seat, a long thread of greenish saliva hanging from her mouth. I unclipped her and took her for a walk, whereupon she threw up again and shot out about a litre of sand-coloured diarrhoea. I cleaned her with a pack of moist fragranced toilet tissues while enjoying the chorus of 'Bake!' that greeted me from my fellow motorists. 'Yes! Bake!' I shouted back weakly, dabbing at my pet's weeping arsehole.

Half an hour later I returned to the car. Anna was listening to something on Radio 4, eyes closed, with all the windows open. I popped Parker on a fresh blanket, clipped her back into her seat belt and we headed off again.

Exeter Services

is, I think, out of all the services on the M5, my favourite. Not only is it large, with a children's play area, grassy knoll and multiple fast-food outlets, it also has a Ladbrokes, should you wish to place a bet on whether the A30 will be gridlocked all the way to Land's End. By the time we reached it the day was fading, and with it our hopes of making it down much further west. The back seat was coated in a toxic combination of poo and puke – pooke, if you will – and the footwell in front of it was swilling with gob. Anna had gone into shock and was now silent, trying to get her head around the fact her beloved car was being destroyed, slowly, from the inside out. It was the same routine as the other services: dog out, moist towelette, water if she wanted it, more shit/sick, moist towelette, 'Oi, isn't that Mel from *Bake Off*?' vomit, moist towelette, 'Oi, Mel, BAKE!' buckle her up and off.

It was pitch black by the time we neared Exeter. All plans had been abandoned. Anna was starting to get a headache from the smell and we both felt distinctly nauseous. We had rowed ourselves hoarse and now fell back into a tense silence.

It was then that Parker detonated.

Yes, detonated. I really don't have another word for it. She went off like a canine grenade. It was an eruption the like of which I have never seen before or since. Every pore in her body leaked something foul. It hit the windows, the driver's seat, the passenger seat – it sprayed every conceivable corner of the car.

Anna broke the silence.

Anna: I'm going to stay in a hotel. Drive me to a hotel.

Me: Please, don't do that. We'll go to our mate Michele's. She's nearby. She'll help.

Anna: Fine. Don't talk to me.

Me: OK.

Anna: I said don't talk to me.

I pulled over. I unbuckled the dog and let her pad around the pavement.

'On your marks, get set . . .' shouted a passing motorist.

'BAKE!' I hollered back, before turning once more to my sopping hound.

'Is there anywhere on or in this car – anywhere AT ALL – you haven't shat?' I screamed partly to the dog and partly to the heavens.

Almost as if in response, Parker turned a rheumy eye towards me and fired a cannon of liquid shit against the wheel arch. It went on and on and on – like something out of a *Little Britain* sketch. Then all went quiet again.

Suddenly I noticed that there were spots of blood all over the pavement, blood over the wheel, blood over the dog. I panicked. I popped her back in her seat and shut the door and drove off like a nutter in search of an emergency vet.

What I *didn't* do was buckle up the dog.

By now it was raining – driving, driving rain. Parker was retching in time to the windscreen wipers. I felt exhausted and teary, but I stayed focused. Just a few more miles until we reached our mate – I could drop Anna off, then get the dog to a vet.

The motorway was busy with all the erratic stop-and-start stuff you get with bad weather. We were going at around sixty miles an hour when Parker, fresh from another rectal sneeze, decided she had had enough. She was ill and upset and she wanted to sit with her mum.

So she did.

Unfettered by a seat belt, she clambered between the two front seats and thence made the attempt to get onto my lap. In doing so, she kicked the gearbox into sudden and shocking neutral. There was a roar, a loss of power, and I struggled to pull us over onto the hard shoulder amid the traffic.

The engine stalled. I tried the ignition. Nothing. Again. This time it turned over. I crawled the rest of the way – power steering ripped, the electrics erratic, the clutch – don't go there.

I don't know exactly what happens when your clutch burns out on a motorway, but I do know how much it costs.

£2,500 (and counting).

There was also £300 on valeting, though some days you can still catch the odd whiff in the air.

As for Parker, she had colitis. I don't know exactly what colitis is, but I do know how much it costs.

£1,200 for a weekend stay at the vet's on a drip. (She is now, thankfully, right as rain.)

And now, whenever we go anywhere, wherever we go – we take *my* car.

It's not only my poor eyesight and tendency towards the erratic which make my driving less than perfect. I also suffer from road rage. Outside a car I pride myself on being a reasonable, tolerant, empathetic human being. Inside one I am an animal. A vile, invective-spewing animal. I have been run off the road. I have stood, nose to nose, screaming at a fellow motorist in the middle of the A406. I am not proud of these things.

In a car I think I am Jason Statham – although, I mean, I don't put on the voice or anything weird like that.* In a car I become this totally focused tank of aggressive fervour. I'm a pedal-to-the-metal nut job. I'm a wheel-spinning high-revving hot-rodder. I steer with the palm of my hand and scream and shout at every single junction. I mean, I *really* think I am Jason Statham – although, I mean, I don't invent scenarios or anything weird like that.† I don't shout, 'I'm the Transporter! Get out of my way,

---

* I do.

† I do.

bitches – I've got to get a pint of skimmed milk from the garage before it closes!'

One day around about four years ago I was in the car heading to the supermarket. Actually, in truth, I don't remember where I was going or indeed if there was any urgency about the trip. It was broad daylight. The sun was shining. It was a bright day – a very, *very* bright day – the sheer, unforgiving brightness of it will become significant later.

The arterial roads near my flat are narrow and lined with Audis. Every day is German Automotive Superiority Day in Hampstead, north London. It was the school run and I'd had a nightmare getting out of my road; I could feel the veins in my neck twisting like rope with the tension. My face flushed. In front of me appeared hazard after hazard – parking lorries, darting kids, dogs off leads.

I started with a few generic 'piss offs', just to warm up, get my eye in. Then I proceeded to work through a couple of light-to-medium-grade slurs on parental legitimacy and IQ. The car in front of me failed to indicate – I let loose a smattering of what the 1970s British Board of Film Classification would deem 'sexual swear words'.

By the time I hit Downshire Hill, some three minutes from my flat, I was ready to kill. I pulled in to let a lorry pass. The driver didn't thank me. He got a middle finger and a 'Screw you, mate' for his trouble.

Then I saw it, a showroom-fresh spanking-new Mercedes – top of the range and glinting in the sun. Its bonnet buffed by a thousand lackeys. From where I sat, engine idling, it appeared to fill the entire width of the road – towering over me at the top of the hill while I waited like a supplicant in an old banger at the bottom.

It came upon me like an electrical storm, hard and fast – a

potent mix of class war and pure envy. I was the last in a long line of Perkinses doffing their caps to their Lords and Masters in a daisy chain of generational oppression, and I wasn't having it.

I wasn't having *any of it.*

This was one game of chicken I could afford to lose, I thought. So what if my car got scratched? It was scratched already. So what if it got written off? Its resale value was maybe a couple of hundred quid. Who cares?

I put the car into first and started up the hill. The Merc didn't tuck in. The obstruction was their side of the road but they didn't tuck in. I casually flicked some double digits and carried on. Second gear now, and still no sign of them backing down. I worked a combo of V-signs and F-bombs as I started to accelerate. They continued forward.

Just one more chance for them to pull in, just one more space – I was now leaning forward, my boiled face randomly spewing every epithet I'd ever heard, like a four-letter fruit machine.

You seismic shit-splat!

You cock-juggling thunder-quim!

You deliquescent dick-cheese!

But they don't take that chance. They're coming straight for me.

We were locked in. No backing down. We now had to try and pass one another on this bright, double-parked, German-lined street. I was slamming my fists on the wheel as our bonnets met . . . and then . . .

Then I pulled out a combination move I'd never tried before – double bird, single bird and multiple Vs. I followed this with a fast-cut series of mimes – gun to the head, noose around neck, machine gun spraying, grenade launching, howitzer firing –

and, just as our windows met, I slowly drew my finger across my neck as if slicing it, and said, 'You . . .

Both of our windows were open, nothing more than a cigarette paper's worth of space between us. And there, at the wheel, Esther Rantzen.

. . . cunt.'

The word dropped into her lap like a hot angry baby.

Esther's face was, for a second, the very model of bland acknowledgement. She was, after all, merely passing another vehicle, slowly, in a London street. She saw me and registered two things. First that it was me, someone she knows from the TV, and second that the person she knows from the TV was miming cutting her throat while uttering possibly the most offensive and certainly the most visceral word in the English language. Something crossed her face – her eyes flickered a little, as if reacting to an alarm sounding in the distance. Later, I thought. Later she would process what had happened. Later she would realize what I'd said and what I'd done.

My hand finished its action across my neck. It dropped to my knees like a stone.

'Hi, Esther!' I said, making the gear-change to jolly as our cars inched past. 'Hi!'

And then I was gone.*

* There is no punchline to this story. Sometimes life doesn't give you one. I'm as sorry as you are.

As I was finalizing the manuscript for this book, I was lent an entirely new perspective on cars, courtesy of the BBC show *Top Gear*. *Top Gear* isn't a show I've ever really watched. For starters it's about cars, so I'm only mildly interested from the get-go.

Anyway, somebody, somewhere made up a story that I was in line to be the new presenter of *Top Gear*. If you didn't already think that was a ridiculous idea, then hopefully the previous chapter has convinced you otherwise. Then the bookies got hold of the story and duly (even though it had no basis in truth) tipped me as favourite for the job. Suddenly, after years of peaceful existence on Twitter, my timeline was full of thick-necked white men in the twilight of their usefulness telling me that I should be dead. The general gist appeared to be, 'Man do car, woman do cake.' One tweeter even went as far as to say they'd like to see me set on fire.

I'd never join a club that would allow a person like me to become a member, said Woody Allen, paraphrasing Groucho Marx. Let me add to that. I'd never join a club that would like to see me burned to death, because that club sounds AWFUL.

So I took myself off social media for a bit.

Then the trolling story became front-page news. I said nothing. I just assumed that somebody, somewhere would say, 'Don't be silly, of course she isn't the next presenter. Have you seen her? She can barely stand up straight, let alone operate machinery.' But nobody did. So the more I appeared on the front pages, the more people thought I was indeed the next *Top Gear* presenter, and the more venom came my way. It became a Möbius strip of indignation.

Sometimes I comforted myself by having imaginary conversations with those journalists in my head.

Me: The thing is, this has all been rather upsetting.

Journo: IT'S DISGUSTING. IT'S PC GONE MAD. YOU'RE A WOMAN, FOR GOD'S SAKE.

Me: Yes. Yes I am.

Journo: ANOTHER EXAMPLE OF THE METROPOLITAN LIB-ERAL ELITE USING POSITIVE DISCRIMINATION.

Me: Listen . . .

Journo: YET MORE BED-WETTING PINKOS DRIVING A RADI-CAL LESBIAN LEFTIST AGENDA.

Me: The thing is –

Journo: WOMEN CAN'T EVEN DRIVE! EVERYBODY KNOWS THEY DON'T HAVE OPPOSABLE THUMBS!!

Me: Please . . .

Journo: COME ON, SHOW ME YOUR THUMBS! SHOW ME YOUR THUMBS!

A month later it all died down. Now all is quiet on my time-line again.

So . . .

I'm putting it out there. I'm the new presenter of *Songs of Praise*.

Come and get me.

I Am Become Cake,
the Destroyer of Midriffs

This is a photocopy of a project I did when I was a girl. I would like to start by addressing some comments to the teacher who marked it.

Dear Teacher,

Thank you so much for your feedback on my project. Here are some of my own notes, made some thirty-eight years after your markings.

Firstly – disappointed? Really? ARE YOU OUT OF YOUR MIND? My baker is making bread on a levitating bench!!!! How many of those do you see in catering situations? Plus, he/ she is doing so while wearing a hat larger than their own torso. Those are tough conditions in which to create the perfect crusty cob.

As for 'Pictures would improve your project' – well, Lady-Whose-Name-I-Can-No-Longer-Remember, you might want to take a look at all those funny things above your comments. Can you see them? They look suspiciously like pictures, don't they? They do to me.

Finally, on the 'interesting' front. You see that bird in the foreground? The picture of the bird? Well, it's not going 'cluck-cluck' is it? If it was, it would be a chicken. But no, this bird is going 'quack-quack' because it is a duck. I am using DUCK's eggs instead of common or garden HEN's eggs. That is one hell of an enriched dough going on there FYI, lady . . .

Anyhow, I do hope you are enjoying your retirement, which I have done a project on below. I'm sorry it doesn't include any pictures.

Yours,
Susan Perkins, aged 45

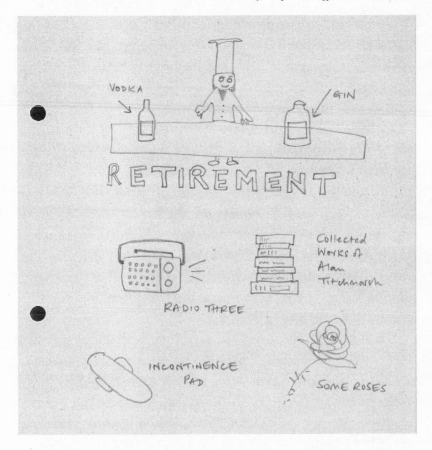

I was six years old when I did that project. We made bread at school, and I LIKED it. I liked it not only because it was messy, but messy in *the best possible way* – because you could actually eat the mess after you'd made it.

I certainly didn't need to do a project about cake to alert my senses to the thrill of sponge. I loved it. I loved it raw, I loved it cooked, I loved it warm, I loved it stale. I loved it so much that Granddad Smith used to trick me by holding out a teaspoon of pale brown goo for me to taste while Mum was baking, only for me to discover upon eating it that it wasn't cake mix at all, but pokey English mustard.

My earliest culinary experience was a batch of rock cakes I baked for my mum in the mid-1970s. The best thing one could say about those cakes was that they didn't breach the Trade Descriptions Act, resembling, as they did, something you might get hit with should you lose your way in an asteroid belt. I had made a schoolgirl error – forgivable only by the fact I was actually a schoolgirl at the time. I had made the mixture according to the recipe, baked it until golden, but then failed to let the cakes cool. Instead, I slung them, piping hot, into a tin and Sellotaped the sides in preparation for Mother's Day morning. I was thirty minutes and one wire rack short of perfection.

My mother welled with pride as she opened the tin – she's always been a fan of the home-made present. That pride lasted right up to the point her teeth started to fracture against the granite-like intensity of the bake.

I didn't need to be any good at baking, since Mum was such a good pragmatic cook – brought up on the commonsensical recipes of the late, great Marguerite Patten and Mary Berry (whatever happened to her?). Mum was, it's fair to say, a master of mass catering – vast tray bakes, bubbling batter puddings the size of double duvets and undulating sheets of lasagne without end. There were usually only the five of us sitting down to eat, but I think the huge volumes of food were pre-emptive, precautionary – in case a coach full of starving football supporters happened to break down right outside the house. In which case, she, Ann Perkins, was ready to serve a piping-hot linear metre of cannelloni directly into the chops of a needy centre forward.

There wasn't an awful lot of spare cash knocking about when we were little, so we often ate soya rather than beef mince, which was freeze-dried and packed into clear plastic bags. It was the colour of sadness and the texture of granola, but could be heated and cajoled back to half-life with tomatoes and stock. It was cheap – though I wouldn't go as far as to say cheerful. I ate so much of the stuff that I'm pretty confident I'm one of the most genetically modified presenters working in television today.

I haven't always been a big eater. I was underweight and sickly at birth, and remained that way until my late thirties when I discovered the Healing Power of Sponge. My indifference to food extended back to primary school during the reign of Sister Mary Dorothy and her right-handed harpies. When I was seven, I developed a full-blown eating disorder. Most food related problems stem from a deep-rooted psychological issue, although mine came courtesy of an unlikely source – *Buck Rogers in the 25th Century*. Remember *Buck Rogers*? Gil Gerard, as the eponymous hero – all teak bloat and enthusiasm, with Jack Palance as a scene-chewing space wacko heading up a nomad cult on Planet Vistula. (Vistula? You can get a cream for that. You're welcome.)

I loved *Buck Rogers*. I believed every word of it. But Buck lied.

Yes, Buck, you did indeed predict the rise of the onesie and the playsuit. And, by God, you looked dapper in both. But no, Buck, the world did not end in a nuclear catastrophe at the close of the 20th century leading to the founding of the Earth Defense Directorate. The worst thing that happened was that a few people got frightened about the millennium bug, stockpiled tins of beans and thought their computers might crash. Oh, and the Wall of Fire which was supposed to light the Thames on New Year's Eve 1999 was pretty shit. A Wall of Shit as it happens.

OK. So one particular episode of *Buck Rogers* – 'Planet of the Slave Girls' if you must know – featured a storyline in which the earth's fighter squadron became totally incapacitated after eating poisoned food. This led me to the totally natural conclusion that even though I a.) wasn't in an intergalactic fighter squadron, or b.) didn't routinely eat weird discs covered in toxins, I too was being poisoned.

Other things that *Buck Rogers* made me frightened of:
gay robots
acid-coated boomerangs
Roddy McDowell

So convinced was I that my food was contaminated, I started to hide cheese sandwiches, spat things into napkins, feigned illness – anything to stop solids entering my digestive tract at the meal table. I was skinny as it was, and after a week of self-imposed starvation it became clear my parents were going to have to stage an intervention. One day, as I sat down for my tea, lips pursed, I noticed my mum and dad staring at each other in an unusually intense manner. She kept nodding at him, as if to say, *Go on, Bert. Get on with it!*

So Bert/Dad got on with it. He leaped from his chair, held my nose and, as my mouth obligingly fell open, rammed the Captain's finest down my gullet. Yep, my dad force-fed me fish fingers, which incidentally is the most alliterative way you can be force-fed. Afterwards my mum said they both cried. 'It was an act of violence,' she said. I didn't say anything because I was still coughing up neon-orange grit and the odd gobbet of cod.

In retrospect, I'm just glad she's never asked me if I think that particular early trauma is one of the things that has made me gay. My mum is deeply cool about me being lady-homo but will sporadically try to link childhood events (where she perceives herself to be lacking in some way) to my sexuality in an attempt to rationalize it.

Mum: When I forgot to bring your jacket with me and you

nearly froze to death in Sainsbury's car park that time, do
you think that had anything to do with your sexuality?

Me: No, Mum.

Mum: When we refused to allow you to go on the school day-trip
to Calais and you had to sit with Karen Rosenberg all day
– who couldn't go because she was an observant Jew – did
that make you gay?

Me: No, Mum.

Anyhow, after Fishfingergate, I ate with gusto. I am in no
way condoning or celebrating force-feeding. I'm just saying
that it worked for me. And it may or may not have made me
gay.

Mum, I'm kidding. Look. See? I was fine. I even did a project
about it.

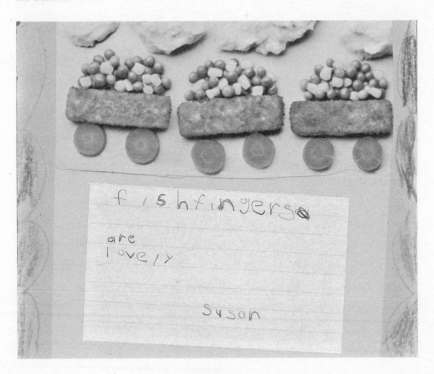

f i s h f i n g e r s

are
lovely

Susan

Sadly, I only got a C grade from my teacher, as there weren't any images of fish fingers in it.

As I hit double digits, Mum started entertaining in earnest. We three kids would sit on the stairs in height order, like myopic von Trapps, and peek through the wood-effect balustrade at the adults below. There would be the comforting peaty reek of Scotch and the rumble of banter, in the days before 'banter' was a euphemism for 'white male doing rape jokes'. These early dinner parties soon evolved into more lavish events – often themed and costumed – culminating in a series of vicars-and-tarts parties. These were all the rage back then, back when there was some form of moral divide between the two camps.

I am still in therapy over the sight of my dad dressed as a 'tart'. He looked like an east-European shot-putter wearing the pelt of Farah Fawcett. Occasionally he would ram a hand down his nylon blouse and adjust one of his balloon breasts, which would sag and pucker over the course of the evening until, around 2 a.m., he would put them out of their misery with the prick of a pin.

Finally, Mum was able to put the mass-catering skills she'd been honing for a decade into practice. Not only that, but she started experimenting with serving suggestions, presenting things in Kilner jars or atop scrubbed scallop shells she got from the fishmonger. She never served the actual scallops, of course – they would have ended up in the bin. Why? Because

'They're foreign muck.'

Dad's answer to anything that wasn't ice cream, sausages or chips was

'Not for me. It's foreign muck.'

Dad's gastronomic conservatism didn't stop Mum though –

she loved to push herself. The most exciting thing that ever happened was one of us bringing home a vegetarian. These were the days where vegetarian meals were just side dishes or listed on menus under 'Accompaniments'.

Mum: Are you saying we never gave you enough vegetables? Do you think that might have made you gay?
Me: No, Mum.

Once I'd left home and the 90s established themselves, the dinner parties faded out. I imagine it was because the kids had grown up and now the parents had to do the same. Either that or my dad's unconvincing and unrelenting transvestism had created a rift between him and his mates. After that, Mum and Dad opted for smaller affairs with only the closest of friends, the sort of friends comfortable with

a. Dad pretending he had an enormous pair of breasts.
b. Mum mainly serving food in seashells.

I remember that my dad's mate Mick would come round a lot. I loved him and his missus. He'd known Dad since they were kids, when they'd ripped around south-east London creating mayhem together. Mick would arrive and then the drinking would begin. And by God, could they drink – bottle after bottle after endless bottle. Sometime around 3 a.m. Mick would fall into the hedge in the front garden on the way to his car. He always drove. Right up to the time they banned him for life.

At the sound of grown man collapsing into hedgerow, we'd wake up.

Me: What's happened, Mum?

Mum: Your Uncle Mick has just had one of his dizzy spells. Now
          go back to bed.

I loved those two. Loved them for reasons I am only now starting to fully understand. I believe that Mick was the only person
keeping the black dog of depression away from my dad after
the cancer pecked at him, until even he retreated for a while
and let it consume Dad at will.

Taking the Époisses

One such evening Eve, Mick's wife, brought round a large
cheese. At the end of the meal the women duly unwrapped its
cling-film shroud and, hey presto, the whole room smelt like
instant arse.

Dad: Christ! What's that? It's awful.

Mick: It's making my nose bleed.

Mum: [*burying her nostrils in her sleeve*] I'll open a window.

There was no way we could eat it – for starters, it was impossible to get it within arm's length of your face without
retching. Any proximity set the whole of your GI tract into
spasm. But it couldn't stay in the room. It was a health hazard
just sitting there, sweating. And so it got moved to the fridge.
Out of sight, out of mind, but very much still in nasal passages.

   Then, at the end of the evening came the fight about who
should take it home.

Mick: I'm not having it in the fecking car.

Eve: I'm not having it in the fecking house!

Mick: And it was a present. A *present*. You can't return it. You can't look a gift cheese in the mouth, Bert.

So we were stuck with it. Stuck with the cheese of doom. God only knows what cheese it was, but after years of making food television my money's on an Époisses. The house was humming for weeks – imagine a boiler room densely packed with wet golden retrievers and you're not even close. The French might not have won a major war for over a hundred years but, I'm telling you, they have been stealth-attacking British households for decades with devastating efficiency.

Every time we opened the fridge, this gust swept over you, like a flatulent bison with giardia. It made my eyes water and my hair rise at the roots. My entire body would stiffen, every atom sending messages to my brain – *This smell? This smell ain't right* . . .

Of course you're thinking, *Why didn't they just bin it?* Well, they could have were it not for the fact that

a. My parents would never ever countenance wasting food.
b. My parents don't like to opt for an easy solution when a complex deadlock is possible.

So there we were, trapped between the Franco-stein horrors of 1990s artisanal cheese production and the moral rigour of 1950s austerity. Something had to give.

Thankfully we didn't have to keep it for long. Mum and Dad soon devised a cunning plan by which they could smuggle the cheese back to Mick and Eve's. The next time they went round for dinner they took the cheese with them. Bold as brass.

Mick:	Oh Jesus, the smell – it's even worse than I remembered.
Eve:	[*shrieking*] Get it out of here!
Dad:	It's a present. A *present*. You can't return it.

And so it sat in *their* fridge for six weeks.

Next dinner, and it was clear the Flynns were going to have to up their game. They brought the cheese to our house, but instead of openly offering it, they hid it behind the curtains. One–nil. Mum and Dad tracked it down (not hard, for reasons made manifestly clear above) and then returned it and hid it under a floorboard. One–all.

That was in 1991.

It is now 2015, and what you need to know is that the game is *still going on*. Same cheese – different hiding places. So far the cheese has been in flowerpots and hedgerows and under beds and in cupboards. Hell, in one particularly successful gambit, my super-square mum excused herself from dinner, went to the bathroom, pulled out a screwdriver from her purse, unscrewed the bath panel and sneaked the cheese in there. Take THAT, Catwoman.

That particular placement took them six months to find. I distinctly remember the call from Mick several weeks after the dinner.

Mick:	Susan, is your mum there?
Me:	No, she's out.
Mick:	OK. Right. OK. Can you take a message?
Me:	Sure.
Mick:	Can you . . . I need you to . . . Oh God. Just ask her – have we got the cheese?

Finally they found it, and the game was on again. It travelled back to us in disguise, and last I heard it had gone back to them rammed into the bottom of a bottle of expensive Scotch. Ooops. I've given it away now. First rule of Cheese Swap, you don't talk about Cheese Swap.

As a family we often talk about the cheese, and at the merest mention of its name that smell rises again in our nostrils.

Me: I've never, never to this day smelt anything like it.

Mum: Mmm. Me neither. [*Pause*] Do you think it might have made you gay?

Me: Possibly, Mum. It's possible.

In the spring of 2009 the then controller of BBC2, Janice Hadlow, asked if I'd think about presenting a cake show. By this time I had become the go-to girl for extreme eating for the minimum wage.

I said, 'That sounds like an awful idea. No one is going to watch it, and I can't imagine anything more tedious. It would be like watching paint dry, except worse, because after paint's dry you can at least hang pictures on it and sit back and admire it, whereas with a cake you just eat it and then feel awful about yourself.'

I said no.

But Janice is nothing if not a persistent soul, and when Janice thinks something is a good idea you listen, seeing as she is pretty much the cleverest person in the whole world. In pitching meetings you'd listen in awe as she riffed on Byzantine art and string theory and why the Hanoverians had such dysfunctional families, and then you'd feel bad for pitching her *The House of Hairy Children** or some such piffle.

Still, I said no.

By this point Janice was probably pretty pissed off, but stuck with it using the most effective weapon at her disposal – making me unemployed. Yep, she rather cleverly made sure I had no other work to distract me. Eventually the thought of dicking about with my best mate overcame my reservations about dragging myself and the nation towards morbid obesity and Type 2 diabetes.

From the outset Mary Berry was a dead cert for judge. I'd already had the pleasure of working with her in the 1950s – when she came on *Supersizers* and cooked a horsemeat steak in Stork. Trust me, that's the sort of first meeting you never forget. The male judge, however (as he is now affectionately known), was less set in stone. The first-round casting process failed to turn up a suitable candidate, but then we remembered this bloke on a cable show several years before, all mahogany and burly, pummelling the living shit out of a wannabe cob.

'Yes! He's great – what was his name?'

'Screw his name,' I replied. 'Let's talk about his *hair*.'

Paul Hollywood's barnet is made up of a series of grey vertiginous spikes, which serve not only to repel invaders but also to test the texture of sponges. It's a technique he mastered while working at the Dorchester. Just one simple bend of the waist and he can skewer the cake on his locks. If there is any residue left on his hair, then the cake is underdone. If the hair comes out clean, it's ready to remove from the oven.

So there we were, the four of us – Mary, Paul, myself and

---

* I believe this is now in production.

Mel – the most ridiculous and over-scrutinized family since the Kardashians. For those who have never seen *The Great British Bake Off*, the show in question, allow me to elaborate. Here's how it works.

I arrive around 8 a.m., impeccably dressed and elegantly coiffured. I then remove these perfect clothes and change into a jam-smeared jacket, ill-fitting low-crotch trousers and muddy brogues while tousling my hair into a wonky cockerel spike – all in an effort to get to the role of 'Sue Perkins'. I have opted to play 'Sue Perkins' as a care-worn scruffy little sugar hog who speaks only in double entendres (see baps, plums, tarts, etc.).

At around 8.30 a.m. my life partner Melanie and I walk into a large tent stationed somewhere in England's green and pleasant land and invite the contestants within to make a perfectly simple, everyday creation. It could be a life-sized statue of Michael Gove in vanilla sponge or a tier of profiteroles that expresses their feelings about nationalism. Simple, everyday stuff. To begin proceedings, I shout the word BAAAAAKE in a strangled and slightly sarcastic manner.

Next it's time for what we have named the Royal Tour, in which either Mel or myself potters around the benches finding out what large-scale adventures in baking the contestants will be attempting. We are joined on this pilgrimage by the show's iconic judging duo, Paul Hollywood and Mary Berry. Their love affair is one of the worst-kept secrets in show business. Paul's job is to listen to the baker's description of the pie / cake / tart in question, leave an ominous pause and then say, 'Mmm. I'll be interested to see if that works,' before walking off, shaking his head. No matter how hard he shakes his head, not a single hair will move. Mary, on the other hand, says very little but sets her eyes to 'Stun'.

My job is to steal and eat as much food as I can. And I can eat *a lot*. My motto: 'If it's at head height or lower I will eat it.' Above head height, I won't touch it. I won't climb for food. I'm not desperate.

For the next four hours I systematically wander round the bakers' work stations, robbing them of ingredients and making them cry because they no longer have enough chocolate to complete their big brown *Schichttorte*. Occasionally I will remove a batter-soaked spoon from my mouth long enough to bellow 'One hour left!' 'Ten minutes!' 'Thirty seconds!' or 'Time's up!' before returning to the bowl like a velociraptor to Bob Peck's face.

After the Royal Tour the other presenter promenades around the benches 'doing emos'. Ostensibly, this is the part where we discover a little more about what makes the contestants tick – their backgrounds, families and personal history. What we're also trying to do, however, is work out how many overwrought puns and how much seaside smuttiness we can squeeze out of the situation. We'll begin with the double entendres: tarts, buns, soggy bottoms, ginger nuts and my own particular favourite, rough puff. Then, when those have been exhausted, we'll move to single entendres – e.g., 'That baguette looks like a penis' and 'Those macaroons resemble tits.'

It's then back to the green room for a couple of tots of rum (medicinal) with Bezza (one of Mary's many nicknames) and a carb-crash in front of the telly. Paul grabs the remote so he can watch a Grand Prix or the Isle of Man TT. We wrest it from his grasp and put on a box set of *Mad Men*. Mary silently endures but secretly wishes for *The Jeremy Kyle Show*, to which she is now addicted. Mel falls asleep, mouth open, within a nanosecond. Mel's capacity for sleep is the stuff of legend.

Several hours later we reappear in the tent. There's the sound of a dozen mixers and the intoxicating smell of lemon zest and caramel. Atoms of icing sugar dance in the air. We sit and wait. Wait for television gold.

And, sure enough, it happens. A baker will drop their bake. That mirror-finish ganache, that tower of biscuits, that scale model of the Parthenon – whatever it might be, crashes to the ground and mingles with a furry floor tile. Suddenly, the entire camera resources of the United Kingdom are on hand to film it. There are more eyes on that spattered sponge than there are trained on the battle-torn streets of Homs in Syria. At some point that baker will do a cry and I will hug him/her until he/she feels uncomfortable and then he/she will do a snot on my blazer. I vow to dry-clean this blazer, but then life gets in the way and I forget. And then the next series comes along; I drag it out of the wardrobe and, hey presto, it takes a small axe to hack off the dried sadness-slime.

Then comes the judging. Paul's judging technique has evolved over the years into the finely honed act it is now. First he embeds his thumb deep into the bake. This thumb is always stained blue, as it has been loitering deep within his jeans pocket for several hours. On removing his thumb, he performs a series of knowing laughs, interspersed with 'underbaked' and 'overproved' barked at random. Mary says very little, but sets her laser eyes to either 'I love you' or 'I'm going to kill you.' When I say Mary says very little, what I mean is that she says very little that is broadcastable on a pre-watershed show. The woman has the face of an angel and the mouth of a docker.

The truth is we're family, with our own unique relationships but united under the banner of love. Paul is Kato to my Clouseau. We constantly try to batter each other with the plastic prop baguettes that litter the tent. He'll sneak up behind me and karate-chop me in the neck with a polymer brioche. I'll clatter him in the knackers with a fake lemon drizzle. It's the love that dare not speak its name. We laugh at his high-performance sports car, which Mel and I attempt either to steal or deface every series. He laughs at my car, but for completely different reasons. He's funny and kind. He's heavy, he's my brother.

Mary is one of the most extraordinary people I've ever had the pleasure of meeting. I love her, and it's a badge of honour that she'd consider me a friend. It's as good as having the Queen as your mate. She is the most unique of souls, walking, as she does, a tightrope between regal dignity and childish mischief. Young at heart and old of soul. In her seventies she went clubbing at Pacha in Ibiza. At the wrap party to series four she downed tequila slammers, forgoing the salt and lemon as a sideshow distraction that needlessly delayed the passage of grog from glass to throat. 'What a palaver,' she said before tossing the fruit over her shoulder and sliding yet another shot down her neck.

And we love the bakers too – we've never had a bad one yet. And by the time we get to meet their families in week ten we feel like we know them because we have spent months listening to their stories and sharing their lives.

Is it strange that the show has been co-opted by the tabloids? Yes. Is that intense ownership of the show sometimes responsible for people saying horribly censorious and humourless things about us? Yes. Is it likely that sections of the above will be taken out of context and printed in a red top in an effort to drum up moral outrage? Of course. You're welcome. Come on, lads. Try proving me wrong.

And yes, sometimes, when the sound is down, the show can look a little like a UKIP recruitment video, with its jingoistic imagery, bunting and green and pleasant landscape. That notwithstanding, I love it. I love the legendary Andy Devonshire, who helms it all so impeccably. I love the production team, the crew, the home economists. It's a treat to come back every year and see the same faces (with ever-bigger waistlines) joining in with us.

Over time it has become the show that it looks like to the general public. But let me tell you, it wasn't always that way.

First series are always hard. And by God this was hard. In its first year *Bake Off* was a touring affair, with the tent dismantled and reassembled in a different part of the UK each week.

For the first weekend we were in beautiful picture-perfect Kingham in Oxfordshire, tent pitched slap bang in the middle of the village green like croissant-obsessed aliens had landed. Roswell-in-the-Wold, as it now resembled, couldn't have been a more perfect spot.

Except.

Except the rain was biblical from the get-go. The heavens opened at 6 a.m. and they stayed open all weekend. The sky moved from black to slate grey to black again. The catering arrived at 7 a.m. in the form of a man called Barry. No gourmand was ever called Barry. There will never be a *Masterchef* champion called Barry. No Barry will accept a Michelin star. That is not the lot of Barrys. Barrys sell cars in Walford, they don't make luncheon.* So, Barry parked up his burger van and all day flipped Shergar steaks on a filthy griddle.

* I am now braced for an onslaught of livid, gastronomically blessed Barrys.

There were no takers.

Oftentimes, when you start a big show like this, there is a period of adjustment while the different agencies involved try to rough-hew the production into the shape they want it. Their idea of what the show is might not tally with that of the broadcasters or the presenters. And so it was with *Bake Off*.

The production company was used to making award-winning, intense and provocative documentaries on multiculturalism and poverty, and took this journalistic ethos right into *Bake Off*. Suddenly the bakers were asked rather heavier, personal questions than they had been expecting.

'I just wanted to talk about my tea loaf,' sobbed one of the contestants under his umbrella after a particularly intense interrogation. 'I just want Mary to come and have a look at it . . .'

'Why *Mary*? Do you have issues with your mother?' asked a producer.

'No, I just wanted her to tell me why it's collapsed in the middle.'

A tense pause for effect.

'Have *you* collapsed. Is it you that's collapsed?'

'Please, please just get Mary . . . I need Mary.'

After seeing not one, not two, but *three* of the bakers sobbing, we decided to take a stand. This wasn't the sort of show we were used to presenting, and so, at 9 a.m. on day two
we walked out.

Yes, there really is no rule by which you can measure my or Mel's ability to commit career suicide. First we exited *Light Lunch* just at the point it was becoming truly successful. Now we were walking out of a show that was to become almost as powerful as *Top Gear*, only without the casual racism, misogynist 'banter' and punching of co-workers.

There were meetings. Many meetings. We all learned lessons. I learned there's no point getting uppity about things once they've been recorded. It's too late by then. If I want change, I'll effect it on the shop floor. So nowadays, if one of the bakers gets upset or overcome with emotion, I simply start swearing and libelling pharmaceutical companies like there's no tomorrow, and I know that it won't get broadcast. I know they are safe. More and more, that's the nature of our job. Pastoral care. Everyone on the show does their bit to make sure that the stressful, silly hand of television touches the contestants enough to change their lives but not so much it bends them out of shape altogether.

That first series was a slog. Not only did we routinely do fourteen-hour days, but we over-recorded to a ridiculous degree. Remember the historical interviews with a woman dressed as an Anglo Saxon warrior princess? The poetry of the Mayor of Sandwich? The pudding throwers of Yorkshire? Nope. Because none of them made it to screen. It turns out that simply watching nice people make nice cakes is all you need, and everything else is superfluous.

The final of series one took place at Fulham Palace in London. The location scouts had excelled themselves; it looked great, the perfect grandiose backdrop for a season climax, plus it was close to home. There was just one thing they hadn't accounted for:

it was on the Heathrow flight path.

Not just on it. *Right* on it. Every thirty seconds, sometimes less, during daylight hours the belly of a jumbo blocked out the sun above us. Added to which the noise was deafening. There was nothing we could do but soldier on.

Mel/Sue: For the last six weeks Britain's best amateur bakers have been whipping themselves into a frenzy, bashing their dough and caramelizing their nuts in an effort to win the title of –

Sudden roar of a Boeing 747 from Addis Ababa.

Director: CUT! [*Waits for quiet*] Go again!

Mel/Sue: It's the final weekend as we reach the conclusion to our search for Britain's best amateur baker. Inside that tent our plucky threesome have donned their aprons, brandished their whisks –

Airbus A380 from Singapore rumbles across the sky.

Director: CUT! [*Waits for quiet*] Go again!

Mel/Sue: It's the moment they've been waiting for – our final trio of muffin makers are bracing themselves for the biggest weekend of their lives. Grab your *kugelhopfs* and –

Boom of a 777 en route from Beijing.

Director: CUT! [*Waits for quiet*] Quick, there's a lull! Go again!

Mel/Sue   [*gabbling*] IT'S THE FINAL! THERE'S THREE LEFT!

Director: Great! Now let's try that piece to camera about the history of the spotted dick.

In the end the noise proved so disruptive that for the entire finale weekend we were forced to trim all pieces to camera down to a few hasty words. If you watch that show back, you'll see everything delivered in desperate, staccato sound bites –

rushed through before the next plane in the Heathrow queue rumbles into view.

Me: Last challenge. How are you feeling?
Baker: Well –
Me: [*cutting in*] Great. BAKE!

By the time we got to the judging the whole thing was starting to feel more like *They Shoot Horses, Don't They?* than a baking competition. There were now only two bakers in the running, so we reckoned we stood a half-decent chance of leaving before nightfall. We were wrong. Just at the point we could take no more, Paul and Mary opted to get all meta on our arses. This meant that the judging for the final of series one took FOUR AND A HALF HOURS.

Yep. You heard that correctly.

FOUR AND A HALF HOURS.

Here are some things you can do in four and a half hours.

Fly to Moscow.

Complete a marathon.

Begin and end a relationship (if you're me).

Give birth to a child.

What Paul and Mary elected to do in four and a half hours is argue over whether or not a cupcake is a cake. Is it a little cake? Is it a muffin? Is it a light bite? More importantly, what *is* cake? It was exactly the kind of ontological badinage television was invented for.

By the time the show finally ended, I only knew one thing.

I never, *ever* wanted to do it again.

But I did. Something about the combination of people, the allure of a tent in green fields, the flap of bunting, pulled me back. Now, after six series, the show is a finely oiled machine.

Plus, with all the new technology – CGI and green screen – and the judicious placing of mirrors we get the whole thing done in twenty minutes.

BAAAAKE! Overworked! Nice buns! I've still got a taste of plums in my mouth! Halfway through! That looks a little underbaked! Ten minutes left! You've dropped your *croquembouche*! Time's up! Here's Mary and Paul! Soggy bottom! And the winner is . . .

In all seriousness, I often get asked questions about the show, so I thought I'd take an opportunity to answer some of the most regularly posed.

FAQs

Sue, what are you and Mel like behind the scenes of Bake Off?

Well, we're exactly like we are on screen, except instead of puns, we make very nuanced literary allusions to Russian novelists.

Is Mary Berry real?

As real as rum and vodka and wine and whisky. Very real.

What does Paul style his hair with?

Let me answer that with another question. Have you seen *There's Something About Mary?*

Why is there a long-running feud between Dapper Laughs and Mary Berry?

Because he misappropriated her catchphrase, 'proper moist'.

Do you bake?

Not really. Here's why. There are really good shops and some of them serve cake. Added to which, I am mates with Mary Berry, so never go hungry.

Has Bake Off *changed you?*

Yes. I am now made up of 50 per cent carbon and 50 per cent lemon drizzle. I can no longer see my feet when I step on a set of scales. And I cannot go anywhere in the world without someone shouting 'BAAAKE!'

Will we see the series two squirrel again?

No, I'm afraid not. After the tabloid furore, the squirrel was forced to go into hiding. He has now been put into a squirrel protection programme under a different name, for fear of reprisals.

Shame! Will there be any more close-ups of woodland genitals?

There is a sheep's udder in series five. I'm afraid that second-ary sexual characteristics are as far as we can go these days without there being a tsunami of manufactured outrage.

Can you remember any of the bakes?

No. I can remember *all* of them.

In my head there's a Rolodex of every single mouthful I've tasted on the show. I'm like a sponge savant, able to recall with breathtaking accuracy the taste of each and every bake: Mary-Anne's Midnight Mocha, Jo Wheatley's Banana Mousse, Ryan's Key Lime Pie – all sorted and available for recall at the flick of a synaptic switch. I am tortured by it.

'My name is Susan and I'm a sugar addict.'

'Hello, Susan . . .'

What will next year's Bake Off *hold? Is there a format change? Could you give us any hints about the first episode?*

OK, but they're going to KILL me for this.

Here's a sneak preview of episode one of series seven.

8.00 p.m. Opening credits. Close-up of tent flaps suggestively swaying in the breeze. Cut away to lambs gambolling in field. Will we see their genitals? Maybe later. For now we move into a kitchen. A child is smearing MARY BERRY in red icing on the walls. The music swells. Suddenly a massive celebratory Hungarian ring swings into view. It covers the child's face. On it we read the legend BAKE OFF.

8.01 Mary and Paul are winched down from the tent ceiling. Collabro sing 'When Will There Be a Harvest for the World'. Mary is rocking a Hillary Clinton-style pantsuit in purple paisley. So is Paul.

8.02 The signature challenge. The bakers are asked to make something that reminds them of childhood. Immediately one of the more senior challengers starts fashioning a representation of the three-day week out of marzipan.

8.07 Sue steals a handful of pistachio nuts from one of the bakers' benches.

8.09 The cry goes up, 'Who has taken my nuts? Who has taken my nuts?' Mel and Sue rush to be first to the double entendre and in doing so Sue is mildly injured by an upturned piping nozzle.

8.12 A twenty-minute VT on the history of the palette knife, voiced by Cherie Lunghi.

8.32 The technical challenge is about to be revealed. Close-up shot of a baker eating his entire hand in fear. A medic is called to attend to the bleeding stump. Mel and Sue fight to make a joke about lending a hand. A deep silence.

8.33 The challenge is announced. The contestants must work together to make a life-sized date and walnut loaf in the shape of Eric Pickles. Time starts now.

8.34 A nine-minute montage of famous spoons.

8.43 The Pickles cake is complete. Mary slowly runs her hand down the soggy sponge seam of Eric's leg. 'What a close texture!' she exclaims. It feels wrong. Very wrong. Time to finally cut away to

8.44 Close-up of lamb's genitals.

8.45 The showstopper challenge. The bakers are tasked with making a batch of biscuits suitable for an up-market wake.

8.46 Staring at ovens.

8.50 Guess the weight of the cake competition.

8.53 Guess the weight of the presenters competition.

8.55 VT insert. Theresa May takes us through her favourite batters.

8.57 Final judging. Who will win star baker? Paul gets into an Aston Martin and handbrake-turns the name of the winner in gravel.

8.59 Collabro sing from their new album, *On all Fours*.

ENJOY.

FIVE

The Rest of the World

The Dalton Highway

In the summer of 2010 I'd just finished recording the first series of *Bake Off*. I was 100 per cent certain it wouldn't be returning* so signed up to do a show called *The World's Most Interesting Roads* instead. Its basic premise was that a couple of telly folk would sit next to one another in a four-by-four, driving across some of the greatest landscapes on the planet, from Nepal to Bolivia to the jungles of Laos. Already I should have been thinking *Why view the brilliance of nature through an insect-splattered windscreen? Why not get out of the car in order to see it in all its glory?* But ours is not to reason why, ours is to do and then get slagged off by A.A. Gill.

I was paired with lovable man-hunk Charlie Boorman, and on first meeting it became clear we were the chalk and cheese of 'Let's do a travelogue.' He liked biking, wearing leather, drinking with the lads and . . . biking. I liked books, puns, 1960s Polish film posters and the odd night at a health spa. I expect the producers thought our differences might lead to some entertaining 'banter' or fighting. But there was no banter or fighting; just a lot of long silences where communication should have been.

We landed at Anchorage, Alaska, late on a gloomy afternoon and headed straight for our beds. Now, when I arrive at a hotel, there are many things I expect to see.

---

* I thank God every day that I am not responsible for my own career.

a. Bored uniformed staff pretending they are on the phone when you check in so they don't have to talk to you.
b. Piles of leaflets for the local waxwork museum and log flume.
c. The mild eye bulge of the concierge when two women request a double room.

What I don't expect to find in reception is a lavishly stuffed and mounted polar bear rearing in my general direction. And that was just the beginning. In every hotel I stayed in in Alaska I'd go to the lobby to make a call and find a mummified musk ox behind me. I'd go get a soda from the machine on the landing, only to find myself in the shadow of a grizzly bear dancing with a couple of Arctic foxes.

If there's one thing I hate more than trophy killing, it's taxidermy. You've killed it. Don't take the piss. Don't fill it with sand and make it play poker with a load of animals that it would have made mincemeat of in the wild, for God's sake.

I was aware that in this state of the Union I was in a minority of one. Saying you don't like slaughtering things in Alaska is like standing up at a UKIP rally and saying you don't think there are enough Polish builders currently working in the South East.

I don't like guns either – they scare the living daylights out of me. I went clay-pigeon shooting once and burst into tears when I hit a target.

Instructor: It's *clay*, Sue – it's not a real pigeon.
Sue: I know. It's just that I've got the idea of a pigeon in my head now . . .

Guns are, however, a part of life in the Last Frontier, so it was inevitable we would film in a gun shop – Jim's Guns, to be precise, one of over thirty licensed firearms warehouses in Anchorage. We walked in. Charlie instantly headed for a high-powered 50 millimetre assault rifle and started talking serial numbers with a man sporting an impressive walrus moustache. I stood there, looking uncomfortable, in the shadow of a rocket launcher.

'Hey there, little lady.'

I immediately froze. I come from a place and time where only serial killers in films say that.

A man in a stained motorcycle singlet and Chris Waddle-inspired mullet stood in front of me. I was distinctly aware that if we had been having this same conversation six feet away, just over the door threshold, I would be speed-dialling the cops around about now.

Ted: My name's Ted. What can I get you? Looking for anything in particular?

Me: No, I'm just . . . browsing. Is that the correct verb? Do you browse through weaponry?

Ted: Sure. Care for a few suggestions?

Me: I dunno. Maybe – what do you have in mind?

Ted: Let me show you something you're going to love.

Unless it's a petition outlawing handguns, Ted, I doubt it.

Ted: OK, so you're out at a swanky party. You're in a little black dress. What do you need?

Me: Spanx? A surgical truss?

Ted: You need . . . this!

Spectacles

Ted brings out a snub-nosed black pistol less than six inches long.

Ted: Smith and Wesson. .38 calibre. Great grip and the recoil won't rip your shoulder out. Pop it in your garter belt and you are ready to go.

Garter belt, Ted? Are we in a fin de siècle *burlesque show?! But Ted is just getting started . . .*

Ted: OK, so . . . aim it at my nuts. Go on!

I really don't want to hold the gun, let alone train it on Ted's little twins.

Ted: Come on, go for the nuts! Come on!

'Come on!' came another voice from the direction of the cash till. I was being heckled by a guy to blow another guy's nuts off.

   I'm a sucker for peer pressure so aimed for Ted's groin and pulled the trigger. After it clicked, I realized that I hadn't even bothered to check whether the gun was loaded or not.

Ted: Feels good, huh? Tell you what's better. The great thing about this little baby is that it comes with a laser sight. Depress the trigger a little. See?

I squeeze my forefinger and a red dot appears between Ted's balls.

Me: That's great, Ted. A laser sight. After all, I wouldn't want my ability to kill a stranger to be compromised by being blind drunk.

Charlie saunters over, carrying a bolt-action Remington rifle.

Charlie: Do you know they sell grenades here? It's awesome!

Me: I'll leave you boys to it. Ted, look after those nuts. Charlie, I'll be waiting by that stuffed lynx in reception.

Our next stop was Whittier, a tiny port city on Western Prince William Sound. You go there to watch the orcas, the minke and humpback whales, or to die of hypothermia. Whittier is about an hour's drive from Anchorage, a little more if you get stuck behind a herd of Dall sheep or some rogue moose. It remains one of the weirdest places I've ever visited. It has a total population of around 220, all of whom live in two abandoned army facilities not altogether convincingly converted into condominiums.

Begich Towers, one of these blocks, is a brutalist beige blot on the landscape, looming large over the smattering of thin trees and ramshackle collection of tugboats and pick-up trucks which litters the railway line. Everywhere there is the grey filth of melting snow. The magical freeze was ending when we arrived, and all that remained was the endless drip, drip, drip of the ugly thaw.

'Well, it's certainly living up to its tag line,' said lovely John, our fixer.

'What's that?' I asked.

'Well,' he continued, 'the saying goes, "There's nothing shittier than a day in Whittier."'

That's how legendarily glum it was. It had its own rhyme. I wondered if that sort of thing could catch on back home.

'There's no point in schlepping to crappy old Epping!'

'A smack in the skull is preferable to Hull!'

The first thing the production team decided to do was split us up. Charlie went off to do something – I forget what. Something manly and charismatic, I'll warrant. I was sent off to meet a weather specialist, the legend that is

Brenda T.

Brenda not only ran the local gift shop (specializing in antlers and leather goods – mainly antlers) but supervised the Whittier weather station. Brenda turned out to be as cranky as she was brilliant.

Me: What's the weather doing, Brenda?

Brenda: Shit if I know. Look at the book, dumb-ass. Anyhow, I gotta go feed the reindeer.

I was in clover. Not only was Brenda thrillingly indifferent, bordering on abusive, but she had ANIMALS TO PET.

We headed down the stairs, out of the army condo and into the snow. Over the road there was a pen, inside which were two reindeer which I

INSTANTLY ANTHROPOMORPHIZED.

They're sad in that pen, I thought. *Look at their sad, sad eyes. They want to walk. They want to graze freely. They're telling me that – they're trying to communicate their sadness through the medium of ignoring me.*

Right, I decided. *I'm going to take them for a walk.*

Me: Brenda?

Brenda: [*snarling*] What?

Me: Can I play with the reindeers?

Brenda: Whaddayamean, *play* with them?

Me: I don't know. Maybe . . . walk with them?
Brenda: Jesus Christ, you Europeans . . .

She opens the gate and purposefully grabs one of the reindeer by the rope that hangs from its neck.

Brenda: Take this one. It's less mean.
Me: What?
Brenda: Come on, come on. This one won't kill ya. Now listen, English. Whatever ya do, don't let go.

With that, Brenda shoved the rope into my hand and trudged off into the snow. Suddenly I was left holding my first reindeer. At this point it's fair to say I had certain expectations.

For starters, I expected the reindeer to look at me with gratitude, acknowledging I had liberated her, pupils swelling in adoration, the way they do in Disney films. I expected her to meander towards me, nuzzle at my neck and gently place her antlers either side of my head, cradling me with her horns. I expected to stand there, gently stroking her, breathing in her scent – the smell of Christmas. 'I love you,' I'd whisper. 'Moo,' she would reply – or something close to that. (My reindeer is a little rusty.)

Well, I didn't get any of that. What I did get was a psycho quarter-ton hot-water bottle with attitude. The first thing the reindeer did once my hand hit the rope was roll her eyes in my direction. Then she started moving. I had expected her to be strong, just not that strong. Also, what I hadn't reckoned on was her sheer speed. Reindeer can hit speeds of up to fifty miles an hour when they want to. And this one wanted to. Suddenly I was running through the slush full tilt trying to keep hold of the rope, until the pace became too much and my arm nearly left its socket. I let go of the rope, and off into the distance hurtled Brenda's reindeer.

'There's a moose loose!' I shouted in the heat of the moment. I regret it. It was neither funny nor the correct species of deer. And therefore even less funny.

I trudged up the three flights of stairs to Brenda's flat.

Me: Brenda?
Brenda: What? Tell me you didn't bring a reindeer up a stairwell?
Me: No. I . . . I've lost her.

Brenda rolls her eyes so hard I can actually hear them rotating in her skull. There is much harrumphing. Finally, she puts on her sheepskin coat, moleskin shoes and beaver mittens – then calls someone on her mobile phone, which is the size of a brick. (I guess it has to be if you're dialling wearing beaver mittens.)

Brenda: Mikey, the English has lost the reindeer. Can you get the boys on it? [*To me*] Jesus, you . . . I should put a bull's eye on you.
Me: Bull's eye? What, like a *target*?

Suddenly I am in an episode of Fargo.
  It is exactly at this moment that Charlie pitches up, looking manly.

Charlie: Hey, I've just been talking with the lads about the head-lamp modifications on the Kawasaki Concours.
Me: That's nice. I've been losing livestock.

We got into the Jeeps and drove in circles round the pale streets. I started to get nervous. Brenda's opening gambit had been mild hostility; I didn't want to know what the next level up was like. After two hours of ducking and diving there was still no sign of the reindeer. Nothing. I ended up back at Begich Towers ready for Brenda to run me through with a souvenir antler. As she came out onto the street to meet me, a patrol car pulled up and a policeman yelled, 'Brenda, you lost a reindeer? Only there's one on the railway tracks . . .'

I'd been saved.

I tried really, *really* hard not to give the reindeer a backstory: 'All these years in that pen, no hope of freedom, year after year – I had to come down here and end it once and for all, while I had the chance.' In my head this scene by the railway tracks was an ungulate end game – a suicide bid, years in the making, with me the unwitting accomplice.

I thought about the train coming and wondered how long it would take me, *Railway Children*-style, to strip down salopettes, tracksuit bottoms, woollen thermals and double-sock combo to my pants, in order to wave them – and realized I would freeze to death way before I'd got through the first layer.

I imagined Brenda on the tracks. A locomotive coming. She turns round. The driver catches the look on her face and shits himself. The train comes to a standstill an inch in front of Brenda's nose. Terrified. She has terrified a train. She's like a character from *X-Men*. She can make anything feel mildly, but thrillingly, disciplined.

We arrived at the railroad, where a small crowd of burly men had gathered. The reindeer was busy chewing a tuft of frozen weed poking from the rails. One of the locals stood opposite the reindeer, braced himself and bellowed.

Local: Screw you!

Spectacles

The reindeer pauses for a moment and looks at us.

Local: Yeah, you – ya big bastard. Screw you!

Another joins in.

Local 2:   Screw you!
Me: How is that helping?
Local 2:   Best way to get 'em. Swear at 'em. Always works, no idea
            why.
Me: Oh.

*I make a mental note, in case any of my First Great Western trains back
home ever encounters a Reindeer on the Line.*

Local 3:   Fucker! [*A man in a visor to my left*] You little fucker!
Local 4:   Fucker! [*A woman from behind me*]
Local 5:   Asshole! [*A kid who's just joined the group*]
Me: Any of you been on the *ET* ride at Universal Studios?
            You'd love it!

*By now the reindeer has taken a few tentative steps towards us. The crowd
redoubles its efforts. I join in.*

Crowd: Asshole! Fucker!
Me: You . . . massive dick!

Sure enough, the reindeer increased her speed towards us,
crossing the railroad and finally submitting to the tether.
Brenda slapped her hard on the butt, emitted a throaty laugh in
my general direction and headed off to whittle something
horny back at the shop.

338

Once the reindeer was safely back in her enclosure, I pottered over to say goodbye. I like to think that the look she gave me, right before she stepped on my toe, was one of pure devotion.

'Thank you,' she said. 'Oh, and by the way, I'm a boy. You can tell from the antlers. Fuckwad.'

We resumed our relentless drive northwards, stopping briefly at Wasilla on the way. Lovely John the Fixer had said he could get me an interview with Sarah Palin at her house as he had an in with Todd, her husband.

En route, Charlie asked me, 'Who's Sarah Palin?'

'She's Michael Palin's wife,' I replied, jokingly.

'Oh,' he said, and carried on driving. I still don't know to this day if he was winding me up or if he genuinely believed me. Either way, we travelled the next seventy kilometres in silence.

Once in Wasilla, we parked at the security station at the end of what looked like a very long, posh driveway. I got out.

'What do you want?' said the robotic voice over the intercom.

'I'm here to see Sarah Palin,' I ventured politely.

'Do you have an appointment?'

'No, but I'm with the BBC.'

In retrospect that might not have helped. It was a little like trying to curry favour with Kim Jong-un by telling him about your work experience fortnight with Sony Pictures.

'Wait there,' said the security Dalek as he went off to check my details.

There was a long pause. I could make out John the Fixer in the distance, gesticulating wildly. The more I looked, the more I realized the frantic waving seemed to be for my benefit. I wandered over to find him finishing a phone call.

Me: Hey, John, security is just checking me out. I think I've man-
         aged to swing it.
John: I just got off the phone with Todd.
Me: Cool!
John: He said you get the hell off his property or he'll blow you
         off.

We'd been travelling for hours before the constant bump of hard core gave way to the smooth icy surface of the Dalton Highway. I'd been droning on about early contrapuntal music and Charlie had been telling me what his watch could do at two hundred metres below sea level when we felt the change. Suddenly we were no longer buffeted by loose chippings. We were gliding.

The highway is some 414 miles long, stretching from Liven-good, north of Fairbanks, to Deadhorse, near Prudhoe Bay by the Arctic Ocean. It is one of the most remote roads in the world. Sometimes the only thing travelling alongside you is the Trans-Alaska Pipeline. It's grimly ironic that this blot on the landscape – an ugly reminder of our addiction to fossil fuels – is the very thing that created the road and, therefore, the very thing that enables us to experience the pure wonder of this part of the Alaskan landscape.

The moment we hit the ice, I knew we'd hit trouble. The road itself is well maintained and robust – you quietly skate along with no hint of trouble. It's steering that's the issue. It's easy to get in a trance state, overwhelmed by the views, the magnitude of the landscape, the barren beauty of it all, and in doing so let your hands relax a little on the wheel. If you veer, even a tad, that's where they'll get you – those fingers of black ice splayed at the road's edge. Hit one and they'll claw you off track and pull you into a snow-lined gulley with no hope of getting out.

We'd been going an hour or two. I'd been expressing my thoughts on Gothic architecture and Charlie had been telling me how, on an expedition, you can make dirty pants like new by simply reversing them. Occasionally he would pause from his anecdotes to give me helpful pointers on my driving.

'So these bike tours, you get a load of grimy lads, couple of cases of grog, make a fire, get some meat on the go, start telling stories . . .

'WATCH OUT ON THE RIGHT!

'Sometimes you'll wake and you'll be in the desert with a mouth full of sand and a tent full of empty bottles and you won't ever know how you got there.

'SUE! YOU'RE VEERING TO THE RIGHT!'

It was warm in the car – rhythmic puffs of hot air gusted from the vents, and my belly was full of cheese sandwiches and bad coffee. Visibility was excellent – I could see for miles ahead. Nothing coming. Nothing going. My muscles relaxed. My famously limited attention wavered.

'The local guy will fix us up with a couple of shots of local whisky, then we're back on the bikes. Your arse gets sore after a while, but you can get a half-decent massage from some of the local girls . . .

'WATCH OUT ON THE RIGHT!'

I had gone into a hypnotic state – snow – road – snow – road – snow. The car drifted too far and suddenly hit a talon of black ice. It became impossible to control the steering. It was over in a flash. Our vehicle, now stationary, was at a forty-five-degree angle in a ditch.

Charlie rolled his eyes. Poor guy. Every moment I remained next to him, his masculine credibility plummeted further.

Not knowing anything about cars, I turned the engine on and ceaselessly revved the engine until the smell of burning rubber overwhelmed us.

Charlie: Shit. Axle might be broken.
Me: Is that bad?
Charlie: Yep.
Me: Oh. Sorry. Can we get a new one?

Charlie said nothing and merely turned his attention towards the horizon.

Suddenly, from behind us, a noise like a vast mechanical exhalation. A giant truck hove into view, stopping gracefully just a few inches from our car. The fenders were sparkling and you could smell the heat of the metal.

The cameras turned to the driver, who was stepping down from his cabin. It was an impossibly handsome man in his early thirties – trimmed beard, piercing blue eyes. I felt my personal polarity shift a little, then settle.

Man: You guys in trouble?
Me: No.
Charlie: Yes.
Man: Need a hand?
Charlie: Yes, please.

I stood there, dumbstruck, as thick, sleek cabling was uncoiled, hooks attached, weights and tensions considered.

Throughout, the trucker worked silently. I couldn't help but notice he averted his gaze from the camera. Fascinating, I thought. Perhaps he has escaped to the wild country after a divorce and doesn't want anyone to find him. Perhaps he is on the run. Perhaps he's worried the publicity will alert his pursuers to his location and he'll be caught again.

(I can't emphasize enough how exhausting it is being me.)

Man: What are you guys filming?

Charlie: Oh, just a documentary for the BBC back home.

Me: Is it bothering you? You want us to stop?

I am trying to make maternal concern sound a little sexy, and failing.

Man: No, it's OK.

Me: I can't help noticing you don't like the camera.

Man: Nah. It's just, you know . . .

Me: What?

I am getting close to finding his secret. I lean in.

Man: It's just . . . well . . . I wanted a break from all that stuff.

Me: A break?

Man: Yeah, we just finished season three of *Ice Road Truckers*, and I needed a bit of downtime before the next one. You know.

In the middle of nowhere – *nowhere* – I had managed to crash a car and be rescued by a bone fide global superstar, Jack Jessee. The only thing that could have made the experience weirder was if we'd been hit by Joey Essex, treated on the scene by one of the doctors from *24 Hours in A&E*, then flown home by Jeremy Spake.

Day six. We'd overnighted in Fairbanks, where I'd caroused with a female roller derby team. Boy those girls can party like it's 1958. Sadly, I had to get up and be in the car ready for filming at the crack of dawn.

I was starting to regret the bit in my contract where it said I would be working 'daylight hours'. The closer to the Arctic Circle we got, the more the days lengthened, until we'd only have a few hours of gentle dusk before I'd be back at the wheel.

After I'd finished a fascinating monologue on Dadaism, Charlie took out his earplugs and we stopped for the night. Our pit stop was one of the most magical on earth. Wiseman. I'd call it a village, but the population was fourteen. What does that make it? A grouping? A settlement? Who knows? The moon backlit the pines and the only thing you could hear was the occasional drift of snow in the mountains. A local hunter had told me that I had to be quiet, because the moose were always listening. And so that night I whispered 'Hello' into the depths of the forest, then told them the hunter's exact location – just in case he had been serious about them earwigging.

The next morning I rubbed my nose with the heel of my palm to get the blood flowing again, ate a stack of pancakes, three eggs and a portion of gravy and biscuits. Then we got back in the bloody car.

It was my turn to drive again. By now Charlie was sick of my driving. He was better at the wheel, capable of focusing on the road for more than ninety seconds without getting distracted by a bird or an animal. Plus I think he hated being in the passenger seat because that meant he had to work the CB radio – and this compromised his masculinity. It wasn't right – two grown men, revealing their coordinates to one another. It was just too intimate.

The CB radio is your best friend on the highway. Once your eyes fail in the endless and unrelenting white, you turn to the radio and listen to your salvation – your voice. It is your voice, and the crackling one in the box that comes back at you, that tell you where you are and how you are doing. And whether or not you are still alive.

The temperature was dropping and a vicious wind started to kick around the tyres. As we passed a lone worker at the side of the road, the director, Ian, travelling in the support car behind, radioed through.

'Charlie! Stop! Let's do a piece here, with this guy. This guy spraying the road.'

I was pretty relieved I wasn't involved. It looked like they were going to be talking about technical stuff, plus the wind chill looked like it could turn the tops of your ears into Frazzles.

I watched Charlie chatting away. Poor Ollie, the best sound guy in the business, was standing holding the boom above him, trying not to faint with the cold.

The highway worker was resurfacing the road with a pressure hose. The water started to freeze as soon as it hit the ground. He was motioning forward violently with his hands.

Ten minutes later Charlie bounced back into the car. The ends of his whiskers were crispy.

'Blizzard's coming in,' he said. 'We need to get out now, else we'll get stuck.'

'Right,' I said, trying to pretend this sort of thing happened to me every day. 'I should probably turn the ignition on then.' (I really am very lacking when it comes to initiative.)

'OK!' shouted Ian. (Shouting was Ian's default setting; he really was very commanding.) 'We're breaking for lunch!'

Me: What do you mean? We can't break – we've got to get out of here! There's a storm coming!
Ian: I know. There are some plastic cheese sandwiches and some cold moose cuts. Oh, and Oreos. [*He adds, as if that will somehow sweeten the deal*]

I got out the car and opened my mouth long enough for my taste buds to get anaesthetized by the chill. Then I tucked in. It's amazing how good plastic cheese and moose can taste when you can't taste at all. I plucked up courage to speak to the gaffer.

Me: Hey, Ian, can I have a word?
Ian: Sure. You want to try some of this bear? It's weirdly fishy.
Me: No. Listen, why are we waiting? Isn't that a bit reckless? Can't we have synthetic sandwiches and wild animal meat at our destination?
Ian: Yes, but . . . Well, thing is . . . they've seen the rushes back home . . .
Me: So?
Ian: And they've decided they're not . . . not . . . *dangerous* enough.

There is a slight pause before I respond.

Me: Dangerous?
Ian: Yes. Dangerous. I can see what they mean. There's no point

346

in having 'dangerous' in the title if nothing dangerous happens. You see?

Suddenly everything around me begins moving very slowly.

Me: Why would 'dangerous' be in the title, Ian?

Ian: Because it is. Because that's what this show is – *The World's Most Dangerous Roads*.

Me: No, no, no. The show *I'm* doing is called *The World's Most Interesting Roads*.

Suddenly, I'm thinking, am I on the wrong shoot? Is there a crew somewhere pottering around a creek admiring rare birds and wondering why Bear Grylls is presenting it?

Ian: Well, it was called that originally, Sue, but the title got changed. That was *ages* ago. We did say. Didn't we? Please tell me someone told you.

Suddenly it all made sense – the total lack of tourist traffic on the road, the locals shaking their heads as we chugged out of town. That lone woman crossing herself at the final junction in Fairbanks, the wooden crucifixes that sporadically lined our route. But mainly this – why would you travel on a road made solely of ice WHEN OTHER PERFECTLY SAFE AND SCENIC ROUTES ARE AVAILABLE?

I got back in the car and ingested something that may or may not have been polar bear. Fast.

Me: [*yelling*] Come on, Charlie. We're off!

I reach over and try to pop his seat belt on.

Charlie has difficulty replying, as a clod of indiscriminate meat has attached itself to the roof of his mouth. He has to use the traction of a handful of crisps to dislodge it.

Charlie: [*mumbling*] Hang on. Gimme a second . . .
Me: WE DON'T HAVE A SECOND! [*I scream, channelling Jason Statham again – before putting the car into the wrong gear and revving the engine to fuck*]

Along the side of the entire Dalton Highway there are delineators. These are white and red sticks positioned at regular intervals along the route, giving you some idea as to the visibility. In clear conditions I knew I could see nearly twenty.

Almost as soon as we were under way, I felt a change. Nothing physical. It was instinctive, limbic. Something wicked this way comes – that kind of thing. After a few minutes the steering became a little harder, the tyres a little lazy. The wind started to smack against the window with more of a scream than a whistle. We were now nearing the highest and most exposed point of the route – the Atigun Pass, as it crosses the Brooks Mountain Range, where the ice road snakes violently to the right and up a long and punishing 12 per cent gradient.

Suddenly, from nowhere, the snow started. Not like snow I knew. The snow I'm familiar with has a simple trajectory – falling simply from top to bottom. It comes from up above, it lands at my feet. Simple. This snow was different. It emerged from everywhere – up, down, left and right – and swirled in huge circles around us. Visibility went from fifteen to five delineators in less than ten seconds. The incoming blizzard turned the air white and then the road white until visibility dipped again from five to two to one. Then nothing. Just a wall of white – nothing but white.

A large drift started accumulating on the front right tyre and I tried steering to correct it, but the back kicked out, and suddenly we were – I didn't know – sideways, maybe? All I knew was there was a ravine somewhere to my right and I did *not* want to fall down it.

In a second the vehicle was wedged solid with snow. Suddenly, and rather magnificently, Charlie went into overdrive. I could smell the testosterone coming off him. Every anecdote, every adventure, every cell in his body had been leading him to this. His hero moment. He jumped out of the passenger seat and fiddled with the tyres (to this day I have no idea what he did, but goddam it, it was TECHNICAL) before pulling me out of the driving seat. This was no time for feminist badinage, so I let him. Charlie was the only one of us who was experienced enough to get that car moving again.

And I was the only one experienced enough to get the entire Ice Road community rocking to my CB skills.

It's amazing what you learn about yourself when you come face to face with death. What I learned is that when I confront my own mortality I like to do it in the voice of Fenella Fielding.

For some reason I began to speak like her. I guess I figured that the only people out there listening were men and that in order to get them to save us I'd need to sound really HOT. Is that the action of a feminist? Oh God, I don't know. I really hope so. It was merely self-preservation. I'm sorry.

As Charlie wrestled with the screaming motor, I was pleading down the airwaves in my husky new accent. Most accidents, I remembered from our safety briefing, are caused by eighteen-wheelers ploughing into smaller vehicles. Eighteen-wheelers can't apply their brakes in these conditions – it's just too dangerous. They'd jack-knife on the ice and career to their deaths.

'Northbound four-wheeler stuck at the Atigun Pass,' I pleaded. Although, with that voice, I might as well have been saying, 'Anyone of you big lads fancy a blowie, on the house?'

I kept on going until the radio crackled.

Man: Hello, little lady.

Oh God, not that again. It must be an Alaskan thing.

Man: How can I be of assistance?

Well, hellfire, I just bagged me a mountain man.

I don't remember much about the man who rescued us, other than he was hugely disappointed when he finally made the connection between the sexy voice emanating from his CB and the goofy nerdulant coming towards him, sobbing. He'd expected an incandescent Emily Blunt; he got Gareth Malone. With tits. I also recall that he was wearing a T-shirt in minus thirty degrees. Honestly. How hard can you be? Alaskans.

Our saviour chaperoned us through the blizzard all the way to our final destination – Prudhoe Bay. By that point night had finally fallen and we were so exhausted both Charlie and I fell into our first proper silence together. For the first time in weeks we no longer fought against it, and instead gave in to the blissful quiet.

We parked the four-by-four next to a row of super-trucks shivering in the fierce crosswind. Daisy chains of cabling connected their engines to batteries so they didn't choke in the cold. Stalactites hung from the fenders and slivers of silver ice nestled in the tyre treads.

The complex at Prudhoe was a vast industrial hangar catering for the itinerant thick-necked strongmen who make their living on the oil fields. We entered a voluminous hall – polished floors, hard lines, long empty steel tables. We hadn't eaten for hours and were starving. We could smell food but couldn't see any. We couldn't see a soul. Then, we realized that on each wall sat a giant vending machine. Not the sort of vending machine I grew up with, those derisory affairs in leisure centres which sent a pack of Discos down a steel chute, rendering its contents dust as it smacked down to earth. These were industrial monstrosities, dispensing every food product known to man: Thai green curry, Singapore noodles, burgers, fries, chow mein, pork balls. You name it, the automated metal claws could get it. We jabbed wordlessly at buttons for hours, and pre-prepared international cuisine rained down from the sky.

When I finally got up from the table I remember feeling the twang of muscles I never knew existed, newly warmed sinews spasming from the shock, I guess. I hobbled to my room, which was on the second floor, past a deserted launderette the size of a tennis court. Huge drums spun and stuttered; inside, endless loops of checked shirts and Y-fronts belonging to the myriad men lodging there. I went past a state-of-the-art gymnasium – treadmills beeping, rows of stationary bicycles flashing. No one running. No one cycling. No one.

Everywhere you looked it was like a Stanley Kubrick film – beautiful, chilly vignettes of the automated soulessness of the future.

Where was everyone? Where had they all gone?

'Is there anybody there?' I shouted. Nothing.

For a brief moment I panicked. What if the BBC commissioners had changed their minds again? What if the show had gone from *The World's Most Interesting Roads* to *The World's Most Dangerous Roads* to *The World's Most Sex-Starved Oil Workers*? Or, even worse, *Redneck Psycho-Killers*.

I remember clearly that my door had four locks. I remember I made use of each and every one of them. I remember a perfect silence save the *thrum* of the launderette and the gym and the canteen, and all those other vast, empty mechanized spaces that carried on beating in the absence of human life. I cried. I cried because for a while I had felt truly under threat, lost and insignificant and vulnerable. I cried for my family and friends and my dogs. And I cried because I missed home. Finally at the end of the road I allowed myself the memory of home.

Then I dried my eyes and rehydrated a lasagne using the mini-kettle.

I hope it was dangerous enough for you.

It felt dangerous enough for me.

The Ho Chi Minh Trail

The second time I got into a four-by-four in the name of television I was at least up to speed on the correct title of the show. Forewarned is forearmed. This time my companion was the effortlessly brilliant Dame Liza Tarbuck. Instead of it being a Boorman-esque pairing (me soliloquizing about Bandura's socialization theory and he about the latest tweaks to the BMW series 3 engine), we bonded over the fact we both love Diana Ross and both like behaving like four-year-olds.

I'm pretty sure we are the first women ever to have self-driven the Ho Chi Minh trail. I *know* we are the first women to have done it singing 'Love Hangover' the entire way. When the film was wrapped, I can only imagine the hell endured by the editors, picking their way through endless loops of poorly harmonized 70s disco with inane interjections about the landscape. I imagine the soundtrack in that cutting room went something like this.

Me / Liza: Ah, if there's a cure for this
I don't want it. [Ooh look there's a pig on the back of that motorbike.]
Don't want it.
If there's a remedy
I'll run from it, from it. [Christ, it's hot – got any sunblock?]
Think about it all the time [Mind that water buffalo!]
Never let it out of my mind

'Cause I love you.

I've got the sweetest hangover [If you had to sleep with
one of the researchers, which one would it be?]

I don't wanna get over.

Sweetest hangover . . .

As opposed to my trip to Alaska, I couldn't tell you *where* I went.
Not a Scooby. It was like a magical mystery tour, but with the
word 'magical' replaced with 'breathtakingly unhygienic' and
'morally questionable'. At no point were we shown a map or
given directions or provided with any information that could
have pinpointed our location. As a result, I can tell you everything
that happened, I just can't tell you *where* it happened.

Liza and I would punctuate the tedium of endless driving
with games – the finest of which was the Water Buffalo Game.
This involved driving into a massive, wet, freshly laid buffalo
turd and seeing how heavily you could saturate the driver-side
camera in shit.

I told you – four-year-olds.

This meant that when it came to viewing the footage back
in London, the editor of the B camera had to listen to us singing 'Love Hangover', punctuated occasionally by a flying wet
dung-ball smacking into the camera. I like to think it's the
video of the track that Diana always wanted to make but was
too creatively blocked to realize.

One day, while travelling through the tiny village of I HAVE
NO IDEA, Liza was at the wheel and spotted a ripe bean-
bag-shaped pile of fresh manure in the road ahead. This was
around the same time I spotted, from the passenger seat, a
young schoolboy, in pristine uniform, walking alongside us.
Liza steered right, and before I could say anything, she had
squarely hit the shit.

Liza: [*roaring with pride*] Bull's eye!
Me: Oh God . . .

In the rear-view mirror we catch sight of the schoolboy, dripping with wet cack.

Liza: [*bellowing*] I am so so sorry!
Me: We're not all like that!

In fact, we are – we are *all like that*.

Though technically a road trip, this adventure turned out to be more of a tour of Asian brothels. Whether the BBC budget was tight, or the production company had spent all the money on GoPros and other camera gadgetry, I don't know. What I do know is that night after night we stayed in rooms that wouldn't have looked out of place in *The Human Centipede 2*.

In the first hotel (definitely a brothel) there was a six-inch gap under my bedroom door. Every hour, on the hour, I'd hear a knock, followed by a thick smoker's cough and a muttering in I DON'T KNOW WHAT LANGUAGE. Each time I would wake up, shout 'No thank you!' in my loudest, poshest voice, then try to bank another sixty-minute kip before it happened all over again.

The room was dank. In the corner, by the open-plan toilet area, stood a black Biffa bin full of stagnant water. Mosquitoes scudded across the surface. I studied it for a while. I was new to Asia and Asian sanitary ware – what on earth was it there for? Eventually I decided it was a kind of makeshift plunge pool, so stripped off, climbed onto a chair and then plopped inside.

Insects nibbled my shoulders. I sluiced then dragged myself out again.

At 5 a.m., after the regular punctuation from wannabe

punters, I woke again – this time to a frenzied squawk, followed by silence, then a pool of blood running under the door towards the bed. It was obviously cock o'clock.

An hour later I got up for breakfast. As always when away from home, I had the vegetarian option – a cloudy soup with morning glory and garlic. Delicious. Delicious right up to the point I drained the bowl and found a chicken's foot bobbing around at the bottom. 'For texture,' said the woman serving.

As we were packing up our things, I muttered over to Liza, who seemed to be trying to get GPS on her phone,

Me: Interesting bathing scenario . . .
Liza: What d'you mean?
Me: Last night. You know – the bath . . .
Liza: What bath?
Me: That massive bin with the scoop in it.
Liza: You mean the toilet water? The water to flush the toilet with?

I swallow very hard.

Me: Yeah. Yeah, that water – the toilet water. Yeah.

You learn fast in Asia.

I have become very familiar with these rooms over recent years – the black mould creeping up the wall, the overhead fan with exposed wiring, the air con that weeps stale water down the walls. The soundtrack is familiar too: the endless scuttle of roaches and geckos. Do you know that big geckos actually *say* 'GECKO'? I didn't, until one spent the entire night doing so right next to my pillow.

'GECKO! GECKO!'

I thought it was Liza taking the piss, but when I turned on

my head torch, I became aware of its enormous dry body scuttling around next to me.

Once we arrived at a hostel (brothel) in I DON'T KNOW WHERE, and the door to my room was locked. Finally a bloke came out, red and sweaty, followed by a young girl. The room smelled of sex and stress. Reception seemed most put out when I asked if they might be able to change the sheets. I didn't sleep. I didn't sleep at all.

At some of the out-of-town places prostitution is a family affair. The mother cooks the dinner, while the daughter stares at the diners and touts for business. It's a dynamic that makes me very queasy, no matter how long I spend in Asia.

I think back on these nights and all I remember is thick heat and the listlessness that comes with it, plastic tables and chairs, the smell of fried garlic, the hum of a fridge full of Lao beer. The sound of men laughing at another table, possibly at you,

very possibly at you.

Several days into the shoot, and after a twelve-hour drive, we arrived at a hostel like the one in *Hostel*. Within minutes there was a power cut. It was the first time I remember being grateful for darkness – just so I wouldn't have to see the inside of my room. As dawn broke, I woke to the sound of Liza knocking at my door. She had the focused mania of the truly sleep-deprived. She hadn't slept a wink and one eye seemed larger than the other.

Liza: Right! We're leaving! We're going home. I've been up all night studying the map and I think I know where we are.

She points to a red squiggle somewhere between Vietnam and Laos.

Liza:	If we get in the car and drive due west, we can get to a checkpoint and get out of here.
Me:	But what will we say?
Liza:	We'll say we've been held prisoner by a documentary crew who won't tell us where we are or what we're doing and that we want to speak to the British embassy.

There's a sudden noise from behind us. It's Ian, the director.

| Ian: | What are you doing, girls? |

. . . he says to the two forty-something women in front of him. We jump.

Liza:	Nothing!
Me:	Nothing!
Ian:	Right, well, let's get on then, shall we?

We hop into the car, ready for the off. The fan blasts hot air into our faces.

| Me/Liza: | 'Don't call a doctor, don't call her momma, don't call her preacher, no I don't need it . . .' |

We set off. The convoy ahead inched forward at a snail's pace, then came to a halt. We craned our necks to see the cause of the delay. There, at the side of the road, was Ian, taking a piss. We stared at him. He carried on pissing, waving us on with his other hand. It really doesn't get more dismissive than that.

From that moment on, the battle lines were drawn. Him versus us. Man versus perimenopause. Whenever he handed us some notes, or moved to direct us, or even give us a friendly pat on the back, the poor guy would hear a chorus of:

Both: Is that your cock hand, Ian?

Because we were following the Ho Chi Minh Trail, the content of the show was naturally very WAR heavy. Everywhere we went, we were encouraged to discuss WAR and all things WAR related. The problem was, whereas the programme-makers might have been keen to talk WAR, the Vietnamese contributors (many of whom had served with the Viet Cong) weren't. It was extraordinary. It was almost as if the conflict had never happened. The locals we met wanted to talk business, the future, the Western world. The Vietnamese were well and truly done with WAR.

But the Americans weren't.

One of the interviews that stays with me most from that trip (sadly heavily edited for transmission) was one we did with a couple of guys who'd been in the Mistys – a US Air Force squadron tasked with disrupting Viet Cong supply lines along the HCM Trail during the war. Flying low, they would identify potential targets, then direct in fighter strikes. These men, now in their sixties, spoke with such emotion and such candour – a world away from the *Top Gun* cocks-out bravado we're used to seeing on our television screens. There was no rootin' or tootin'. No fist pumps. No 'Yee-haw'. They were thoughtful and humble and more than once their eyes filled with tears as they told their story.

Every day these two men would set out in their planes. Their regular tour took them over a particular mountain top and thence down into the valley beyond. Every day, on that mountain top, they would see the same kid, in his teens, rifle in hand, on sentry duty for the Viet Cong. Every day they would look down at the kid, and the kid would look up at them. They saw each other at the beginning of each and every day, these sworn enemies, and yet, for months and months on end, they failed to fire upon each other. They could have blasted that kid off the rock. The kid could have fired a shot that punctured their fuselage and brought them down. They didn't. He didn't. Some telepathic agreement existed from the get-go – that one would not hurt the other. Every other plane, and every other man further down that valley, was fair game. That kid killed other pilots. Those pilots killed many, many other kids.

After the war ended some Mistys returned to Vietnam, not only looking for news of missing comrades but also, in a spirit of reconciliation, to meet those who had once been their targets. In the course of this, the two pilots came face to face with that boy on the hilltop. They learned about his family and about those he had loved who had not been so lucky in the face of the American arsenal. It was an emotional exchange. They still keep in touch.

That conversation brought home to me so clearly how heavily the Vietnam War hangs in the American psyche, and how lightly it is worn by the Vietnamese. For the Americans, I guess, it remains *the* unwinnable war, or at least it was until Afghanistan and Iraq exploded again.

Even though a map was never forthcoming, I do know that we passed from Vietnam into Laos the next day. I didn't need a piece of paper to tell me that – the landscape did it for me. I have never experienced an atmospheric and visual change quite like the one that greeted me at the border – like two different worlds stitched together by nothing more than a makeshift barrier and a security kiosk. In crossing that line, we passed from revving motorcycles, shops and high-pitched chatter into an ancient land of peace and tranquillity. Buffalo wallowed in red mud at the side of the road. Dense forest stretched as far as the eye could see. Even the light was softer, clouded by the breath of the myriad trees beneath.

Laos is a land with a deep contradiction at its heart. Its enduring beauty is forged by horror. The reason the trees have not been felled in their millions, like they have in Vietnam, is that is unsafe to do so, due to the tons of unexploded ordnance that remain in the ground from the WAR. In essence, those exact same bombs are safeguarding the beauty of the natural environment. How screwed up is that?

We were joined at the border checkpoint by five government shadows, representatives of the Lao People's Revolutionary Party, the only legal political party in the country. The head dude looked a little like Fu Manchu, but less jolly. He had grey pegs for teeth and zero laughter lines – I imagine because there had been no laughter in his branch of the LPRP. Ever.

As with their neighbours over the border, the Lao people don't dwell on what has been. They are resilient and resourceful. Every village we visited had houses built on stilts. Those stilts were made from empty shell cases dropped from American war planes. On the roadside small teams of women with wicker baskets picked shrapnel from the bushes. To venture even a metre from the cleared track is to take your life in your hands. Only a week before, a family of four had been blown to smithereens while playing in the land at the back of their house only a stone's throw from where we were passing.

We got out of the car on a whim and went to talk to the women. We wanted to know what that kind of exhausting and hazardous work felt like to do. As we approached, the government officials got out of their vehicles and approached them too. We asked the women a question. They waited for Fu Manchu to answer it. They repeated his answer, which was then translated for us.

They told us just how much they *loved* their work.

Despite constantly being around the props of WAR, none of these experiences had been especially dangerous, so the team decided to up the ante. This was, after all, as I had learned to my cost in Alaska, a show called *The World's Most Dangerous Roads*. The next morning Ian informed us that were heading off to the Sepon Mine, where we'd shadow a private UXO (unexploded ordnance) clearance team.

Liza: What's going on?
Me: Apparently we've got to go and stand on some bombs.
Liza: He's not giving up, is he?
Me: Nope. He won't stop until we're actually dead.
Liza: [*pause*] I don't want to stand on bombs.
Me: Neither do I.
Liza: Well, I'm not doing it. I mean, I'm not Ross Kemp.

So Liza, rather wisely, opted to stay at the base of the mine, whereas Lady Schmuck here crawled up a vast pile of rubble to meet the head of the UXO team.

Me: [*breathless*] So who is this guy anyway?

Ian: He's an ex-special forces Swede called Magnus.

I immediately perked up. Magnus is a name that automatically invokes excitement in me. I have never met an underwhelming Magnus. This Magnus certainly did not disappoint. He was eleven feet tall, cooler than a skinny dip in Naimakka and with a body that looked like a thousand hammers wrapped in velvet.

I noticed that whenever he got close, my skin flushed and my voice shot up an octave. Damn – what is it about us women? The more remote and unreachable a person is, the more we want to save them. And so the more stubborn Magnus was with his answers the more I fell into his sex web.

Me: So, Magnus, where have you worked?

Magnus: Everywhere. Everywhere that is hell. Iran, Iraq, Afghanistan, Sudan, Bosnia, Kosovo. Sudan was the worst . . .

His eyes are trained on the ends of the earth as he speaks.

Me: Do you get to go home much?

Magnus: Home?

Me: Yes.

Magnus: Ha! [*A single, mirthless laugh*] I don't really ever go home.

I bet you don't, you damaged Nordic mega-hunk.

Magnus: I have a cabin in the woods. It is very simple. Sometimes I return there. Alone.

[*Take me there! Take me there, you nomadic, lost soul!*]

363

Me: Do you . . . do you not have a partner?

Magnus: No. A wife. Once. But there is no room for love when
          you face death every day.

[*I am in love with you! I am IN LOVE WITH YOU, you remote, disconnected mess of a man.*]

Magnus: But . . .

He holds the pause for what seems like minutes. I lean into him expectantly.

Me: Yes?

Magnus: I do have . . .

Me: Yes . . . [*I whisper breathlessly*]

Magnus: . . . a cat.

And with that our relationship is over.

Now the possibility of a romance had disappeared, I was far
more able to focus on the job in hand. Magnus walked me up
what appeared to be a mountain of aggregate. We then took a
cordoned-off path to the left, overlooking a large depression in
the ground.

I stared down.

It is one thing to read that Laos is the most bombed place on
the planet (over two million tons of ordnance were dropped on
it by the Americans during the Vietnam War); it is quite another
to see it with your own eyes.

In the crater down below was one of the most depressing
sights I've ever seen.

A small clearance team was painstakingly working, not only
horizontally, across the ground, but vertically down to the hor-

rors beneath. The first layer had revealed unexploded phosphorus bombs, pineapple 'bombies' and 250-pounders, the second layer 500-pounders, then, going deeper still, all the way to the vast 3,000-pounders. The scale of the work, and its grindingly slow and meticulous nature, was beyond imagination. Magnus stood at the top of the ridge and calmly informed me that approximately 25 per cent of Laos's villages are still contaminated with unexploded devices from wartime raids, which rained death from the sky, on average, every eight minutes, twenty-four hours a day for nine years.

Ian looked pleased – he had got WAR chat – whereas I felt saddened to my core. For all the team's hard work, it was clear this project was a mere drop in the ocean.

And, then, just at the very point I needed to laugh, I looked back down to see Liza staring up at me, holding a pillowcase she had just personalized with a felt-tip pen. It simply read, 'I AM NOT ROSS KEMP.'

By now, Ian had figured that out of the two evils presenting themselves to him –

- spending another week with us lunatics
- serving time in an Asian prison for our murder

– the latter was preferable. Now that his plan to blow us up had failed, he decided that the next best thing was to drown us in a river. That morning we woke to find an old man in orange robes coughing on the steps of our hostel.

Me: What's he here for?

Ian: A monk's blessing.

Me: Oh. What for?

Ian: It's D-Day.

I had no idea what D-Day involved, but it sounded like something I might want to get blessed for. Liza and I were duly seated on plastic chairs outside our rooms and wrapped casually in thin skeins of cotton by the monk's second in command.

A large bucket of water was placed beside us.

The monk approached, hacking. His skin was like greaseproof paper. There was more muttering. We respectfully bowed our heads in prayer. Now was not the time for 'Love Hangover'.

Suddenly, out of nowhere, the acolyte threw the entire bucket over us. And then, as soon as it had begun, the ceremony was over.

Me: Do you think there was *any* element of the religious about that?

Liza: It was like he was washing a step!

I got up. The water had fairly and squarely sluiced my groin, and nowhere else. I had a blessed vagina. Finally, I had a blessed vagina.

We spent the next hour in damp knickers, driving to the top of a hill. Below, a river raged. We drove down again until we arrived at its banks.

Laos river crossings are often perilous, as the riverbed can be uneven and pocked with bomb craters. Instead of the depth being consistent all the way across, you can find the rock from beneath giving way so you end up totally subsumed by water. The traditional way to undertake a river crossing by car or bike is always to walk it first, bamboo stick in hand, prodding into the murk beneath and gauging the depth. Only this way can you be sure that your car won't sink into a surprise hole.

We stood at the water's edge. It's fair to say neither Liza nor myself was raring keen to take part in what amounted to an Asian wet T-shirt competition. I drew the short straw (again). I slowly waded into the current, stick in hand. To the left of me I could see villagers eviscerating a chicken, and seconds later its alimentary canal floated past me like a bloody question mark. I had barely gone three or four metres when my footing disappeared, and I was plunged in up to my neck. Our guides sat on the bank muttering and shaking their heads. Even Fu Manchu, our communist watchman, seemed keen that we proceed no further – unless the thumbs-down sign means something totally different in that part of the world.

Ian, however, sensed this had the potential to become a properly *Dangerous Road* and excitedly shouted encouragement from the bank. He finally had the chance to *literally* kill two birds with one stone.

I found my footing again, but a mere ten metres in my stick was spirited away by the current. I could feel the rip tugging at my shins. I pressed my toes into the wet rocks underneath to steady myself, but there was simply no way I could carry on without being swept downstream.

'I can't tell how deep it is out here!' I yelled as I inched my way back to the safety of the bank. Ian said nothing, but simply stared at us. It felt a little like a dare. And, as you know, I can't resist a dare.

'Come on, let's do this,' I said in a voice not unlike that of Jason Statham.

Ian carried on staring, before lifting his arm and waving us on.

'Is that your cock hand, Ian?' we chimed in unison.

We slammed the doors shut. The engine purred into life.

'Whatever happens,' said Liza, brightly, 'we laugh. OK? However bad it is, we just laugh and laugh.'

So we did.

Liza put the car into first, hit the biting point and then stepped hard on the accelerator. We launched into the water. First the tyres were slicked, then coated, then submerged. For a while it felt like they had no traction at all, and that we were merely floating. The water came up to the window on one side, but we kept on laughing – my hand on Liza's hand like an aquatic Thelma and Louise. We laughed all the way until the tyres gained purchase again and we were safe on the other side. Fu Manchu's face broke into a smile as he stared across. Thumbs up. Thumbs up. And on we went.

Me / Liza: Ah, if there's a cure for this
             I don't want it [Do you think they use pigs as currency
             here?]
             Don't want it.
             If there's a remedy
             I'll run from it, from it. [I don't know where I've got it
             from, but I've got a terrible rash on my arse . . .]

Our go-to guy in Laos was a man called Huang, whose main contribution to the project came in the form of an unfeasibly giant tub of cashew nuts (hereafter known as Huang's nuts). When I say giant – I mean, it was a foot-and-a-half Tupperware tube. You could lose your arm in there. After the endless inedible tangle of street noodles, they were a welcome change – although, as the week wore on, and the more nuts were eaten, the harder it was to get those remaining from the bottom. In the end you were mainly dredging up hard commas of other people's skin and bacteria.

As we ventured further into the jungle, approaching I DON'T KNOW WHERE, the roads became skinny. The hills got steeper and the car grumpier. We made it to the outskirts of a tribal village, whereupon we got stuck in a giant pothole. The engine screamed as we tried to rev our way out of it, but the wheels were embedded in thick red clay. We got out and pushed, but our flip-flops sank deep in the goo. The tyre tracks filled with buffalo piss, with mozzies skating on the surface. In the end we had to get the government guys to help us back to some hardcore where the wheels could get purchase.

We puttered past the village – by the wooden stilt houses, a family of pot-bellied pigs, a cluster of chickens. As we left the clearing, the track became treacherous again and we slowed to a near standstill. Suddenly out of the forest came two men, bare-chested, skin gleaming, carrying baskets full of chicken guts. Both had large, sharp machetes in their hands. Liza was driving. They approached my side of the car. One raised his machete.

'Hello, boys!' roared Liza, who had not yet seen the machetes.

'Oh God, help us,' I muttered, because I had.

The men leaned through the open window into the car. I could smell fresh sweat. I could hear my heartbeat. Time to die.

And then, suddenly, the atmosphere changed, moving from

proper peril to utter calm. The reason? Well, the two tribes-
men had just caught sight of Liza's breasts and were now
transfixed by them. Why wouldn't they be? They are, after all,
the best breasts in show business.

'So, lads . . . Huang's nuts?' she said breezily, proffering the
deep tub of cashews.

Fifteen minutes later, after a lot of gawping, nodding and
eating, we finally left. At our next pit-stop the producer saun-
tered over to us, somewhat surprised.

P: Gosh, they were friendly!
Me: What do you mean?
P: Well when we came for the recce, they came after us with
     knives! We had to put our foot down and get out of there . . .
     didn't think we'd make it!

Much to the disappointment of those around us, we completed
the Ho Chi Minh Trail safely. We didn't get blown up. We didn't
drown. We didn't get macheted by rogue hill-tribe warriors.
After another seven hours of driving, we hit a tarmacked road,
and from there we cruised to GOD KNOWS WHERE. I do
know that by now we were back in Vietnam, propelled by the
promise of a final night's sleep in a proper hotel. It had only
been a fortnight and yet it seemed like an eternity since I'd slept
on something that didn't look like an exhibit in an episode of
CSI Asia.

The spa hotel was brand new, with polished slate and
waterfalls and stuff. I looked around – paranoid – for some-

one selling their body or their sister's body or their daughter's body. Nothing. I looked for mould on the wall. Nothing. I listened for the sound of blaring transistors or the scream of chickens. Nothing. Just the faint whisper of pan pipes and the light scrape of muslin on toned thigh as a receptionist walked past. If Kelly Hoppen did prisons, this was the sort of place they'd be. Incarcerated. In taupe.

I read through the list of treatments and chose their Vietnamese Massage, which was, apparently, 'famous'. I was led into a cool room, where I peeled off my clothes and lay on a bed, face down, placing my head in what looked like a large cotton polo mint.

Two hands pressed either side of my spine.

Heaven.

Then four hands.

Interesting.

It didn't matter.

Finally, a happy ending.

Epilogue

I am sitting in my parents' garden. The grass is warm. Parker is snuffling beside me, occasionally shooting me a cloudy, sightless glance.

I have returned from months away travelling in Asia. I am a gyroscope of stress, still adjusting to the sheer luxury of my surroundings – the calm, the cool, the peace.

The kitchen door swings open and Dad stands in the doorway. Behind him hangs a grey plastic mask that looks like something out of *Halloween*. It's a relic of his radiotherapy sessions for yet another bout of cancer – this time in the throat, poor sod. He is looking a little worn, and his voice cracks when he speaks, but amid the agony of recuperation there is an unexpected gain – Dad is joyful again. Finally, after endless dances with death, after sixteen years with the black dog, he wants to live.

He wanders out into the sunshine, brandishing a fitness tracker armband.

Dad: Breaking news – I've done my stats for the year. I've walked exactly 1,056 miles.
Me: Not bad!
Mum: [*from within*] Bert! Careful on those steps! You'll fall, and that'll be your hip shattered again.
Dad: I've never shattered my hip!
Mum: Yes, well, you've shattered everything else. It's just a waiting game.

Spectacles

*She follows him outside, Marigolds on. They lean against each other. I don't
know who is supporting who. Dad continues . . .*

Dad: I've walked 2,790,361 steps in total. Do you know what that
          averages out at?
Me/Mum: No.
Dad: 7,645 steps per day.
Mum: That's very good.
Me: Very good.
Dad: It's amazing to see how far you've gone, isn't it?

I let the weight of that sentence settle a little before answering.

Me: Yes. Yes, it is.

*And then it hits me. This travelling, this endless momentum – it's for them
– for my mum and dad, who haven't been able to go anywhere for such a very
long time. Finally, after years on Pause, they are moving again. Now, finally,
maybe I can stay still.*

Me: You should put those on your graph, Dad. On the com-
          puter. Just think – by the time you've walked into your
          study, you'll have walked a couple of dozen more steps.
Dad: Good idea. I'll do that.
Mum: I'm coming with you. I don't trust you not to do yourself a
          mischief.

*And off they go, the pair of them. This weird, two-pieced jigsaw that looks
like it couldn't possibly fit together as neatly as it does.*

I love you, I think as they disappear from view.
   I think it, but I don't say it.
   I love you.

Acknowledgments

There are an awful lot of people to thank. Because I am my parents' daughter, I have catalogued them for easy reference.

Shit-Kickers

Louise Moore, who *made me do this*, Saint Jess of Leeke, who turned patience into an art form, and Jess Jackson, who now understands that my interpretation of 'media ready' is 'I've managed to put my trousers on the right way round'.

My agent and friend, Debi Allen (gives one hundred per cent, only takes fifteen – bargain).

The Fantastic Four – Charlene, Jess, Lucy and Linda at DAA.

Good Samaritans

Joshua Reznak at Mill Lane Vets, and his wonderful nurse Lindsey, for helping me make one of the hardest decisions of my life.

All the brilliant, battle-worn souls who work in the NHS, with particular shout-outs to the doctors and nurses of Mayday, Treliske and West Cornwall hospitals.

Shelley Silas, who once saved me in the rain.

Game Changers

The teachers who inspired me: Lora Sanson, Clare Boyle, Mrs Green, Carol Schroder, Professor Janet Reibstein, Jan and Dennis Cassidy, Neil Cowley and Paul Lewis.

Those at the BBC and beyond who've mentored me and

gifted me inspiring and life-changing adventures, with special thanks to Janice Hadlow and Charlotte Moore.

Rufus Roubicek and Pauline Law, who gave us our first breaks in telly.

Dawn and Jennifer, who gave us our first proper writing gig.

Kith and Kin

My surrogate families: the Giedroycs and the Szilagyis. I make a point of only hanging out with people with unpronounce-able surnames.

Mary Berry, Paul Hollywood, and the entire *Bake Off* team.

My dearest friends; Emma, Nicola, Sarah, Gemma, Neil, Andy and Michele.

Lord Donald and Master Noggin.

Mel, my partner in crime – specifically crimes against comedy.

And lovely Spanner, for not minding me spending hours at my desk in my pants screaming 'WHHHHHYYYYY'.

But most of all, it's for The Family Perkins, whose story this is – even though they might not recognize it.

Permissions

If you enjoyed

SPECTACLES

you might like to read the following
titles by the same author . . .

ALL ABOUT MYSELF

Susan.

MILK . by Susan Perkins

A good cover.